Culture and Society in the Asia-Pacific

Culture and Society in the Asia-Pacific

Edited by Richard Maidment and Colin Mackerras

London and New York

in association with

The Open University

First published 1998 by Routledge
11 New Fetter Lane, London EC4P 4EE

Simultaneously published in the USA and Canada
by Routledge
29 West 35th Street, New York, NY 10001

© The Open University 1998

Edited, designed and typeset by The Open University

Printed in the United Kingdom by Alden, Oxford and Northampton

British Library Cataloguing in Publication Data
A catalogue record for this book is available from The British Library

Library of Congress Cataloging in Publication Data
A catalogue record for this book has been requested

ISBN 0-415-17277-2 (hbk)
ISBN 0-415-17278-0 (pbk)

1.1

18192B/dd302b3preli1.1

CONTENTS

Preface   viii

Chapter 1   Diversity and convergence in Asia-Pacific society and culture   1
Colin Mackerras, Richard Maidment and David Schak

    1.1   Introduction   1

    1.2   The Asian way   1

    1.3   Diversity in societies and cultures   5

    1.4   Convergent forces in the Pacific   8

    1.5   Conclusion: tradition and modernization   11

Chapter 2   The old and the new   15
J. Kathirithamby-Wells

    2.1   Introduction: Asia-Pacific integration   15

    2.2   The pre-modern era *c.* 1500–1800   16

    2.3   The colonial era, *c.* 1800–1945   19

    2.4   The new era, 1946–   28

    2.5   Conclusion   36

Chapter 3   Population   39
Terence T. Hull

    3.1   Introduction   39

    3.2   Peopling East Asia and the Pacific Rim, 5000 BC to AD 2000   44

    3.3   Expansions, conquests and empires   46

    3.4   Demographic revolutions   49

    3.5   Demographic tensions   53

    3.6   The struggle for decent demographic futures   58

    3.7   Conclusion   63

Chapter 4   Migration and the diaspora communities   65
Lucie Cheng and Marian Katz

    4.1   Introduction   65

    4.2   Migration and the nation-state   67

    4.3   Diverse experiences or diverse narratives?   69

4.4   Types of diasporas   72

4.5   Migration patterns, types of diasporas and diasporic
identities   74

4.6   Changing configurations   77

4.7   Emerging diasporas: a transnational professional/service
class?   84

4.8   Summary and conclusion   86

Chapter 5   Race, ethnicity and language   89
Anthony van Fossen

5.1   Six degrees of separation   89

5.2   Principal ethnic groups   90

5.3   The case studies   92

5.4   Summary   111

Chapter 6   Religion   115
Julia Day Howell

6.1   Introduction   115

6.2   Which religions?   116

6.3   Religions: coming or going in modern East Asia?   121

6.4   Emergent patterns in East Asian religion and spirituality   131

6.5   Conclusion   138

Chapter 7   Education   141
John Hawkins

7.1   Introduction   141

7.2   Motivation and values in East Asian education   146

7.3   Conclusion   158

Chapter 8   Women's movements in the Asia-Pacific   163
Chilla Bulbeck

8.1   Introduction   163

8.2   Comparing the status of women   164

8.3   Women's movement activism   171

8.4   The international traffic in women   179

8.5   Conclusion   181

Chapter 9   Pacific images   185
Stephanie Taylor

9.1   Introduction   185

9.2   The nature of images   186

9.3   The relevance of images to the study of the Asia-Pacific   187

9.4   The image of emptiness   188

9.5   The primitive islands of love and happiness   194

9.6   Changing images of place   198

9.7   The power of images to construct relationships   201

9.8   Conclusion   205

Chapter 10   Asia-Pacific cinemas   **207**
Mary Farquhar and Linda Erlich

10.1   Introduction   207

10.2   The significance of film   207

10.3   National cinemas in three locations: Hollywood, Japan
and China   209

10.4   Backgrounds   209

10.5   Narrative   215

10.6   Aesthetics   220

10.7   Conclusion   226

Chapter 11   The culture of politics   **231**
Stephanie Lawson

11.1   Introduction   231

11.2   The idea of culture   234

11.3   Culture and the state   237

11.4   The Asian values debate   245

11.5   Conclusion   249

Acknowledgements   **253**

List of contributors   **255**

Index   **259**

Series preface

The five volumes in this series are part of a new Open University course, *Pacific Studies*, which has been produced within the Faculty of Social Sciences. The appearance of *Pacific Studies* is due to the generous and enthusiastic support the course has received from the University and in particular from colleagues within the Faculty of Social Sciences. The support has been especially remarkable given that this course has ventured into relatively uncharted scholarly waters. The potential risks were readily apparent but the commitment always remained firm. I am very grateful.

There are too many people to thank individually, both within and outside of the Open University, but I must record my appreciation for some of them. Within the University, I would like to acknowledge my colleagues Anthony McGrew and Grahame Thompson. *Pacific Studies* could not have been made without them. Their role was central. They were present when the course was conceived and they lived with it through to the final stages. They also made the experience of making this course both very enjoyable and intellectually stimulating. Christopher Brook and Bernard Eccleston made an enormous contribution to the course far beyond their editorial roles in two of the books in the series. They read the successive drafts of all chapters with great care and their perceptive comments helped to improve these volumes considerably. David Goldblatt and Jeremy Mitchell, because of their other commitments, may have joined the Course Team relatively late in the production process, but their contributions, especially to *Governance in the Asia-Pacific* have been much appreciated. Michael Dawson played an especially important role in the production of *The Asia-Pacific Profile* and his calm and genial presence was valued as always. Jeremy Cooper and Eleanor Morris of the BBC were responsible for the excellent audio-visual component of *Pacific Studies*. Anne Carson, the Course Manager of *Pacific Studies*, was consistently cheerful and helpful. All of the volumes in this series have been greatly improved by the editorial craftsmanship of Stephen Clift, Tom Hunter and Kate Hunter, who have been under great pressure throughout the production of this course, but nevertheless delivered work of real quality. The striking cover designs of Richard Hoyle and Jonathan Davies speak for themselves and the artwork of Ray Munns in all five volumes has been most impressive. Paul Smith, whose recent retirement from the University will leave a very real gap, made his usual remarkable contribution in providing unusual and interesting illustrations. Giles Clark of the Copublishing Department was a constant source of encouragement and in addition his advice was always acute. Our colleagues in Project Control, especially Deborah Bywater and David Calderwood, were far more understanding and helpful than I had any right to expect. Lene Connolly of Print Buying and Pam Berry of Text Processing did all that was necessary to ensure that this series was produced on schedule. Anne Hunt and Mary Dicker, who have been responsible for so much of the work in this Faculty over the past several years, performed to their usual exacting standards by preparing the manuscripts in this series for publication with remarkable speed and accuracy. They were very ably assisted by Chris Meeks and Doreen Pendlebury.

Pacific Studies could not have been made without the help of academic colleagues based in the UK as well as in the Asia-Pacific region. This series of books has drawn on their scholarship and their expertise but above all on their generosity. I must record my appreciation to all of them for their participation in this project. The Course Team owes an especially large debt to Dr Gerry Segal, Director of Studies at the International Institute of Strategic Studies, who was the External Assessor of *Pacific Studies*. He was both an enthusiastic supporter of this project as well as a very shrewd critic. His wise counsel and tough advice have greatly improved the volumes in this series. It has been a pleasure to work with Professor Colin Mackerras, Director of the Key Centre for Asian Studies and Languages at Griffith University in Australia. Griffith University and the Open University have collaborated over the production of *Pacific Studies*; an arrangement that has worked extremely well. The success of this collaboration has been due in no small part to Colin. Over the past three years I have come to appreciate his many qualities particularly his immense knowledge of the Asia-Pacific region as well as his patience and courtesy in dealing with those of us who know far less. I would also like to thank all of those colleagues at Griffith who have helped to make this collaboration so successful and worthwhile, especially Professor Tony Bennett, who played a key role during the initial discussions between the two universities. Frank Gibney, President of the Pacific Basin Institute, was always available with help, advice and encouragement. It was one of the real pleasures of this project to have met and worked with Frank and the PBI. This series has also benefited considerably from the enthusiasm and insight of Victoria Smith at Routledge.

The production of *Pacific Studies* was helped greatly through the assistance of several foundations. The Daiwa Anglo-Japanese Foundation awarded this project two grants and its Director General, Christopher Everett, was a model of generosity and support. He invited the Course Team to use the attractive facilities of the Foundation; an invitation which was accepted with enthusiasm. The grant from The Great Britain Sasakawa Foundation was also greatly appreciated as was the advice, encouragement and the shrewd counsel of Peter Hand, the Administrator of the Foundation. Mr Tomoyuki Sakurai the Director of the Japan Foundation in London was always interested in the development of *Pacific Studies* and

I have no doubt that this resulted in a generous grant from the Foundation. Mr Haruhisa Takeuchi, formerly Director of the Japan Information and Cultural Centre, was most supportive during the early stages of this project and his successor at the Centre, Mr Masatoshi Muto has been no less helpful. Finally, I must record my thanks to the British Council in Australia for their assistance which was much appreciated.

Richard Maidment
Chair, *Pacific Studies*
Milton Keynes, March 1998

Griffith University preface

Pacific Studies is the first major project in which Griffith University has been involved with the Open University. It is a great honour for Griffith University to participate in this major international scholarly project and especially with a university with the reputation of the Open University. As a member of Griffith University I regard it both as a privilege and pleasure to co-edit this volume on the society and culture of the region.

The process of developing this book has been arduous but rewarding. It has necessitated the co-ordination of ideas and the ways in which they are presented. It has involved several international meetings of the authors, several international visits, and numerous commentaries on the chapters. One of the visits I made to England, in the autumn of 1996, was through the assistance of the British Council, for which I thank them.

I should like to thank Professor Richard Maidment for his activism, hard work and co-operative spirit in the preparation of this volume. It has at all times been a great pleasure to work with him. I would also like to thank the contributors for their hard work and co-operation and for their willingness to accept the criticisms and suggestions which the process of compiling a volume such as this entails.

Griffith University has been uniformly supportive in this endeavour. Apart from a generous grant specifically for the project, it also helped by giving teaching relief to individuals to enable the preparation of the chapters. I should like to thank the Deans of the Faculty of Humanities, Associate Professor David Saunders, and of the former Faculty of Asian and International Studies, Associate Professor Bill Shepherd, for their co-operation and support in those various aspects of developing this project.

Colin Mackerras
Brisbane, March 1998

Culture and Society in the Asia-Pacific: preface

I would like to thank all the contributors to this volume for their enthusiasm and generosity with their time and effort. In particular I would like to record my appreciation for my co-editor, Professor Colin Mackerras, who was a model of tact, efficiency and above all erudition. Gerry Segal, the External Assessor of *Pacific Studies*, made several acute observations and suggestions which greatly improved the final manuscript. Stephanie Taylor read the entire book and her comments were valued. Mike Dawson stepped in at the last moment and ensured that there were no problems over the production of the book. Stephen Clift and Tom Hunter edited this volume with their usual sensitivity and effectiveness. Finally, Anne Hunt and Mary Dicker prepared successive drafts of the manuscript with their usual meticulous efficiency.

Richard Maidment
Milton Keynes, March 1998

CHAPTER 1

Diversity and convergence in Asia-Pacific society and culture

Colin Mackerras, Richard Maidment and David Schak

1.1   Introduction

To a large extent interest in the Asia-Pacific has focused on its recent economic dynamism. Yet the cultures and societies of the region are a source of considerable interest. They offer a rich tapestry of peoples and religions, languages and traditions. They also provide spectacular examples of several disjunctures between change and continuity, between the strength of history and modernization, and between local conservatism and external influence.

This volume aims to introduce, analyse, and to some extent explain the processes of cultural and social change which have taken place in the Asia-Pacific. As much as, or perhaps even more than, with the economic and political factors the past is relevant, in part because it is important in itself but also as a consequence of its influence and impact on the present. This book makes no claim to be comprehensive, but it does examine several social institutions and cultural processes which have formed a central element of almost all human societies. It examines those special social phenomena which influence peoples and communities, including those that are central to the process of modernization such as education, as well as those traditional institutions like religion. In the field of culture there is a chapter on the cinema which is a particularly powerful medium in the Asia-Pacific. In addition, the book also considers the role of ethnicity and race.

1.2   The Asian way

One of the most important debates in the Asia-Pacific revolves around the notion of the 'Asian way'. Is there something about the Asian way of thinking which might explain why Asian societies and governments so often differ in their attitudes from elsewhere? What is very clear is that several Asian leaders, notably Dr Mahathir of Malaysia and Lee Kwan Yew of

Singapore, have frequently appealed to the notion of the Asian to attack the behaviour and views of Western governments and individuals.

An area which brings this debate into particularly sharp focus is the one about human rights. Several East Asian countries claim that their history, culture and experience give them a somewhat different approach to issues of human rights. Indeed, the Asian Regional Preparatory Meeting for the World Conference on Human Rights, held in Bangkok in March 1993, issued a Declaration which made this very point. While accepting the idea of universal human rights spelled out in the UN Charter, the Bangkok Declaration said that human rights 'must be considered in the context of a dynamic and evolving process of international norm-setting, bearing in mind the significance of national and regional particularities and various historical, cultural and religious backgrounds' (quoted in Awanohara et al., 1993, p.17). On the other hand, the distinguished Indian Professor, Amartya Sen, has described the 'greatest cliché about Asia' as 'the claim that "Asian values" are opposed to human rights'. He argues that the ancient literatures of Asia 'placed as much emphasis on the importance of freedom at the individual level as corresponding Western classics' (Sen, 1996, p.46).

These two views may not actually be as starkly opposed as they appear. Even countries which subscribe to the values of human rights may differ in interpreting them. Whereas Western philosophy tends to stress civil and political rights, most East Asian countries lay greater emphasis on economic and social rights. So a country where the economy has made great strides in recent years, with raised standards of living for the vast majority of its people, would come off quite well in Asian definitions of human rights, even if it failed to follow a system of Western liberal democracy and did not protect free speech or a free press.

A good illustration is the suppression of the student movement in Beijing during 1989. The Chinese government argued that it was not suppressing non-violent demonstrators but 'quelling a counter-revolutionary rebellion' aimed at the overthrow of the Chinese Communist Party. It claimed that its action caused far less pain to society at large than would have occurred had the CCP been overthrown, and that this would probably have happened had the student movement been allowed to continue. In this scenario, the rights of a few individuals paled beside the rights of the many; such individual rights were merely causing trouble, and thus were hardly rights at all anyway.

The response in the West to the actions of the Chinese government was very different. There was widespread condemnation and disapproval. Interestingly, while there was great concern within East Asia over the affair, in general, Asian governments were not nearly as critical of the Chinese government actions as were those of the West. Public opinion is more difficult to gauge, but may also have reacted less strongly than in the West.

Human rights are also involved in issues concerning the family and women. Indeed, a powerful slogan of the women's movement is that 'women's rights are also human rights', but this is a slogan that has had a far greater impact in non-Asian societies. Despite some similar trends, there remains considerable difference in attitudes towards such matters between the West and the countries of East Asia. Many women in China, Japan, Malaysia and Indonesia regard Western feminism as unnecessarily negative over the family system and irrelevant to their particular needs, as well as an indulgence they can ill afford. The belief that many important gender differences derive from nature, not culture, is considerably more widespread in the countries of East Asia than in those of the West.

In general most Muslims regard their religion as highly supportive of women and protective towards them. After all, the Koran (1995, p.76) puts a high priority on commanding people to 'honour the mothers who bore you'. But there is a view for Western feminism to be rather suspicious of Islam for what is seen as its attitude towards women. A specific issue is that of abortion. Many Western feminists regard the right to abortion as part of a woman's freedom to choose whether or not to reproduce; a view which is abhorrent to Islam.

Another area in which the countries of East Asia have generally adopted a different priority from the West is over the environment. In 1993 the weekly *Far Eastern Economic Review*, among the most significant of journals on the affairs of Asia, published the results of a major survey it had undertaken on a range of business matters. It found that no less than 22 per cent of Malaysian respondents admitted to being likely to ignore laws aimed at curbing pollution, while Indonesians followed at 18 per cent (*Far Eastern Economic Review*, 1993, p.52). The explanation for this attitude may lie in two factors: economic underdevelopment and resistance to being told what to think and do by the rich industrialized countries. Highly industrialized countries use especially high levels of resources in virtually all sectors of society. The Earth Summit held in Rio de Janeiro, Brazil, in June 1992 revealed these resentments by the poorer nations. According to one observer, 'For Asia's poorer nations, the Earth Summit provided strong evidence that the US, Japan and other industrialized countries are far more preoccupied with specific environmental issues than with relieving poverty'. And when Malaysia refused to bow to US pressure for a stronger statement on deforestation and earned itself the title of 'bad boy' from the USA for its efforts, its delegate commented simply: 'So be it ... We don't want to be pushed aside and be bullied like we have been for the past 45 years' (Schwarz, 1992, p.61).

A social area in which Western and Asian views tend strongly to diverge is in education. In Western countries, the emphasis is generally on debate and argument and the fostering of individuality. Although some people still believe strongly that too much individuality and egalitarianism break down school authority, society at large value these qualities. Certainly most people regard the role of the government in education as being restricted to providing finances and facilities, and would accept ideological control of the curriculum only if absolutely fixed.

In Asian countries, on the other hand, education is more likely to be seen as a vehicle of the state. While this does not necessarily mean that the state exercises absolute control over the curriculum, its degree of influence is generally considerably higher than in the West. In Asian countries the emphasis of education is on 'nation-building', however this may be conceived. In China and Indonesia, for instance, what matters in the 1990s is to make the country modern and strong, not to foster the individual. In Thailand, as in Japan, the education system must assist national economic development, and the more effectively the better. On 20 August 1994, the Thai Education Ministry was reported in the *Bangkok Post* as calling for 'more professionals in the areas of science and technology to strengthen the country's development'.

The strong tendency in Asian societies is to regard teachers with respect. The student or pupil is expected to treat the teachers with a deference that is not observed in Western schools. The teacher in Asian societies belongs to a higher, and thus more venerated and trusted, age group, in addition he or she knows more and should be looked up to simply by virtue of holding the status of teacher. In societies with Confucian traditions, such as China, Japan and Korea, the teacher is expected to receive special respect from students, because both society and education must establish a hierarchy in which disciplined recognition of one's place in the scale is part of training as a human being.

The generally greater acceptance of hierarchy in Asian, as opposed to Western, societies also affects such socially significant areas as employment and labour relations. In the first place, the relationship between the state and business is a very pronounced feature of contemporary East Asia, and perhaps is one of the reasons behind the region's success. Many observers believe that this is because, in contrast to many Western countries, the government goes out of its way to side with business and not its employees, and resists such obstacles to rapid and sustained growth as the exponentially rising social welfare bill.

In virtually all the countries of the Asian nations of the Asia-Pacific the relationship of the employer to the employee is considerably more paternalistic than is general in Western countries. In Indonesia and Thailand the emphasis on hierarchy and status makes the employer or supervisor seen specifically as a father figure, while in Malaysia personal patronage is frequently a factor in promotion and pay rises. In Japan, the supervisor is expected to socialize with subordinates and to enjoy an almost familial relationship. Moreover, large companies reward commitment and loyalty from their employees. Such factors lead some observers to believe paternalism in Japan to be 'institutionalized' (Milner and Quilty, 1996, p.114).

In general, trade unions are weaker and less effective in the countries of East Asia than in the West. At the end of the 1980s, rates of unionization were relatively low: 17 per cent in Hong Kong, less than 5 per cent in Thailand, 14 per cent in Malaysia and 17 per cent in Singapore (Milner and Quilty, 1996, p.114). In Indonesia, Singapore, Thailand and Malaysia the trade union movement has very little autonomy from the state, while in socialist countries, such as China and Vietnam, there is even less. In Japan, unionization is comparatively high at 26 per cent and enjoys a higher degree of autonomy than elsewhere in East Asia. But one of the distinctive features of Japan is the predominance of unions in large companies and government bureaucracies with the unions being confined to a single company or workplace and covering the full range of occupations there. The result is that unions are likely to restrain those demands with the potential to damage the competitive position of their companies.

An area of considerable importance for contemporary international relations is that of business ethics, and in this field too there are stark differences between Asian and Western countries. Some of these are cultural. For instance, the peoples of East Asia are much more liable to give prospective business partners or clients gifts in order to seal a business arrangement than would be the case in most Western countries. Two academic observers have summed up the tension in values between the West and Asia in the following broad way. Being Australians, they refer specifically to their own country, but their comments are equally applicable to other Western countries.

> The liberal ideological package – a tradition of debate, freedom and individu-alism, a stress on equality, and abhorrence of a too vigorous official nationalism – seems to be more, not less, influential when Australia is contrasted with Asian countries. That such values are so well entrenched is a reminder that they are products of a long history, in some cases reaching back through the Enlightenment and Renaissance in Europe, and further still to the origins of the Christian and classical tradition. In this sense Australian society cannot be regarded as young. The fact that Australians react as they do, in an apparent knee-jerk fashion, to official killings in China or Indonesia, or to government ethnic discrimination in Malaysia or Fiji, is a consequence of inheriting this deeply-rooted liberal tradition.
>
> (Milner and Quilty, 1996, pp.11–12)

Milner and Quilty are certainly not saying that peoples of different cultures cannot understand each other. There are different histories, different experiences, and, for the most part, different economic and industrial levels and it is hardly surprising that they have led to a variant set of priorities, different values, and different ways of looking at the world.

To some extent, then, the Asian way is more than merely mythical in the sense that on a range of issues people from the various countries of East Asia tend to think differently from those of the West. But it is necessary to say that differences in views represent trends only. They are very far from absolute. There are different ways of seeing things in all countries, and given the range of cultural backgrounds and histories it would be absurd to point to any view shared by all countries, let alone all people, in East Asia.

1.3 Diversity in societies and cultures

So no discussion of the Asian way can overlook the fact that the societies of East Asia display an enormous variety of differences, as indeed do those of

Western countries. There are individuals and movements in opposition to government views in virtually all countries. In Indonesia, the democratic movement of the former President Sukarno's daughter Megawati was the source of quite serious anti-government disturbances in 1996. Even in China, where the government's reputation is of intolerance of dissent, there is an environmental movement strong enough in the 1990s that many officials take it seriously. Groups advocating Western views of human rights exist in Thailand and most other countries of East Asia. In the mid 1990s 'people power' is emerging even in China, creating a diversity between the old-fashioned Party rule and an emerging civil society.

> It is almost as if there are two Chinas. The China of steel-fisted Communist Party rule ... is still there. It remains uncompromisingly harsh on political dissent and other overt challenges to its authority. But it is being progressively whittled down by forces unleashed during nearly two decades of Deng Xiaoping's economic reform. Another China has emerged – and is expanding by the day. It is a freewheeling society where people make decisions for themselves, air their grievances openly, change jobs, start their own companies, hire the workers they want and decide which schools to send their children to.

(Crowell and Hsieh, 1996, pp.28–9)

While it is still the human rights abuses which get noticed in the West, they are certainly not the only developments that matter.

A good example of a relatively small but extremely diverse country is Malaysia. In 1994 Malays and other indigenous peoples made up 59 per cent of the total population of just under 20 million, in the remainder were two major originally-immigrant groups, 32 per cent of the total being Chinese and 9 per cent Indians. The Malay, Chinese and Indian cultures are extremely different from one another, with their Islamic, Confucian, Hindu and other backgrounds, they do not mix easily. There has been much traditional hostility towards the Chinese who, with their entrepreneurial skills, have tended to exert economic influence out of proportion to their numbers. Indeed, ethnic rioting in 1969 led to the reinforcement of the Malay domination of the government.

A large country such as China is highly diverse geographically, ranging from the deserts of the far west to the arid mountains of Tibet, from the tropics of the south-east to the plains of the north-east. It has 56 state-recognized nationalities, the Han comprising about 91 per cent of the people according to the October 1995 sample survey of 1 per cent of the population. The remaining 9 per cent are as different from each other as from the majority Han, and include Tibetans with a highly religious culture and Uygurs who are Turkic by language and culture with a strong belief in Islam. And, as discussed above, there is also the dimension of emerging political diversity.

Turning from diversities within societies to those among countries, we find that there are native differences in religion, language, economy, values and world view, family structure and relationships. These include gender issues and political structure, to say nothing of art forms, cuisine and dress. There are differences in tradition and, as well as history, in the physical appearance of the people. However, we can identify a number of what we might call 'culture areas' in the Asia-Pacific. The Pacific Islands are usually divided into Melanesia, Micronesia, and Polynesia on the basis of language, political and social organization, and physical characteristics (see **Eccleston *et al.*, 1998, p.249**). In South-East Asia, there are two basic linguistic groups, Austronesian and Austrasiatic speakers. Geographically, the division is between peninsular and island South-East Asia. Influences vary from place to place, with Indian culture and Hinduism exercising an impact over Burma/Myanmar, Thailand and Bali (Indonesia), and China over Vietnam and to a lesser extent Thailand. Islam is the major religion in Malaysia, is strong in Indonesia, and in parts of Burma/Myanmar, Thailand, and the Philippines. Buddhism is the strongest religion in Thailand and is an important one in Vietnam.

Although we saw earlier a sharp difference between the West and East Asia in terms of business ethics, it is very striking that the countries of East Asia are sometimes further away from each other in such matters than they are from Western countries. A case in point is attitude towards usury or interest. The medieval Christian church forbade this practice, and for many centuries the ban remained an obstacle to capitalist development in the Catholic world at just the same time as Protestant countries, such as Britain, Germany and the Netherlands, were rapidly gaining political ascendancy through industry and capitalism. The result was the disappearance of the traditional ban on usury.

In Asia, Islam is a strong opponent of usury. The Koran (1995, p.46) ordains that 'God has permitted trading and made usury unlawful'. It mentions usury in several other places, condemning it and linking it with cheating. In general, Islam forbids any kind of speculative transaction unless the material benefits accruing to the parties can be predicted exactly. Precise interpretation of the Koranic passages varies in practice with Indonesia's first Islamic Bank, the Bank Muamulat Indonesia, taking the most rigid view that all interest must be condemned, while others adopt a more liberal stance.

While Confucianism specifically placed merchants at the bottom of the social ladder, the Chinese have for centuries been famous for entrepreneurial skills. Certainly prohibitions on interest and profits have been confined to the radical Cultural Revolution decade (1966–76) engineered by Mao Zedong. In the 1980s his successor Deng Xiaoping propounded that 'to get rich is glorious'. The result was that, with the Cultural Revolution safely denounced in 1981, profit-making blossomed in the 1980s and has continued to do so in the 1990s.

We often hear of Asians as 'group oriented' as opposed to the supposedly individualist Westerners. Any such generalization needs much more detailed explanation than a simple label can give. The Chinese have historically been strongly oriented toward family, kin, and other groups based on long-term association but Chinese society is uncohesive and either fearful or hostile toward strangers. The Japanese have a weaker orientation toward family but form stronger ties with groups in the wider society.

The philosopher Francis Fukuyama has observed differences among various societies according to the levels of social trust that exist within them. He categorizes familistic cultures as 'low-trust' because people in general find it difficult to trust each other outside the context of the family. Among the countries of North-East Asia those most strongly influenced by Confucianism come into this category and include Chinese communities, such as the PRC, Taiwan and Hong Kong. Those where the firm or company has shown itself especially powerful within society have succeeded in establishing a basis of trust apart from the family, Japan being an example, despite the Confucian influences it has undergone.

Korea is a problem for Fukuyama and he devotes considerable attention to it. He concludes that South Korea, like China, is 'a familistic culture with a relatively low degree of trust outside kinship' (Fukuyama, 1995, p.145). On the other hand, the large corporation is nowadays known as a crucial aspect of the South Korean economy. Fukuyama's 'answer to this apparent paradox is the role of the [South] Korean state, which deliberately promoted gigantic conglomerates as a development strategy in the 1960s and 1970s and overcame what would otherwise have been a cultural proclivity for the small- and medium-size enterprises typical of Taiwan' (Fukuyama, 1995, p.128).

The other Asia-Pacific country to draw substantial attention from Fukuyama is the USA. He challenges the popular conception that Americans are individualistic by tradition, preferring to see them as communitarian but antistatist. This makes the USA a high-trust society, because people form strong groups outside the family, but oppose strong state intervention. At the same time, he sees a contemporary drift towards an extreme rights-centred individualism – a radical departure from its past communitarianism – and warns that such a trend holds more peril for its future than any competition from other countries (Fukuyama, 1995, pp.307–21). The obsession with individual rights, exemplified so well in the increasingly extreme litigiousness of society, tends to undermine the spirit of responsibility to the community which must provide a sensible balance to the individual. The implication is that 'trust' and 'social capital' are declining in the USA, which could produce a negative impact on the economy and prosperity of the nation.

1.4   Convergent forces in the Pacific

Let us turn now to the forces operating in the Asia-Pacific that are creating similar social and cultural patterns within the region as well as with the rest of the world. These forces are industrialization, capitalism, travel and migration, tourism, communications, and the global media.

First, however, it is important to note that the societies and cultures in the Asia-Pacific have never been static. Archaeological evidence suggests, for example, that the 'great leader syndrome' which Europeans encountered over the last two centuries has not always been there. Perhaps it was the death of a particularly dynamic leader that caused the devolution of the system, or perhaps a disease that affected production and thus population numbers. Change is continuous and what can be observed about change since European contact is that its pace has quickened considerably.

Undoubtedly the first set of influences that affected various societies was migration. Humans have been moving in this region for a very long time, making their way across Asia, conquering less advanced societies and occupying new territories. In just over 1,000 years China expanded from a small area of the north-west to occupy at least outposts in most of the area that is China today. Various peoples migrated into South-East Asia from south-western China and Tibet over the past 5,000 years. China itself has been invaded several times from inner Asian peoples, including the Tartars, the Mongols, and the Manchus. Chinese dominated Vietnam for much of the first millennium, spreading Buddhism and Confucianism as well as their culture and government institutions.

The settlement of Australia, the islands of South-East Asia and those of Melanesia, Micronesia and Polynesia demonstrates the ability to travel by sea, although settlements of the more distant island groups in Polynesia were almost certainly accidental rather than planned with deliberate navigation. At shorter distances, however, travel was planned and purposeful. In Melanesia, there were trading rings between many island groups, the best known in the West, thanks to the work of anthropologist Bronislaw Malinowski, being the kula ring. This was an annual trade in which trading partners exchanged prestige goods between the various islands in the chain. Large white arm shells went in one direction and red shell necklaces in the other. Along with this trade in prestige goods there was also trade in more utilitarian goods.

In the past several centuries, well after the settlement by the 'native peoples', came visits by Europeans, the Spanish, Portuguese, Dutch and English, and where they established some permanent presence, they began to effect profound changes on the native systems, establishing trading posts, colonies, and missions. Chinese also came as traders and labourers. In the past two centuries, some Europeans settled in their colonies and brought their language plus their medical, education and political systems with them. They also imported labour in some places, for example, there are sizeable Indian minority ethnic groups in Malaysia, Singapore and, especially, Fiji. The largest proportion of the population in Hawaii is of Japanese descent, with those of European descent second. Singapore is a European creation with a majority Chinese population in an area otherwise dominated by Malays.

In the Pacific Islands people from the poorer islands migrated to the wealthier, such as Hawaii, or to the USA, Australia and New Zealand. Tongans are now to be found from Australia, New Zealand and Singapore in the west to Los Angeles in the east, with active communication and movements of Tongans maintaining this far-flung people as a community.

Another phenomenon is tourism. Tourists from the developed world now play a very important role in the economies of the Asia-Pacific. They also impose strong pressures on the societies they visit, especially on small ones in which tourism is a particularly large component of the economy. Natives learn foreign languages and with them some version of the outside cultures. Native traditions are repackaged – or reinvented – to explain them to or make them more appealing to the guests. The demand for prostitution has direct effects on those who participate in it and often on feelings toward the tourists, the prostitutes and the dignity of the native culture. It also has a potential effect on the health of the native population, opening it up to HIV and AIDS, as well as other diseases.

Tourism also has developmental effects. Foreign exchange enters the economy and tourists bring something economists call the 'demonstration effect'. They demonstrate a life-style and level of consumption which may be completely foreign to the host country but one which locals may regard as prestigious and desirable. This triggers spending on imported goods rather than saving which the host country needs to continue developing. Tourism skews development along paths that might not be in the country's long-term interest.

Industrialization has also revolutionized economies in unprecedented ways and the effect on people's lives has been profound. Traditional ways of life do not reflect arbitrary choices made on the basis of abstract cultural principles but result from coping with the economic necessities of life. The traditional Chinese desire for many sons, for example, with the idea that many sons mean prosperity, was appropriate when most Chinese farmed small plots of land and when for such people having a greater supply of labour was their only hope of getting ahead. With industrialization and migration from farm to city, this is no longer true. Many children mean higher costs for the parents and perhaps less money available for education or medical care.

Migration to the city changes social life in many ways. Members are separated from their kinship groups. Local ceremonial life is disrupted. Extended family households become less common, although kin networks may remain intact. The relationships between the generations and the genders change. In urban areas, people are marrying later and having fewer children than their mothers and grandmothers did.

In Indonesia, formerly matrilineal groups such as the Minangkabau are tending toward bilaterality and life in the mother–father–children model nuclear family. Urban Chinese are also becoming bilateral in their kinship interaction such that for social and mutual aid purposes the wife's kin network is becoming as important as the husband's. In China grandparents are choosing to live on their own rather than with their sons and are reluctant to be child minders for their grandchildren, wanting their independence instead.

Thus, family systems are changing, a natural thing to social scientists who see the family as a central institution in the adaptation of individuals to their social, political and economic environment, but a threat to many ordinary people who see the world as they know it – and as it should be – crumbling around them. This instigates reactions and nativistic movements.

Nationhood is another homogenizing force. China, Japan, and Vietnam have had continuous, complex, centralized rule and national identity for many centuries. Many groups in East Asia have experienced centralized rule from time to time, Thailand being a contemporary example. However, other Asian nations did not assume their present shape until relatively recently. In the Pacific Islands, most peoples (Tonga and Hawaii excepted) experienced nothing like nationhood until colonialism and had no experience with self-government until the last half-century.

Recent nationhood has signalled extensive changes. Modern government, based on a bureaucratic model, changes the way people are or are supposed to be governed and the roles of those in government and the public service. Accompanying these developments are other changes to the economy, the education system both in how and what students are taught, and the influence of science and modern medicine on peoples. New nations also face the task of ensuring national loyalty, which means new requirements of citizenship, and in nations made up of many different peoples such as China, Indonesia, Papua New Guinea and Malaysia, mechanisms to unite peoples who see themselves as different from, and are often antagonistic toward, each other.

Mass media can have a homogenizing effect both within a nation and, with the spread of movies, videos and satellite television, throughout the Asia-Pacific as well as the world. Imagine an Iban from Sarawak watching soap operas or music shows from the Malaysian capital, Kuala Lumpur. The language is different, and the music style almost certainly reflects the majority culture, perhaps with some outside influences from Japan, China, or the USA. The life-styles of those in the soap operas are probably urban and middle class. All these factors constitute pressures on the local language, traditional culture, and life-style.

Also worthy of mention are modern communication techniques such as facsimile and the world wide web. They are noteworthy because of their speed and accessibility as well as the breadth of information available. Much of what was communicated to the outside world prior to, during, and immediately after the June 4 Incident in Tiananmen Square in 1989 was via fax. The internet plays a role in opposition politics in Indonesia, as the middle-class intelligentsia maintains contact through computers. Moreover, while governments may not like the potential these technologies have for dissent and the organization of that dissent, they are extremely difficult to police short of denying access altogether, which is very problematic.

1.5   Conclusion: tradition and modernization

This chapter has emphasized the enormous variety of family life, religions, life-styles, as well as in the economies and polities of the region. It has also drawn attention to the profound changes which modernizing processes have occasioned, especially industrialization. Modernization can be

Disney's The Lion King *reaches Beijing*

reversible in some ways, but the likelihood is that the processes of
modernization and the profound transformation it brings will continue.
This does not mean that traditions disappear. What is happening is that
tradition and modernity coexist and influence each other. But
modernization creates a far greater impact on tradition than the other
way around. What this means is that in the long term many traditional life-
styles will tend to give way to the modern.

One very important dichotomy is that between the city and the
countryside. It tends to be the most urbanized countries where
modernization has its greatest impact, Japan being the best example.
Within individual countries it tends to be the cities where modernization
takes deepest root and where change is most rapid. Family relationships
have changed far more quickly and drastically in the cities of China than in
its vast countryside.

Sometimes it is quite difficult to determine precisely what is modern
and what is traditional. Forces regarded as being part of a tradition can
modernize themselves very effectively while maintaining a traditional
essence. Although the spread of industry and modern communications
has tended to weaken traditional cultures, they can impact in precisely
the opposite direction to maintain traditional values. Very old religions
show no sign of extinction because of modernization. On the contrary,
religions such as Islam are stronger in the modern world. They retain their
essential traditional beliefs, but that does not prevent their adopting

practices, technologies and ideas which are consistent with the contemporary age.

It is also notable that just at the time when urbanization, which characterizes the industrial age, is spreading and weakening the distinctions between cultures, the notion of national and cultural identity is being reinforced. This is happening all over the world, including in the countries of the Asia-Pacific. It is also very much a factor affecting minority groups within larger states. The result is that the power of identity can re-emphasize or reinvent differences at the same time as modernization tends to spread similar cultural patterns all over the world. This suggests that the stronger traditions are very unlikely to die out. Just as those modernizers who believed that science would render religion irrelevant have been proven wrong, so cultures and cultural identity will prove to be equally resilient.

References

Awanohara, S., Vatikiotis, M. and Islam, S. (1993) 'Vienna showdown', *Far Eastern Economic Review*, vol.156, no.24, pp.16–22.

Crowell, T. and Hsieh, D. (1996) 'People power', *Asiaweek*, vol.22, no.42, pp.28–33.

Eccleston, B., Dawson, M. and McNamara, D. (eds) (1998) *The Asia-Pacific Profile*, London, Routledge in association with The Open University.

Far Eastern Economic Review (1993) 'Managing in Asia, ethics and other issues', vol.156, no.37, pp.33–55.

Fukuyama, F. (1995) *Trust: the Social Virtues and the Creation of Prosperity*, New York, Free Press.

Koran (1995) 5th rev. edn, with a parallel Arabic text, translated with notes by Dawood, N.J., London, Penguin.

Milner, A. and Quilty, M. (eds) (1996) *Australia in Asia, Comparing Cultures*, Oxford, Oxford University Press.

Schwarz, A. (1992) 'Environment, back down to earth, global summit fails to live up to ambitions', *Far Eastern Economic Review*, vol.155, no.25, pp.61–2.

Sen, A. (1996) '50 years of Asian achievement', *Far Eastern Economic Review*, vol.159, no.41, p.46.

Further reading

Bellwood, P. (1978) *Man's Conquest of the Pacific: the Prehistory of Southeast Asia and Oceania*, London, Collins.

Campbell, I.C. (1990) *A History of the Pacific Islands*, St. Lucia, University of Queensland Press.

Evans, G. (ed.) (1993) *Asia's Cultural Mosaic, an Anthropological Introduction*, New York, Prentice Hall.

Harris, M. (1995) *Cultural Anthropology*, 4th edn, New York, HarperCollins.

Henningham, S. (1995) *The Pacific Island States: Security and Sovereignty in the Post-Cold War World*, London, Macmillan.

Hodder, R. (1996) *Merchant Princes of the East, Cultural Delusions, Economic Success and the Overseas Chinese in Southeast Asia*, Chichester, Wiley.

Mackerras, C. (ed.) (1995) *Eastern Asia*, rev. edn, Melbourne, Longman Australia.

Sandhu, K.S. and Mani, A. (eds) (1993) *Indian Communities in Southeast Asia*, Singapore, Times Academic Press and Institute of Southeast Asian Studies.

CHAPTER 2

The old and the new

J. Kathirithamby-Wells

2.1 Introduction: Asia-Pacific integration

The integration of the old and new worlds during the last half-millennium marks a spectacular leap in human history. Nowhere has this process been more complete than in the Asia-Pacific. The current Asia-Pacific era had its antecedents in the expansion of Atlantic commerce and European domination during the post-Columbian era, some four centuries ago. Post-Second World War decolonization brought profound economic changes which helped shift the gravity of industry and commerce from the North Atlantic seaboard, anchored in London, Amsterdam and New York to the western Pacific Rim, centred on Tokyo and Hong Kong. Given the industrial growth of East Asia and Singapore during the last three decades and the natural and human resources of South-East Asia, it is envisaged that the Asia-Pacific will lead global commerce into the twenty-first century.

South-East Asia's natural resources, cheap labour and markets for manufactures which fuelled capitalist formations during the colonial era, have been integral to the 'East Asian Miracle'. Within the framework of these developments, South-East Asia has experienced astonishing growth. Demographic setbacks, under regimes of repression such as in Democratic Kampuchea and East Timor, have been an exception rather than the rule. Natural population increases, arising from hugely reduced mortality through improved health and medical services, have received an added boost through government policy, in some instances. Malaysia, for example, has set high population targets in the interests of boosting labour services for industry and for engineering politically desirable ethnic ratios. The exigencies of food, energy, land and urban accommodation for the fast expanding populations pose formidable problems in the region. They increase latent ethnic and religious tensions. They put additional strains on an environment, already affected by extractive industries, like timber logging, mining and marine fishing, and the construction of mega hydro-electric dams to support the exponential growth of local industries. These problems are compounded by the crisis of modernization which threatens cultural and institutional traditions which are an essential heritage of the region.

This chapter will trace some of the processes of change brought by the region's interaction with the West over almost half a millennium, exploring the extent to which past traditions and experiences have impacted on the present.

2.2 The pre-modern era *c.* 1500–1800

The galleon trade

In contrast to the Atlantic explorations in search of new land and places for migration, the voyages of the Pacific were motivated by the quest for trade aimed at the acquisition of gold and spices. Following the discovery of the New World by Christopher Columbus in 1492, Ferdinand Magellan pressed further west to discover the Pacific route to the Philippines and the Spice Islands. When the Spanish occupied the Philippines in 1570, the capital, Manila, became the terminus for the west–east galleon trade centred on the Mexican port of Acapulco. From the European perspective of the world economy, for which the Americas became the *periphery,* Asia remained an *external arena* beyond the Pacific. In reality, however, the vast amounts of Mexican silver injected into the Asia-Pacific region by the galleon trade, in excess of an average of seventeen tons per annum, initiated a commercial revolution which gained momentum over the next half millennium (Barrett, 1990, p.248). The increased circulation of currency and the European demand for goods triggered rapid monetization and a commercial boom, with extended market networks and expanded production.

Agricultural revolution

The galleon trade came to an end during the early nineteenth century, but its role in the transference of cultivars from the New World to the western Pacific Rim had a revolutionary impact on agriculture and augured a dynamic era of socio-economic change. In South-East Asia, in addition to cassava and maize introduced by the Portuguese, sweet potato which found its way by the Pacific route, added to the mix of crops planted in forest clearings by shifting cultivators who ideally accommodated non-intensive cash cropping to subsistence cultivation and collection of forest produce. Gradually, as cash-cropping for luxuries gave way in the Indonesia Archipelago to state-managed monocultivation of pepper, the finer spices and tobacco (the last introduced from the New World), crops of maize, cassava and sweet potato helped sustain populations earning insufficient returns from cultivating commercial crops to purchase imported rice. It also helped tide over drought, famine and periods of social and political instability. Maize, cassava and sweet potatoes which were suited to poor agricultural conditions and rudimentary cultivation, would appear to have also improved the life-style and boosted the population of less advanced tribal communities. Among the Hmong, Kachin and Wu of mainland South-East Asia, for example, it allowed movement to higher elevations. By strengthening the subsistence base of upland communities, New World starch staples permitted the cultivation of cash crops, ranging from poppy at high latitudes, aromatic benzoin (*Styrax spp.*) and cinnamon at the intermediate levels, and pepper and New World tobacco on the lower slopes. Widely consumed throughout the southern Pacific Rim tobacco, like salt, expanded internal markets of exchange, multiplying the points of contact between coast and interior communities.

In China, enterprising Hokkiens trading with the Philippines introduced New World crops like sweet potato, maize and groundnuts which transformed subsistence agriculture in the commercial hub of South China. These crops were soon cultivated in areas unsuited edaphically and altitudinally for paddies and helped supplement rice in local diets. As elsewhere in the Asia-Pacific, new crops such as sweet potato and maize freed up a proportion of land and labour from rice cultivation, for cash crops. In China, cultivators rapidly pushed into the hills, cropping tea for export and sweet potatoes for subsistence.

The age of commerce

The expansion of production both for consumption and export lent new vigour to traditional networks of trade within the Asia-Pacific, expanding the trade in luxuries. Indian cloth and opium found ready sales in South-East Asian bazaars which, in turn, sold a variety of sea and jungle products to cater to Chinese gastronomic and pharmaceutical needs. European capital and ships infused new vigour into Chinese business and indigenous production networks.

The full spectrum of international commercial transaction, incorporating old and new aspects of production and business was represented, for example, in the maritime centre of eighteenth century Jolo (Sulu). Sea cucumbers or bêche-de-mer (*teripang*) and birds' nests collected by Sulu slaves for their masters were sold by Chinese middlemen to European 'country trade' servicing the Canton trade. A parallel trade in deer skins and eaglewood from Thailand and silks from China secured Japanese silver for European merchants to supplement American silver imports for their trade in Asia. New and expanded markets also helped sustain and improve traditional technologies in Indian cloth, Japanese silk and Chinese ceramic production and boat-building. Dutch and English *East Indiamen* carrying Chinese tea found a convenient and profitable ballast in blue and white ceramics produced in Fujian and Guangdong. Some well perfected technologies reached neighbouring regions through migrant communities and trade networks to become indigenized to the production of elegant Vietnamese and Thai ceramics, as well as South-East Asian junks fashioned out of teak in the shipyards of north Java and Bangkok.

The ethics of commerce

Besides lending new vigour to old commercial centres, European participation in the Pacific trade provided the impetus for political integration
and state formation in the trading world of South-East Asia. Commercial
power became a potent source of wealth. As international trade expanded,
the respectability of commerce became everywhere evident. In South-East
Asia, the rulers of maritime areas commonly functioned as merchants while
port administrators combined official functions with trade. In the
Theravada Buddhist Thailand profits from trade were invested, in part, in
earning merit points (*sakdina*) through temple endowments and acts of
charity and facilitated the social integration of wealthy Chinese merchants.
In island South-East Asia the ubiquitous Muslim trader who acted also as a
messenger of the Prophet, was accorded a high place in local society while
the learned among them often graced the courts of indigenous rulers.

In China where merchants had stood low in the old social order,
society's perceptions of merchants and their trading activities rapidly
changed. The commercial elite made efforts to reconcile profit seeking with
righteousness and service to society. They channelled some of the new
wealth to philanthropy and community service in compliance with the
'Confucian moral imperative of paternalistic social responsibility'. In China
during the Qing dynasty (1644–1911), foreign trade previously constrained
by official tributary trade, was endorsed through the appointment in
Guangzhou (Canton) of the *hong* merchants as the official brokers. After
1842 there was further accommodation to foreign trade and the *hong* were
fast replaced by compradors or Chinese contractual employees of foreign
trading firms. Men of status and education, they combined the roles of
cultural brokers and business agents, some of whom rose to be
entrepreneurs in their own right at the treaty ports.

In Japan, under the Tokugawa, the samurai who were unable to sustain
themselves as a warrior class, turned to trade, upgrading the status of the
merchant in the process. The Japanese thinker, Ishida Baigan, who
preached enlightenment at the turn of the seventeenth century and was
himself a merchant by profession, considered the samurai as bringing to
the *chonin* (the townsmen or business community) the virtues of the
warrior (*bushido*), namely, honesty, diligence and economy. At the same
time, economic rationalism, enshrined in the concept of *shimatsu*,
contributed to the development of a high level of accounting and business
skills, including double-entry bookkeeping and a complex credit system for
the rice trade. A rice exchange was in operation in Osaka in 1730, well
before the founding of the London stock exchange.

Throughout East Asia, lineage and the family provided the basic
structure for business with the positive features of facilitating capital
raising, maximizing trust and loyalty and providing long-term planning
over the generations. These institutional features of East Asian business
were replicated within the network of Chinese diasporas in South-East Asia,
integral to the functioning of the local economies. In Japan, modern
economic development has been attributed to the family enterprise, the

zaibatsu, despite US attempts after the Pacific War to reduce their influence. In Taiwan, an estimated 97 per cent of business firms today are family based.

2.3 The colonial era, *c.* 1800–1945

Socio-economic transformation

East Asia's receptiveness to trade facilitated the inroads of European capitalism and colonialism. In China, by the 1830s tea exports reached a record 100 million pounds as against some 5,300 pounds of the more valuable opium imports (Fairbank, 1989, pp.273, 286). Imperial China proved unable to draw its merchants and lower officials away from the illicit trade in opium imported by Europeans. Imperial commerce at the key positions of Manila, Batavia (the present Jakarta), Hong Kong and Singapore became the refuge for Asian entrepreneurs and China's surplus population seeking new opportunities. New plantation crops in the form of South American tobacco and rubber and Arabian coffee provided the foundations for the colonial economy in the region, superseding the traditional trade in luxury produce (see Table 2.1). Indigenous rulers, where they continued to exist, exchanged effective power for titular status. Ruling elites were absorbed into colonial bureaucracies, trading social influence and material perks for fixed salaries, within defined, stable and legally constituted, rather than competing hierarchies. Functioning as indispensable agents of colonial governments, they formed a vital link between new colonial administrations superimposed on old village structures such as the *barangay* in the Philippines, the *desa* in Java and the *kampung* in the maritime Malay world.

The peasantry, though assured of greater political stability under Western regimes, was less able to wield 'the weapons of the weak' in the form of social protest, rebellion and flight. Traditional elite-turned colonial-officials, whose status under the old regimes was underpinned by personal influence and public accountability, were compromised by colonial patronage. They helped convert traditional tribute payments, the collection of which had been subject to political and economic fluctuations, to a system of regulated taxation. In early nineteenth-century Java, about 70 per cent of peasant labour was involved in the Dutch cultivation system in which tax was computed in export crops, largely sugar and coffee. In Vietnam, in addition to the traditional land rent, the colonial regime added new tax burdens on basic items of consumption such as rice, wine and salt, aggravating peasant discontent. Increased populations brought a huge pressure on land, particularly in the Red River (Song-koi) Delta. The impressive export figures for rice realized under the colonial economic regime in no way suggested sufficiency at home, or a remission in peasant tax burdens.

Table 2.1 *South-East Asian primary production, 1937–40 (metric tons)*

	British Malaya and Borneo	Burma	French Indo-China	Nether-lands East Indies	Philippines	Thailand	Total	% of world production
Abaca	1.2	–	–	–	183.0	–	184.2	95.6
Cassava	–	–	–	7,759.0	–	–	7,759.0	80.0
Cinchona	–	–	–	10.4	–	–	10.4	80.0
Coffee/ Copra	–	–	1.5	62.4	3.0	–	66.9	7.0
Coconut products	116.0	–	10.0	506.0	54.0	–	686.0	73.0
Kapok	–	–	–	20.0	–	–	20.0	70.0[1]
Maize	–	–	565.0	2,037.0	427.0	7.0	3,036.0	80.0
Palm oil	46.0	–	–	238.0	–	–	238.0	47.6
Pepper	–	–	–	20.0	–	–	20.0	70.01
Petroleum	1,000.0	1,000.0	–	7,400.0	–	–	9,400.0	4.5
Rice	324.0	4,940.0	3,945.0	4,007.0	2,179.0	1,771.0	17,165.0	98.0[1]
Rubber	501.0	8.0	61.0	432.0	–	38.0	1,040.0	85.2
Sugar	–	39.0	43.0	547.0	1,076.0	19.09	1,724.0	21.01
Tea	–	–	0.7	67.0	–	–	67.7	17.0[1]
Teak[2]	–	475.0	–	400.0	–	189.0	1,064.0	95.0
Tin	77.0	2.0	1.6	40.0	–	13.4	134.0	65.0

[1] Percentage of world exports.

[2] Cubic metres.

Source: Tate (1979, p.25)

Less visible but substantial revenues were extracted by colonial governments with a large wage-earning labour force, such as in Peninsular Malaya and Indonesia, from gambling and opium farms. These institutions which had been previously the monopoly of rulers, were reorganized and licensed to Chinese bidders. In Peninsular Malaya, where just 20 years following British intervention in 1874 some 55 per cent of the world's tin was produced, the mines became a lucrative source of tax on leisure and consumption. Tin mining operators, keen on recovering some of the capital invested in wages, were the main licensees for the collection of tax on opium and gambling, linked to prostitution. It is calculated that during the early phase of British administration these revenue farms, as well as those for alcohol and pawnbroking, provided a third of the finances for building roads and railways to service the tin and rubber industries.

In Thailand, Buddhism bridged the cultural divide between the Thais and Chinese, allowing for gradual integration. In contrast, Chinese economic dominance in Peninsular Malaya introduced an economic cleavage which exacerbated the religious gulf between them and the autochthonous Muslim population. The Malay peasantry was, in fact, encouraged by the British to produce rice for the needs of an expanding Chinese labour force engaged in the export industries, but did not hesitate to pursue other economic options. Malay indigenes were little inclined to work in European-owned rubber plantations, manned largely by Indian indentured labour. Nevertheless, carrying forward an earlier tradition of raising pepper for export alongside slash-and-burn cultivation, they successfully cultivated South American rubber as a cash crop alongside growing subsistence rice. Peasants adopted a similar mix of activity in east and south Sumatra, improving their incomes substantially over immigrant Javanese engaged solely in good production. Rubber trees were tapped endemically in tune with cycles of maturing and price fluctuations. Profits they earned, particularly in the post-First World War boom, helped improve living standards through investment in food, clothing, bicycles and sewing machines. Despite the widespread cultivation of rubber by the Malays there was no government effort to encourage investment in the related processing industry which was monopolized by Chinese. Instead, the Malay rubber smallholder was regarded as a competitor to the European plantation investor and, in the face of the price slump, the Stevenson Restriction Scheme was introduced in 1922 to help curb smallholder rubber enterprise.

Merchant capitalism

Despite the widening gaps of ethnicity and the social ills bred by colonialism and capitalism which in specific instances resulted in social collapse, the economy of the region expanded by leaps and bounds from the early twentieth century to the onset of the Great Depression in the 1930s. With the previously unsettled delta areas of the Mekong, Menam and Irrawaddy drained, settled and planted, South-East Asia produced about 70 per cent or more of the world's rice exports, while Malaya and Indonesia jointly produced about 75 per cent of the world's rubber consumption (Steinberg et al., 1987, p.230).

Throughout the region the new cash economy lubricated internal market networks; but the simultaneous loosening of patrimonial bonds brought other social ills. Liberated from slavery and clientage, many found themselves cast out to the bondage of Chinese tax farmers in the Spanish Philippines and Dutch Indonesia. Surplus populations, resulting from a combination of factors such as the introduction of smallpox inoculation and the termination of wars under colonial rule, increased pressure on scarce agricultural land in Java. Hundreds were forced into indentured labour under dismal conditions in the European tobacco plantations of east Sumatra. In central Burma, land hunger forced migrant populations to the plains of the Irrawaddy following the British annexation of the country in 1852. Here, in addition to the rigours of land reclamation, the ravages of malaria and disease to plough animals and crops, smallholder peasants fell victims to Chattier money lenders. Land and produce pledged as security for agricultural credit advances threw them into spiralling poverty and, as often as not, left them dispossessed and eking out a subsistence as tenant farmers. The burden of colonial taxation had its parallel in independent Thailand in the form of feudal corvée of forced labour obligations.

The Chinese, in contrast to the indigenous peasantry, put their unfettered labour and freedom of movement to wage earning within the dynamic environment of nineteenth century urban growth. Free of the wider social obligations of the indigenous peasant communities, Chinese *kongsis*, were essentially clan and family-based work forces with the common objective of wage earning and capital accumulation. Apart from investing profits in trading, shipping and retailing, they established a lead in applying simple technologies for tin mining, rice and sugar milling tapioca and timber processing. The increased volume of export produce soon warranted their adoption of improved technologies through the adoption of Western machinery for agro-industries. Private European capital investment became as dependent on Chinese enterprise as colonial regimes on Chinese services and industries. The latter-day corporate giants in East Asia, such as Jardine Matheson, Guthries and Fraser and Neave had their origins in merchant houses with their financial capitals in Singapore, Hong Kong and Canton (Guangzhou). The thrust of US capital investment, westwards to the Pacific Rim was particularly evident in the Philippines. Together with the British, they forged links with Chinese mestizo merchants and retailers whom they furnished with capital and merchandise, especially textiles and machinery, siphoning off sugar, abaca (Manila hemp), coffee and tobacco for overseas markets.

The liberal economy which backed European merchant capitalism was based on the bed-rock of expanding production and consumption to which indigenous societies proved increasingly responsive. Released from the constraints of old political and social orders, values began to rapidly change. As one writer put it, 'The concomitant values propelling growth were the newer ones of individualism and acquisitiveness rather than the old customary obligation' (Elson, 1992, p.142). Colonial regimes espousing *laissez faire* policies offered expanding opportunity for enterprise in the way of land tenure, irrigation, flood control and transport infrastructure. In Cochin China the French undertook monumental earthworks laying, by the turn of the century, more than 1,300 kilometres of canals in the Mekong delta which doubled rice acreage. Indebtedness amongst peasantry was often the result of higher expectancy in standards of living. Imports of cotton goods, an all-time index of prosperity in South-East Asia, grew six-fold in Burma between 1873 and 1914. Sugar, with its high cost of machinery, became the leading industry in Java, where exports rose to 3 million tons by 1930. In Negros and Central Luzon (Philippines) the industry experienced steady growth under a sizeable export quota in the protected high-price US market. Reflecting the dynamic economic change in South-East Asia was the spectacular leap in population, from an estimated 55 million in 1870 to 145 million in 1940. There was a proportionate rise in urban growth. During the first three decades of this century, the 3–4 per cent urban growth in Bangkok and Rangoon, and more than 5 per cent in Batavia (Jakarta) and Bandung, was outstripped by the sharp rise in urbanization in the Philippines from 12.6 to 21.6 per cent between 1918 and 1939 (Elson, 1992, p.169).

Reform and modernization

The all-pervading influence of commercial growth in the maritime regions of the Pacific affected independent as much as colonial regimes. Awareness of the external world brought by commercialization proved the hand-maiden to self-awareness and the search for national identity. In the Malay-Indonesian world these trends were reinforced by increased contacts with Arabia resulting from Singapore's spectacular growth, steamship navigation and the availability of cash, particularly amongst the trading communities. Soon, local Muslim communities found themselves under the influence of the powerful reformist Wahabi movement. In Java, the movement for reform fed on peasant unrest and culminated in the Java War (1825–30), waged as a *jihad* (holy war), both against the Dutch and the *murtad* or apostate Javanese. In Sumatra an active trade had grown in the export of coffee and gambir (extracted from the bark of *Uncaria gambir*) from the Minangkabau interior and pepper from the north and east coasts to Singapore and Penang. Here again, Wahabi influence, through commercial networks, spread the belief amongst religious elite that increased wealth brought moral corruption. The Acehnese poem, the *Hikayat Ranto*, lamented the loss of Islamic values amongst the pepper growers of north Sumatra (Drewes, 1980, p.15).

> Though engaged in trade many pious people practise usury.
> They traffic in opium and in money, so that they always make a profit.
> Though having a security in hand, they take interest, and this is usury, my brother.
> They cut off a part of the opium they already weighed out, and this is a great sin.

Islamic reform in central Sumatra coalesced in the Padri orthodoxy, advocating the eradication of gambling, cockfighting and the consumption of alcohol, opium and betel nut and tobacco. A long, drawn out conflict with the Dutch (1821–38) led to the imposition of colonial control but, ironically demonstrated to Dutch authorities the futility of shoring up against free trade and commercialization. Besides the ships of freebooters and English country captains, US vessels engaged in the Pacific run contributed significantly to pushing free trade in the region. By making higher bids for produce at independent ports, Americans successfully undermined the Dutch commercial monopolies. In fact, during the course of the nineteenth century, the USA emerged as the principal nation trading in Sumatra, exporting a vast array of tropical products. These included plantation pepper, tobacco and the tanning agent, gambir, as well as forest products such as bamboo, patchouli (*Pogostemon cablin*) for perfumery and the dye, dragon's blood (from *Dracaena draco*).

The Dutch for their part, finding themselves unable to hem the expanding tide of free trade and internal discontent, finally yielded to a more liberal economic policy under the rubric of the Ethical Policy (1870–1919), which included a welfare programme. Apart from boosting the economy with the revenue which doubled between 1899 and 1912, the Ethical Policy sowed the seeds of national integration by introducing Dutch education for the elite *priyayi* or official class and founding the Steamship Navigation Company (*KNP*) which brought the far flung islands of the East Indies closer than ever before.

The onrush of commerce and business in the region induced the independent regimes of South-East Asia to initiate their own programme of economic and ideological reforms. In Thailand, the urgency for reform was felt particularly after the Burney (1826) and Bowring (1855) treaties with the British which threatened the institutional foundations of monopoly privileges on which the economy of Thailand rested. These changes were, however, anticipated by internal economic reforms and strengthened regional trade with China. Thailand's encouragement of Chinese enterprise brought the production of tin, pepper, sugar and gambir for the Chinese market boosting, at the same time, the traditional exports of eaglewood, beeswax, rhinoceros horn and cardamom. Reclamation of marshland in the Menam Chao Phraya Delta, using Chinese wage labour, further resulted in a sharp rise in rice acreage with exports to China to meet the needs of a rising population. Bangkok's new line of trade with Singapore proved equally important, particularly for the supply of Western arms. Expanding trade was backed by the extension of canals which served the dual purpose of communication and drainage. A Thai merchant fleet with square-rigged vessels gradually replaced Chinese junks. A fundamental economic reform was the loosening of clientage. Reduced corvée obligations, with the option for settlement in specie or produce, finally freed Thais from economic bondage, allowing them the opportunity to engage in free enterprise. This and the abolition of royal monopolies by the mid nineteenth century gave Thailand the semblance of a modern state.

Thailand's economic reforms were matched by intellectual reorientation. The move was initiated by Prince Mongkut, during the reign of King Rama III (1824–51), through a programme of religious reformation for resorting of Buddhism to its universalism. 'The subtle mental revolution' was aimed at preparing the ground for Thais to open their minds to Western scientific knowledge and rationalism without sacrificing their own culture and tradition. Investigation into Western religion and science, involving dialectical exchanges with Westerners as recorded in the first Siamese printed book, the *Kitchnukit* (*The Book Explaining Various Things*), constituted an integral part of the reform programme.

Comparable efforts at reform were attempted in Burma by King Mindon Min (1853–78). He encouraged Western learning and technological innovation with the introduction of river-steamers, gun boats and telegraph lines. He had less success with modernization than the rulers of Thailand as he failed to make any fundamental change in Buddhist mentality and was unable to come to grips with marrying the old and new in the political economy of Burma.

In Vietnam, progress towards change and modernization stemmed from the desire for liberation from Chinese influence and the search for a national identity. The ineffectiveness and decadence of seigniorial rule, combined with a corrupt bureaucracy within which mandarins purchased offices, fostered a new spirit of questioning and revaluation of traditional Confucianist values. Significantly, anti-mandarin elements coalesced in the central location at Tayson which serviced the important areca nut trade between the coast and interior. The movement was led by three brothers, the eldest of whom was himself engaged in the trade. The Tayson who took control of the south in 1778 initiated an important period of reform aimed at the liberation of commerce and industry. To facilitate trade, a unified currency system was introduced.

Symptomatic of the increased circulation of cash was the growth of wage labour in the main commercial centres of Hanoi, Fai-fo (Quang Nam), Binh Hoa and Saigon, well in advance of parallel developments in Thailand and Burma. Mining was activated and shipyards, military workshops, paper and printing-works established. These developments, in combination with tax reforms and the liberation of maritime trade with China, made the 35 year regime of the Tayson an era of important commercial growth which saw the emergence of a pre-capitalist merchant community. These advances were lost during the succeeding Nguyen dynasty. The aristocratic and the bureaucratic classes were reinstated and the royal monopolies over mines and the export of forest produce and silk and bronze manufactures was restored. A close control was also imposed over guilds and artisans. Apart from the break in commercial development, the mounting problem of landlessness created agrarian unrest. The ruling Nguyen dynasty tried to contend with the problem by merely strengthening its military capacity. But it failed in its attempts to fashion steamships, fortifications and the army after the Western model, exposing the unadaptability of the Confucianist tradition of education to new needs and challenges in Vietnam. As Nguyen Truong To, the Catholic priest from Nghe-an, observed in the 1860s:

> Look at Japan and Korea ... If instead of directing our efforts and time to polishing our style or to embellishing our calligraphy, we were to study current affairs – battle plans, for example, or the methods of building citadels and firing cannons – we should probably be in a position to resist our enemy.
>
> (Hodgkin, 1981, p.120)

Search for identity and self-determination

Growth, heavily dependant on commodity export and vulnerability to market trends, exposed the South-East Asia region to the worst effects of the Great Depression, with a drastic fall both in the quantity and value of exports. The crippling of trade meant that large numbers previously engaged in the hard-hit rubber and tin industries in Peninsular Malaya took to food growing, clearing extensive areas of primary forest in the process. In Cochin China the price of rice in 1934 was approximately a seventh the price five years earlier. Under the increased burden of the Depression, old grievances surfaced as revolts and rebellions, inspired by a longing for a return to an ideal past. In Sarawak, hit by the falling price of forest produce, the Dayak leader, Asun, organized resistance against restrictions on free access to the woods imposed by the Brooke administration. Hsaya San, a former Buddhist monk and leader of the south Burmese revolt in 1930, defended the sanctity of traditional life as it related to the forest where he established his 'capital' and championed the cause of the peasantry through the *wuntnanu athin* or own race societies fostered in the villages by the General Council of Burmese Associations. A splinter organization of the Young Men's Organization and representing the younger and more activist majority, it was representative of nascent political organizations throughout South-East Asia which presaged the new era of nationalism. In Indonesia as well, religious scholarship, in the form of Islamic Reform organizations linked to the middle East, championed indigenous interests before the emergence of a new generation of Western educated elite. The latter, raised in Dutch Native Schools, swelled in numbers from 20,000 in 1915 to 445,000 by 1940 (Steinberg *et al.*, 1987, p.303).

Like the Dutch educated Sukarno who founded the Indonesian Nationalist Party in 1927, young nationalists and reformers throughout Asia imbibed ideas for reform and national liberation through Western education. Vajiravudh (ruled 1910–25), the Thai ruler who advocated cultural nationalism, was Oxford educated and a prolific writer who translated Shakespeare and Molière. Malaysia's first Prime Minister, Tengku Abdul Rahman, read law at Cambridge. Vietnam's nationalist leader, Ho Chi Minh, trained in the Chinese Whampoa Military Academy, and was widely travelled. France and Moscow had a profound influence on the ideology he shaped for Vietnam.

Expanding US interest in the Pacific, in tandem with Christian missionary activity, was a major factor in the spread of Western education, particularly in East Asia which, in turn, influenced intellectual ferment in South-East Asia. With the fast pace of industrialization at home, the USA saw opportunity for marketing cheap manufactures in the western Pacific rim as well as entering the Western scramble for a slice of the Chinese commercial melon. The foundation for Western education in China was laid largely by Protestant missionaries, about half of whom were Americans. The USA invested part of its share of the 1908 Boxer indemnity to China in founding the Qinghua (Tsing Hua) College in Beijing. Soon, a steady stream of Chinese students on scholarship went to America where their numbers totalled some 5,500 between 1921 and 1940. Trained largely in the sciences and business economics, they came to form the non-revolutionary wing of the Chinese intelligentsia. Many of them made significant contributions to science. With Rockefeller support, they opened the doors to new discoveries, including Peking man (an early human species) and the ancient Shang capital of Anyang. Typical was James Yen, a graduate of Yale and a member of the YMCA, who launched his Mass Education Movement to solve the problems of the peasantry through elementary education and agricultural science. Chiang Kai-shek himself used YMCA methods for his New Life Movement (1934–37) aimed at China's regeneration through reviving the ancient virtues of righteousness and integrity (Fairbank, 1989, pp.460–2). In the case of Korea, American influence was received indirectly via its imprint on the Japanese model which Korean reformers aspired to emulate.

Ironically, as nationalism gained pace in Asia with the aim of casting off Western imperialism, Russian expansion into the western Pacific Rim, with the extension of the railway to Vladivostok, saw a counterpart American thrust into the western Pacific Rim. Resulting from the war with Cuba, US occupation of Hawaii, Guam and Manila had not only strategic but also profound cultural implications. In the Philippines (1901–41), the USA launched an educational programme more comprehensive than that of any other colonial power. Concerned more directly with increasing production and consumption, the older colonial powers offered limited Western education, largely for training indigenous administrators, while vernacular education was aimed at turning out disciplined citizens. The US government in the Philippines, on the contrary, appreciated the danger of an ignorant mass falling victim to a small and powerful elite leadership. Within the course of the first two years of occupation, the USA brought out more than a thousand teachers with the result that, by 1920, there were nearly a million children receiving English education.

In areas outside the American sphere of political influence in the Asia-Pacific, Christian missionaries played a significant part in extending Western education beyond state-sponsored initiatives. They made a particularly significant contribution towards broadening information in the vernacular by introducing the Roman script, such as the *rumi* for Malay and the *quoc ngu* for Vietnamese. By facilitating printing, the roman script vastly expanded the influence of the vernacular press amongst the masses. Within Muslim communities in Malaya and Indonesia which lay outside the scope of missionary activity, traditional Islamic education emanating from the Middle East and firmly rooted in rural villages, provided a potent alternative for the new political awakening. On the whole, metropolitan tertiary education, whether in Cairo, Tokyo, Lisbon, Amsterdam, Moscow or Cornell were effective eye-openers, paving the way for the growth of nationalism in the region. The example of Western superiority which Japan was rapidly challenging, provided a model for political aspirants committed to the cause of nationhood. By the 1920s Manuel Quezon, at the helm of *ilustrados* (the indigenous educated elite), championed Filipino nationhood. In Burma, the secular nationalist movement of the Young Men's Buddhist Association followed the path of political agitation beginning with the Rangoon University strike in 1921.

In Peninsular Malaya where the indigenous aristocracy formed a significant core of the English educated elite, national sentiments were less rooted in resentment of the British than concern over the fast progress being made by domiciled alien Chinese and Indians, compared to the Malay peasantry. It was considered inappropriate for Chinese to be placed on an equal footing with indigenes in view of their patriotic ties with China and their involvement in the Kuomintang and communist movements. In fact, early Malay nationalism surfaced in the form of a strong move amongst Malay rulers and political leaders to press for government action for curbing Chinese immigration in favour of Muslim Javanese.

Similar anxiety amongst Javenese about their economic status paved the way for Indonesian nationalism. Muslim merchant entrepreneurs in competition with indigenized Chinese (*peranakan*), found common identity in religion and culture. Their views were given political expression through the Budi Utomo, formed in 1908 by Dutch-educated Javanese officials (*priyayi*) and the Syarikat Islam, founded in 1912 by the prominent Surakarta *batik* merchant, Haji Samanhudi. Originating from a growing sense of community, these organizations articulated the search for a Javanese identity, based on secure economic and cultural foundations. They felt Chinese competition to be, at once, a threat and a stimulus. By 1922, however, a small group of students educated in the Netherlands saw fit to launch the *Perhimpunan Indonesia*, or the Indonesian Association, transcending ethnic, class and territorial divisions, to give Indonesian national identity expression for the first time.

In Vietnam, as elsewhere in South-East Asia, nationalism in its early beginnings was an elitist movement which took in peasant concerns without their direct involvement. It was also characterized by the strong attraction to external ideological influences. Japan's triumph in the war with Russia (1894–95) and China (1904–5) and its emergence as a modern state impressed disaffected Vietnamese scholars and students. In the absence of political patronage from Tokyo, however, the Vietnamese revolutionaries were inspired by Chiang Kai-shek's Kuomintang movement. Kuomintang ideology which incorporated adaptations of Leninist Russian doctrines, influenced formulation of the nationalist dogma of the *Quoc dan dang* party, founded in 1927. Communism, both in China and Vietnam, represented another phase of Western influence but provided a catalyst for adapting the old to the new.

2.4   The new era, 1946–

Japanese imperialism and the emergence of new states

Though the Second World War and the Japanese occupation brought profound changes to the Asia-Pacific, long before the event Japanese influence had already set a model for Asian modernization, boosting indigenous political confidence. As far as Japan was concerned industrialization placed it in competition with the Western powers for markets in the region into which, by the 1920s, Japanese business and enterprise was making fast inroads. Japanese retail shop owners, clothes merchants, barbers and photographers filtered into the country towns from the capitals of South-East Asia where Japanese comfort women were a familiar phenomenon. By this time, there was even a Japanese newspaper, the *Java Nippo*, printed in Batavia, and Japanese scientists were already joining their Western counterparts in exploring the region.

The beginning of the war with China in 1937 increased Japan's need for South-East Asian natural resources. The industrial structure was such, that, more than rubber and tin, Japan needed iron, coal, oil, nickel, bauxite and timber. The need for natural resources became an important incentive for promoting, under the banner of 'Asia for Asians', 'The Greater East Asian Co-prosperity Sphere', encompassing East Asia. Increased secularism in the region and the common quest for economic and political liberation provided fertile ground for Japanese anti-Western propaganda such as amongst the early Burmese nationalists led by Aung San who received Japan sponsored military training in Hainan with the aim of overthrowing British rule. Whatever Japan's ulterior motives, it evoked for the first time a sense of regional and cultural identity, transcending ethnic and religious barriers.

As it turned out, the Japanese regime in South-East Asia (1942–45) proved economically a disaster with the dislocation of the export economy on which the region was totally dependent. Politically, too, it fell seriously short of the high hopes the Japanese had raised amongst indigenous leaders. Curiously, however, the enormous hardships experienced and the cruelties suffered, particularly by the Chinese, at the hands of the Japanese military, taught South-East Asians an important lesson in self-reliance. The spell of external power and protectionism, built through a prolonged era of colonialism, was finally broken. Japanese efforts to win local confidence resulted also in their patronage of nascent nationalism, allowing local leaders to gain political experience and form armies. On the part of the masses, thousands previously engaged in export industries which collapsed under the Japanese had to live by their wits. Subsistence food-growing became the norm, combined with a variety of other means for earning a livelihood which included petty trade, black marketeering and serving as Japanese informants. In the case of Peninsular Malaya, hundreds of Chinese went underground to join the communist guerrilla movement (MPAJA).

An important outcome of the Japanese Occupation was the fact that their anti-Chinese policy allowed indigenous communities, hitherto marginalized by Chinese competition, a breathing space for business initiatives. A large number of Malays, for example, quit salaried occupations to try their hand at business. Moreover, Japanese business which followed hard on the trail of the Japanese army for tapping local resources, such as timber, introduced a new business ethos, linking private and public interest, which post-war independent regimes in South-East Asia later adopted as a norm. The concept of *jinmyaku* (literally 'veins of humanity') or networks of personal ties which the Japanese introduced into the Co-prosperity Sphere during the Second World War, and used in the post-war period for business lobbying, has been reciprocated in modern business organizations within newly independent regimes (Hatch and Yamamura, 1996, pp.132–3). It had a particular appeal for them in that it allowed the traditional linkage between the ruler and commerce to be carried forward into modern business organization.

Old and new in the post-war era

Japanese influence while serving as an important catalyst for the post-war transformation of the region, did not push out earlier influences and cultural traditions which had helped shape the identity of the new nation-states. The diversity of peoples and their way of life are neatly integrated into the political economy of the South-East Asian states, characterized by their widespread market networks and international trade. Though Western colonial regimes, engaged in intensifying production, found it imperative to firm-up boundaries through territorial integration and administrative centralization, they left intact the efficient functioning of existing hierarchies and structures of production related to class and ethnicity. It is the restructuring of society within the framework of new concepts of state and nation, along the lines of modern socio-economic development, that continues to offer modern leaders the greatest challenge.

Ethnic and cultural diversity is not a modern phenomenon, given the commercial orientation of the region. Competition for political and resource control between adjoining tribal communities such as the Shan and Mon, Vietnamese and Khmer, Filipino and Moro, has been a constant theme in South-East Asia's past. However, these conflicts and cultural differences continue to remain, despite the incorporation of vertical divisions of language and ethnicity within the economic class stratification of the modern era.

In contrast to the rural areas which have been generally the preserve of the indigenous people, the urban areas of South-East Asia were the domain of alien communities. This neat structuring of the political economy was gradually eroded, in the Philippines and Burma/Myanmar for example, by the penetration into the rural economy of merchant and capitalist enterprise. At the same time, disinheritance of land, population expansion and the search for new opportunities and wage labour have, in recent decades especially, accelerated the process of urbanization. Concepts of democracy, citizenship and nationhood have compounded the problem of class and ethnic conflicts, with minority and marginal communities and alien domiciles (especially the ubiquitous Chinese), no longer contented to remain on the peripheries of political life. The concept of linguistic and cultural homogeneity consistent with Western ideas of nationhood raises a particularly serious problem in a region where diversity has been synonymous with identity. Given these complicated problems, the new nations of South-East Asia have been quick to tailor Western political ideologies, whether democratic, socialist or communist, to their domestic political agendas.

A popular comment on contemporary South-East Asia is the pervasiveness of authoritarian rule whether in monarchical Brunei, republican Singapore, communist Vietnam or military Burma/Myanmar. In contrast Laos and Cambodia, which emerged as new nation-states, were unable to establish centralized authoritarian rule and have proved the least stable. Leaders in South-East Asia have consistently defended maximum government, marital law, press censorship and even detention without trial as necessary tools for maintaining political stability and generating the necessary climate for social reform and economic growth. The effectiveness of such rule is guaranteed throughout the region by means of concentrating power within an elite group, synonymous with the plutocracy in the Philippines, the Malay aristocracy and bureaucracy in Malaysia, the army in Burma/Myanmar and Indonesia and communist party leadership in Vietnam. These linkages between the ruling group and the elite, bound by patron–client networks were renovations of the traditional order. In Cambodia, Prince Sihanouk exploited the prestige of the monarchy for political reform towards introducing popular government. The *Sangkum Reastre Niyum* (Popular Socialist Community) he founded in 1955 was synonymous with his charismatic personality. Family and kinship ties, important in the pre-modern era, were strengthened by education, status and wealth which permeated politics and extended into the bureaucracy and the army in Laos and Malaysia.

Family influence in politics, strong in the Philippines and in Indonesia, was reinforced by business ties. It struck a common cord with the East Asian business culture, realizing the earlier Japanese aim of a Pacific Co-prosperity Sphere. Commercial monopolies, controlled by rulers and chiefs during the pre-modern era, were translated into privileged licences for investment and industry, enjoyed by the ruling elite and their families. In oil-rich Brunei, the Consolidated Fund provided in the 1954 constitution was abolished after the aborted coup of 1962, making the finances and reserves of the country virtually the personal wealth of the Sultan. In the Philippines, public funds lined the pockets of Ferdinand Marcos and his political cronies. The business success of the Suharto family's Cendana holdings which has operated with the advantage of tax privileges, is common knowledge. Those at the helm of power, in turn, diverted some of these privileges to the army, the bureaucracy and technocracy to purchase loyalty. The tradition of group privileges known in traditional society was given wider interpretation within the context of Malay dominance in the form of capital grants, trade concessions and special access to education and the administrative service for *bumiputra* (the indigenous people). Party membership, election campaigns and voting are related less to political ideology as personal ties and loyalties. Parties in the Philippines, for instance, are described by one author as 'fiefdoms allied together'. Even in communist Vietnam, these features had their parallel in party leadership and loyalty. Modern democratic processes, based on vote-winning by parties through competitive social agendas, has been downplayed by South-East Asian authoritarian regimes in favour of culture-specific national ideologies for securing the loyalty of the masses. Sukarno's *Pancasila*, embodying the concept of 'unity in diversity', has proved the overarching force of unity in the face of changing political fortunes and social crisis. In Burma, Aung San's idealism for a plural society could not be reconciled with Buddhist dominance but shared some common ground with the equity of mankind enshrined in the Buddhist socialism founded by U Nu and, later, capitalized by the military. The trinity of 'nation, religion and king' has been embodied in the constitutions both of Thailand and Malaysia. In secular Singapore the prosaic ideology of a 'clean society' has served equally well.

In appealing to the nation as a wider 'family' all of these ideologies drew on Asian values of kinship and patrimonial leadership. Tengku Abdul Rahman, Malaysia's first Prime-Minister and a prince to boot, was widely referred to as *Bapa* (Father of) Malaysia. Though the 1932 revolution removed the Thai monarchy from a direct role in politics, traditional ceremonies linking the monarchy and Buddhism with the popular masses were revived in the 1950s by Field Marshal Sarit Thanarat. In Malaysia, the constitutional monarch who continues to wear the traditional honorific: *Paduka Seri Baginda*, literally, 'Under the Foot of the Fortunate One', enjoys the same sacred status as the Emperor in pre-war Japan whose genealogy, believed to derive from the Sun Goddess, was faithfully memorized by school children. Reminiscent of pre-modern political processes, compromise is widely sought in Thailand and Malaysia as a preferred alternative to confrontation between competing power groups, with the monarchy serving as a neutral reference point for maintaining national unity. The modern media, particularly television, is recognized as an essential accoutrement of information and modernization and, as such, is controlled by South-East Asian governments for the purpose of widening the base of traditionally rooted concepts of power and charisma. These influences are widely manifested in ceremony and ritual, embellished in modern times by new wealth.

Carrying over the pre-modern tradition of state monopolies enjoyed by merchant rulers and elite, South-East Asian states have also been drawn inexorably to a policy of state intervention and central planning for the economy. State corporations have been created for the development of utilities, energy and industry and include Malaysia's Federal Land Development Authority, PERNAS (State Trading Company), Indonesia's Pertamina (state oil corporation) and the Philippine Sugar Commission (Philcoa). Strongly linked to government political agendas, the state corporations are yet another manifestation of South-East Asia's politics of commerce. Government economic initiatives have vastly assisted growth as demonstrated in the case of Malaysia. The Prime Minister, Mahathir bin Mohamad's 'look East policy' and direct appeal to Japanese industrialists led to the establishment of Matsushita's first factory in 1972. It was quickly followed by a series of similar investments, supported by easy rapport and, in some cases at least, direct and personal channels of communication with the government.

Though central planning has facilitated funding and aid for development, government entrenchment in trade has been shown to be double-edged such as in the arms-for-aid scandal relating to the UK's Overseas Development Administration (ODA) funding for Malaysia's Pergau Dam project in Kelantan during the Thatcher government. One is reminded here of a bygone era when beleaguered rulers in island South-East Asia made desperate appeals to British monarchs, beginning from the time of Queen

Elizabeth I, for assistance with arms and ammunition in return for commercial privileges. Though considerations of self-preservation previously curbed the sale of Western arms to indigenous rulers, lesser restraint has been exercised in the post-war era of new nation-states, with the consequent escalation of conflict and guerrilla warfare generic to the region.

The role of women

The integration of old and new has been evident, not least, in the important role played by women in the making of modern South-East Asia. South-East Asian women, though not accorded equal status with men, have enjoyed a greater socio-economic freedom than women in other East Asian countries. Mobility, derived from habits of slash-and-burn shifting agriculture and widespread trade and peddling, contributed to the active role played by women outside the home, complementing the activities of men. While men felled trees and cleared, drained and irrigated the land, interspersed by periods away from the village to take up wage labour, women cultivated crops, producing sufficient for substance and bringing the surplus to the market. Here they used their skills at controlling domestic budgets for commercial speculations. The withholding of produce to push up market prices was often a decision made by women. Women are also known to have effectively registered their protest against the high price of imported cloth by reviving their skills at weaving.

A young woman student, in traditional dress, parks her moped outside the Gadjah Mada university in Jakarta

Though excluded from religious office, they were popular spiritual intermediaries in the village and household. In the face of political crisis women, Buddhist and Muslim, were trusted as power holders and guardians of peace. Queen mothers invariably took over as *de facto* rulers who protected the thrones of minors. Women serviced not only harems but also the royal bodyguard. Those of wealth and nobility, with access to capital and influence, were often entrepreneurs in their own right and complemented the role of female peddlers, ubiquitous in the market place. In the course of business both interacted with foreigners, conducting transactions and serving as money changers with consummate mathematical and linguistic skills.

Under European economic domination, modern taxation and reliance on manufactured imports brought women increasingly into wage labour, largely in plantation agriculture where they established their skills in the dextrous tasks of tapping rubber, cropping tobacco and tea picking. Others sought to supplement household incomes through increased participation in petty trading and entry into the urban service sectors of domestic labour and food catering. The variety of roles they fulfilled, both in the domestic and public sectors have enabled them to make the transition to the modern era with relative ease. Even Islam has not succeeded in putting serious restraints on South-East Asian women who have faced little discrimination in education, business and politics. They continue to be valued for their specialized roles in manufacturing, ranging from cigar rolling and embroidery to the production of microchips. The participation of rural and urban women in business ventures, varying in scale and variety, has been impressive during the post-war era of development. A few have risen to be captains of business and industry. It is widely known, for example, that the late wife of President Suharto, Ibu Tien, was the brains behind the family's business investments. In Malaysia, women have served in important ministerial posts like those of Finance and Home Industries.

On the down side, modernization and urbanization in South-East Asia has also increased the ills of prostitution and concubinage. Women still work for lower wages and incomes than men. Through circumstances of poverty and deprivation, many continue to be part of the culture of resistance in defence of simple customary rights for access to forests for food and fuel, their activities ranging from guerrilla warfare to evasion of the law in day-to-day affairs. Often, they share the risks with men in hiding illegal timber, taking care of tips or pay-offs. Furthermore, by adding wage-earning and public duty to domestic chores, South-East Asian women have increased their work burden. Nonetheless, through maintaining a good measure of personal freedom and economic independence, an increasingly large number marry late and fewer remain under the charge of fathers, brothers and husbands. They continue to exercise a powerful moral influence at home, restraining their partners from gambling and drinking and inculcating the values of discipline and education amongst their children. The latter is a significant function of women even in Japanese society where women have been ascribed a notoriously subordinate status.

Past traditions in the face of new challenges

South-East Asian nations are oblivious to the fast pace at which their natural resources, particularly timber and marine products are being unsustainably exploited. 'Green gold' (timber) has since the 1970s become a major source of export revenue in the region. Out of 25 million cubic metres traded in the international market in 1986, 21.4 million cubic metres originated from the region (Collins *et al.*, 1991, p.53). Estimates for 1988 give a total production of 76 million cubic metres for Indonesia, Malaysia, Philippines and Thailand with a total of US$5.47 billion in export earnings.

But rightly or wrongly, this stems partly form a rapid shift in the economic emphasis to manufacturing in which they recognize a more stable future. The spectacular switch to industrialization without earlier experience of export manufacturing comparable to the reputation of India and China for cloth, silks and porcelain production, emphasizes the region's traditional sensitivity to global market forces. In the same way that South-East Asia built its early international trade through harvesting marine and forest produce to meet the culinary and pharmaceutical demands of China and adapted, later, to large-scale plantation agriculture and mining to meet the expanding demands of Europe, its modern-day industrialization may be seen as a response to market trends.

Ironically, while governments are set on targets for industrialization, traditional strategies of survival have been driven harder by the crisis of disinheritance and poverty brought by loss of customary land, livelihood and way of life. Shifting cultivation, ideally beneficial to man and environment, is no longer sustainable because of reduced rotational cycles brought by land hunger, compounded by the loss of forests to plantation industries. Cassava which thrives on poor soils and is cultivated as a cash crop for the manufacture of starch, continues to account for large areas of slash-and-burn cultivation. In Thailand, entrepreneurs in search of quick cash returns invest in cassava cultivation which follows the trail of logging tracks and takes up broad road fronts, contributing to soil impoverishment and invasion by the pernicious *Imperata cylindrica* grass. Palm oil, in contrast, has been established as a permanent plantation crop in many parts of Island South-East Asia proving, in recent years, a more successful dollar earner than rubber. But, like all other forms of economic activity which have involved deforestation of watersheds, slop land and river fringes, has contributed to the erosion, desiccation and siltation of water courses. Furthermore, the processing both of cassava and palm oil continues to pollute rivers with effluents in the face of insufficient legal provisions to regulate and check well entrenched practices by manufacturing industries.

The cash economy, once essential for the purchase of luxuries, has now become vital for subsistence. Aid for eradicating poverty is directed to transforming traditional ways of life, no longer sustainable. Capital and the introduction of simple technologies for fresh-water prawn farming and trawler-fishing have been funded by external agencies and governments for generating cash but without investment in the broadening of knowledge about long-term effects of coastal and maritime exploitation on habitat, biological cycles and productivity. In the Philippines, for example, the mangroves which stood over 450,000 hectares in 1920 had shrunk dramatically to some 146,000 hectares by 1980 (Ganapin, 1987, p.60). Loss to human settlement, industrial sites, agriculture and salt ponds was not compensated, as expected, by the gains made through aquaculture which contributes to only 10 per cent of the country's fish production. Sustainable regimes of production and consumption evolved over time by the peasantry were maintained through inviolable codes of customary conduct, religious beliefs and ritual which disguised underlying rationale. By contrast, modern technologies appropriated from external sources are neither understood fully nor protected from abuse by customary taboos (*tabu)* and neatly sum up the modern crisis of conflict between old and new in South-East Asia. Anomalies arising from the bizarre grafting of old practices on to new institutions without proper rationalization permeates contemporary life in South-East Asia. Throughout the region, the prevailing business spirit has drawn the affluent urban population even closer to spirit and ancestor worship. Much as Tokyo's dark-suited corporate heads put their trust in *shinto* worship, Malaysian businessmen and speculators pin their fortunes on worshipping at the most auspicious *kramat* (cult shrines). In the Royal Plazza, in the middle of Bangkok, businessmen regularly lay offerings at the statue of Chulalongkorn, Thailand's modernizer par excellence, praying for continued prosperity and success with their commercial ventures. At the same time, the efficacy of a talisman distributed by a Buddhist monk is believed to seal the fate of Thai political candidates.

2.5 Conclusion

The radical shift from pre-war passivity within the framework of colonial production to post-war dynamism within the spiral of growth in East Asia demands the expansion of mental vistas, beyond the limits of market exigencies. Just as print and tertiary education provided the impetus for nation-building in East Asia, it is likely that the fast broadening base of university education, if matched by the free flow of information, can provide the scientific basis for twenty-first century developments. In a region divided by race, religion and language, trade continues to be the cohesive force. Commerce dictates political relations more than political ideology in East Asia and culturally anchored personal influence dominates inter-personal and corporate relations more than legal provisions. Whether traditionally anchored perceptions of family and community responsibility, successfully translated into business ethics, will address the broader interests of public good related to the current environmental and population crisis remains to be seen.

References

Barrett, W. (1990) 'World bullion flows' in Tracy, J. (ed.) *The Rise of the Merchant Empires*, Cambridge, Cambridge University Press.

Collis, N.M., Sayer, J., Whitmore, T.C. (1991) *The Conservation Atlas of Tropical Forests*, London, Macmillan.

Drewes, G.W.J. (1980) *Two Acehnese Poems: Hikayat Ranto and Hikajat Tengku Di Meuke: Bibliotheca Indonesica, 20*, The Hague, KITLV.

Elson, R.E. (1992) 'International commerce, state and society' in Tarling, N. (ed.) *The Cambridge History of Southeast Asia: The Nineteenth and Twentieth Centuries*, Cambridge, Cambridge University Press, pp.131--93.

Fairbank, J.K. and Reischauer, E.O. (1989) *China: Tradition and Transformation*, Sydney, Allen and Unwin.

Ganapin, D.J. (1987) 'Forest resources and timber trade in the Philippines' in *Forest Resources in the Third World*, Penang, Sahabat Alam Malaysia.

Hatch, W. and Yamamura, K. (1996) *Asia in Japan's Embrace: Building a Regional Production Alliance*, Cambridge, Cambridge University Press.

Hodgkin, T. (1981) *Vietnam: The Revolutionary Path*, New York, St. Martin's Press.

Steinberg, J.D. *et al.* (1987) *In Search of Southeast Asia: A Modern History*, Sydney, Allen and Unwin.

Tate, D.J.M. (1979) *The Making of Modern South East Asia: Volume 2, The Western Impact and Economic and Social Change*, Kuala Lumpur, Oxford University Press, p.25.

Further reading

Chowdhuray, A. and Islam, I. (1993) *The Newly Industrialising Economies of East Asia*, London, Routledge.

Das, D.K. (1996) *The Asia-Pacific Economy*, New York, St Martin's Press.

Hicks, G.L. and Redding, S.G. (1983) *Industrial East Asia and Post-Confucian Hypothesis: A Challenge to Economics*, Hong Kong, University of Hong Kong East Asia Studies.

Jacobs, N. (1957) *The Origins of Modern Capitalism in East Asia*, Hong Kong, Octagon.

James, W.E., Naya, S. and Meier, G.M. (1988) *Asian Development: Economic Success and Policy Lessons*, Madison, Wisconsin.

Kathirithamby-Wells, J. (1992) 'The age of transition: the mid-eighteenth to the early nineteenth centuries' in Tarling, N. (ed.) *The Cambridge History of South-East Asia, vol. I*, Cambridge, Cambridge University Press.

MacIntyre, J. and Jayasuriya, K. (1992) *The Dynamics of Economic Policy Reform in South-East Asia and the South West Pacific*, Singapore, Oxford University Press.

McVey, R. (1992) *South-East Asian Capitalists*, Ithaca, New York, Cornell University Press.

Owen, N.G. (1992) 'Economic and social change' in Tarling, N. (ed.) *The Cambridge History of South-East Asia: the Nineteenth and Twentieth centuries, vol. II*, Cambridge, Cambridge University Press.

CHAPTER 3

Population

Terence T. Hull

3.1   Introduction

Human populations have spread across the world and grown at an unprecedented rate during the twentieth century. This has been nowhere so dramatic as in the Asia-Pacific, where at the close of the millennium almost half the total human population resides. The concentration of people is in China, the most populous nation in the world, followed across the Pacific by the USA, and in South-East Asia by the most populous largely Muslim country in the world: Indonesia. These three countries combined are notable for the great cultural contrasts they provide, and for the heterogeneity of their citizenry. In fact, when looking at the varieties of ethnic groups present in each, it could be argued that they should not be studied as the huge nations they are today, but the various regional and ethnic communities which have come together to form these units. It is certainly at the regional levels that the dynamic forces of society, economy, and culture merge to shape demographic behaviour.

However, if the heterogeneity of nations, communities and peoples is an inexorable element defining the divisions of societies, there is an equally prominent surge which seeks to define commonalties in various groupings of nations as a step toward establishing meaningful regions. Continental land masses which provided simple water-bounded definitions in the last century are less the focus of attention than the groupings defined by economic links, political similarities, cultural heritage and, more recently, shared dreams. It is in this context of imagining new regions, that the notion of the East Asia-Pacific is coming into its own. Defined loosely as the nations sharing the hemisphere, they are defined as a sort of 'photo-negative' concept of a continent. Rather than a large land mass surrounded by water, this region is described in terms of a large water mass surrounded by land. The Pacific, the greatest of the world's oceans, laps on the shores of East Asia; Australia, New Zealand and the other states of Oceania; and the nations of North America. Table 3.1 lists most of these nations and their populations, and shows how national populations contribute to the various sub regions, and to the population of the Asia-Pacific as a whole.

Table 3.1 *Population of the Asia-Pacific, 1995*

	Population (thousands)	Percentage of region	Percentage of the Asia-Pacific
Selected countries of East Asia	*1,905,960*	*100.0%*	*78.4%*
Brunei	285	0.0	0.0
Burma/Myanmar	46,527	2.4	1.9
Cambodia	10,251	0.5	0.4
China	1,221,462	64.1	50.2
East Timor (political)	814	0.0	0.0
Hong Kong	5,865	0.3	0.2
Indonesia	197,588	10.4	8.1
Japan	125,095	6.6	5.1
Korea, North	23,917	1.3	1.0
Korea, South	44,995	2.4	1.8
Laos	4,882	0.3	0.2
Malaysia	20,140	1.1	0.8
Macau	410	0.0	0.0
Philippines	67,581	3.5	2.8
Singapore	2,848	0.1	0.1
Thailand	58,791	3.1	2.4
Vietnam	74,545	3.9	3.1
North America	*386,387*	*100.0%*	*20.5%*
Canada	29,463	7.7	1.2
Mexico	93,674	24.2	3.9
USA	263,250	68.1	10.8
Oceania	*28,549*	*100.0%*	*1.2%*
American Samoa	54	0.2	0.0
Australia	18,088	63.4	0.7
Cook Islands	19	0.1	0.0
Fed. States of Micronesia	124	0.4	0.0
Fiji	784	2.7	0.0
French Polynesia	220	0.8	0.0
Guam	150	0.5	0.0
Kiribati	79	0.3	0.0
Marshall Islands	54	0.2	0.0
Nauru	11	0.0	0.0
New Caledonia	181	0.6	0.0
New Zealand	3,575	12.5	0.1
Niue	2	0.0	0.0
Northern Mariana Islands	47	0.2	0.0
Palau	17	0.1	0.0
Papua New Guinea	4,302	15.1	0.2
Pitcairn	0	0.0	0.0
Solomon Islands	378	1.3	0.0
Tokelau	2	0.0	0.0
Tonga	98	0.3	0.0

Table 3.1 *Population of the Asia-Pacific, 1995 (contd)*

	Population (thousands)	Percentage of region	Percentage of the Asia-Pacific
Tuvalu	10	0.0	0.0
Wallis and Futuna	14	0.0	0.0
Western Samoa	171	0.6	0.0
Vanuatu	169	0.6	0.0
Asia-Pacific total	*2,432,376*		*100.0%*
Asia-Pacific as portion of world	*42.6%*		
World total	**5,716,426**		

Source: United Nations (1994)

Though largely a 'league table' of nations, this table reveals a variety of important insights into any consideration of human settlement around the Pacific Ocean. Most important, perhaps, there is need for caution in considering the list of nations in Table 3.1. An alternative would be to present a map of population density showing the spread of people across the landscape. This would show heavy shading of dense concentrations of people on coastal cities, and up fertile river valleys. The islands of Java, Bali, and much of Japan would be seen to be heavily peopled, in contrast to the vast empty regions of Australia and western China. Where desert is land without water, the Pacific can be imagined as a vast expanse of water without land – with equal consequence of scarcity of habitable area. Such a map is instructive, in general, and for some reason, it is often more important to consider nation-states as the key units for consideration of population size, growth and quality. Even in an age when people talk of globalization, nations remain the units at the negotiating tables, the regulators of markets, the protagonists of territorial disputes, the arbiters of local conflict, the proponents of culture and socialization, and the prime claimants of social loyalty and fealty. As Table 3.1 highlights, though, the two and a half billion people of the Asia-Pacific are organized into nations of widely different demographic size, and this difference is magnified further by differences of economy and culture.

No consensus exists about which nations should be included in a list of Asia-Pacific countries, or even if only portions of some countries, like China and the USA, should be regarded as part of a region defined by the Asia-Pacific. Almost any list is bound to attract complaint as being either too exclusionary, too exclusively concerned with nation-states, or too synthetic in the description of commonalties. For our purposes, the list attempts to err on the side of including the micro states of the Pacific Ocean, while excluding the nations of South America which have traditionally been oriented more to Europe than East Asia in terms of tradition, trade and culture.

The regions of the Pacific Rim tend to have greater meaning than the concept of the sum of the parts. East Asia had nearly two billion people in 1995, with the majority being in China. (Because the figures are from

Large populations create transportation problems. One solution the Tokyo underground has found is to employ 'pushers' to push people onto the trains during the rush hour

official UN publications, which do not recognize Taiwan as a separate state, they include the 20,000,000 people of Taiwan in the figure for China.) With this huge population, China's demographic experiences of fertility, mortality, and people's welfare have a determinant impact in defining the demography of East Asia, and a very influential impact on any assessment of world experience. By contrast nations such as Singapore and even Japan may stand as models for others to study or emulate, but changes in their fertility or mortality has little impact on the demography of the region or the world. In reading the two columns of percentages we can get some sense of the degree to which each nation influences the demography of their immediate region and the Pacific Rim as a whole.

Across the Pacific Ocean the nations of North America are similarly dominated by one large nation, the USA, which has over half the population of the group. Mexico's population is just under a fifth of the total, while Canada has 30 million. It is on the eastern side of the Pacific that the concepts of regionality become very problematic. The USA, Mexico and Canada have promoted common interests in trade (through NAFTA), and grappled with a variety of issues surrounding their common borders, yet all three are intent on preserving their distinct national interests, and particular culture, in the face of potential influence from abroad. Even the USA, which is regarded by other nations as having a hegemonic influence on mass communications and consumer trends, feels the threat of foreign countries in the form of cheap imports, immigrant numbers, and political de-stabilization. As such these North American nations tend to emphasize their own identities rather than claim to being a part of an East Asia-Pacific region.

Societies in Oceania present a contrast with the large nations of East Asia and North America. Australia and New Zealand are both countries with a strong British heritage but also have very important indigenous and non-British migrant populations. The fact that together they represent over three-quarters of the regional population makes them the strong, but highly contrasting, definers of Oceania identity. The other quarter of the region's population is made up of Melanesian, Polynesian, and Micronesian peoples who have a strong affinity with common Pacific Islands cultural traditions. When looking at this group it is important to remember that the islands of Hawaii, which are a state of the USA, have a population of nearly one million, a portion of whom have strong orientation to and family ties with the other Pacific Islands. While Australia and New Zealand are populous by standards of the region, they are insignificant when their population' numbers are compared to the Asia-Pacific as a whole.

Around the Asia-Pacific, then, is a circle of nations which together constitute over 40 per cent of the world's population, but they range from the most populous nation on earth, China, down to the least populated political entities like Pitcairn island. There is little sense of community among the nations in this categorization, and various political, trade or cultural groupings set many of these nations in marginal demographic positions. The small island states of the Pacific share many cultural and political interests, but are dependent on large neighbours or colonial links for much of their economic support. The largest nations of China, the USA and Indonesia see the necessity of linkages on the basis of their greatness, but share little by way of cultural, social or political identity. For all these reasons the concept of 'population' in this region is particularly problematic. Instead we need to think of the history and dynamics of a large number and variety of human groups who traversed and settled the lands around the Pacific, producing the detailed mosaic of nations and communities we see there today.

3.2   Peopling East Asia and the Pacific Rim, 5000 BC to AD 2000

Looking deep into the history of populations, it is always important to remember that the first humans left little evidence of their lifestyles, and virtually no indications of their numbers. Their successors left products of their labours – tools, houses, art – which indicate more about how they lived. In the East Asian and Pacific Rim areas there is archaeological evidence that settled agriculture developed five to seven thousand years ago. Remains of irrigated rice cultivations indicate relatively advanced technological innovations, but we have little knowledge of the daily lives of the inventors, nor do we know much about the organization of their society.

At best, according to McEvedy and Jones in their *Atlas of World Population History* (1978), we can guess that between 10,000 and 400 BC the population of East Asia rose from around one million to 80 million humans, with most clustered in small settlements reliant on farms and domestic animals in tropical and temperate regions, and small numbers hunting and gathering in the peripheral regions in an arc from the Ural mountains to Honshu island in Japan. These foraging peoples probably numbered no more than a few hundred thousand.

Small tribes with beliefs tied to the forests, seas and skies, the culture and language they passed on through oral tradition formed the foundation of modern civilizations. With population growing only slowly – perhaps taking over a thousand years to grow from 115 to 185 million across the vast continent and coastal archipelagos – the oral tradition must have been family based, with a few surviving children being adopted by uncles and aunts as high rates of mortality both carried away a large portion of newborns, and many of the women and men of childbearing age. It would be the rare member of the tribe who lived into old age. Small wonder that the elderly and the ancestors would be the object of veneration and the subject of inspiration. Figure 3.1 gives some indication of the long period of relatively stationary population numbers prior to the initial jump in numbers a thousand years ago. It is also notable that the growth of population by 60 million over a thousand years contrasts with the 90 million China alone adds to the world population every year in the 1990s.

It was relatively late in the development of civilization that humans began to record their experiences, in the written myths, stories and accounts, a few of which survive to the present. We can look back on those records and make some guesses about the size and structures of the societies which produced them but it is virtually impossible to validate such estimates. The self-conscious recording of population numbers, and comments on births, deaths and movement of people came about only recently as more formal histories were etched into stone, or written on paper. But these were more for the use of rulers intent on exercising control over subjects, than they were for the edification of the general public, and so the sketchy and isolated records which were kept were often lost to later

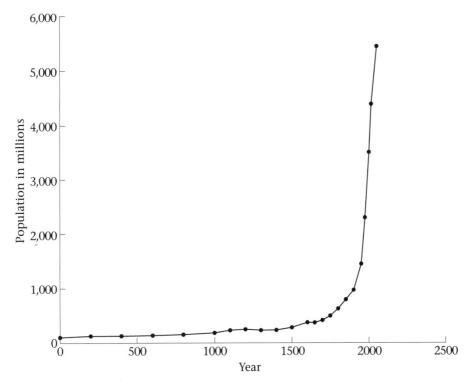

Figure 3.1 *Population of Asia AD1 through 2050*

(Asia in this graph refers to total continental Asia, including the subcontinent and West Asia.)

Source: McEvedy and Jones (1978)

generations as weather, discord or purposeful destruction eliminated the few or even single copies of statistics. Moreover, systems of population enumeration designed as instruments of social control were obviously subject to error as subjects tried to avoid being counted in an attempt to gain some freedom from autocratic manipulation.

Printing presses, multiple records, and education for and about common people are only a few centuries old, and formalized procedures to routinely count populations arose in the nineteenth century to improve the accuracy of population estimates. Thus the picture shown in Figure 3.1 should be read as a rough reconstruction of reality, rather than an accurate record of history. Yet such warnings about the shaky foundations of demographic science are more designed to make us cautious rather than deny the effort to understand the growth of population numbers over the ages. Even rough guesses are useful in tracing the rise of human populations in East Asia and the Pacific Rim, and those guesses combined with our recent efforts to systematize population research give a good basis for imagining the most likely trends in population over the last two millennia.

So Figure 3.1 tells us that the long trend of relatively stable population which accompanied the rise and fall of great historical East Asian civilizations must have been a time when birth and death rates remained in rough balance at high levels. Historical records telling of famines, devastating wars and plagues indicate the constant threat of excess mortality. Since mortality weighs most heavily on the newborn it is likely that women would lose many of their children, and families would be relatively small, even though childbearing might be frequent. But the fact that fertility was high does not mean it was uncontrolled. Throughout East Asia and the Pacific Islands, cultures prescribed long periods of abstinence following the birth of a child, to give the mother a chance to recover her strength and ensure that the newborn obtained sufficient nutrition and care. Women of the region also used a wide range of herbs and practices to prevent conception and procure abortions, thus keeping fertility well below the biological maximum. Finally, for the mass of the population, patterns of marriage and the likelihood of early widowhood meant that the potential reproductive life of many women was curtailed, thus further restricting family sizes. Over centuries the distinctive cultural groups of the region vied for territory, trade advantage, and maintenance of group strength and solidarity, in the face of heavy pressure of individual mortality. It is little wonder that the histories of these groups were so marked by the rise and conflict of a variety of religious conceptions setting the groups in their natural environment, and seeking protection from the supernatural.

3.3 Expansions, conquests and empires

Around 1650 the world changed, and over the following 300 years mortality fell, fertility rose, and there was a population growth of historically unprecedented magnitude. By the middle of the twentieth century the population of East Asia had added one billion people, and by the end of the century another two billion would be added. For the Asia-Pacific, such massive population growth poses important questions for both historians and governors. How could such massive changes come about? How can limited ecosystems sustain such numbers?

In the seventeenth century the intrusion of European populations brought massive changes to the economic and political structures of the Pacific Rim, and saw the decimation of many indigenous groups, the subjugation of the survivors, and the establishment of important trading linkages among the communities of the region, and beyond. From the late eighteenth century the region was swept up in an unprecedented population growth which has led to the multiplication of numbers in increasingly shorter time periods as the rate of population growth rose from close to zero to over 2 or 3 per cent per annum in many places. In many important ways the population growth and later the efforts to control population numbers have been some of the most important legacies of the colonial experience.

Two examples of the complex interaction of colonial policy and population change are to be found in the islands of Java, which came under

Dutch control in the centuries after the establishment of a commercial base in Batavia in the early 1600s, and Fiji, a mid Pacific island group which was ceded to the United Kingdom in 1874. In both cases we find the strange mixture of exploitation and protection of native peoples by rulers presuming cultural superiority based on their military power.

Java has been regarded as the classic example of both the beneficial impact of good government promoting population growth, and the demonstration of dangers of overpopulation. Evidence for the former claim was gathered in the early twentieth century to justify continued Dutch control over the resources and products of the world's largest archipelago. Though Java was less than a tenth of Indonesian land, the population had increased at a rapid and rising rate through the nineteenth century, from the 4.5 million counted by Raffles in 1815 during the brief period of British control at the end of the Napoleonic wars, to 29 million in 1900 to be over two-thirds of the national population. The rate of growth was unprecedented, nationalistic Dutch historians quickly attributed this to the beneficial effects of agricultural developments, health care programmes, and the peace and security brought by colonial rule.

Not surprisingly seven decades later nationalistic Indonesians and a new generation of Dutch historians re-examining the data found that such pride was built on shaky foundations. Widjojo Nitisastro (1970) catalogued the many reasons for scepticism about welfare improvements, pointing out that the Dutch had themselves prosecuted some of the bloodiest wars of the island's history, and had extracted wealth from a country whose people went hungry and died of curable diseases. Moreover, the population figures on which the claims of growth rested were questioned, with demographic forensics suggesting that the Raffles census may have missed a third to a half of the population of 1815 Java, thus implying a lower rate, and perhaps a more uneven rate of growth than the Dutch apologists might have preferred.

Ironically, in 1900, as the Dutch were claiming praise for the growth rates, the government was simultaneously fretting about the problem of 'overpopulation' in Java. Around that time they embarked on various measures to relieve the pressures of population on resources in an attempt to improve the welfare of the largely agriculturally dependent Javanese. Their strategy was four fold: increase agricultural productivity, promote development of manufacturing industry, build infrastructure to enhance the productivity of Java, and, most notoriously, systematically move Javanese farmers to other islands to set up agricultural colonies. Indonesia today bears the burdens, and enjoys some of the benefits of the population policies of the early 1900s. Rail and road systems, educational institutions, industries, and hundreds of Javanese villages established in other islands in the 50 years prior to independence continue to set the pattern of modern Indonesian development. Today many of these are regarded as accomplishments of independence, and there is some truth in this claim, but the roots of these developments in the colonial experience are also important. Rather than alleviating population pressures, for most of the century developments were accompanied by increased population growth rates, until finally in the 1950s and 1960s Indonesia experienced the highest rates of growth in history. At that stage government and people alike changed direction to adopt policies of fertility control. None the less, well before the end of the twentieth century the population of Java had exceeded 100 million people, and this number will continue to grow well into the next millennium.

The small islands of the Pacific were virtually all colonized between the time of Napoleon's defeat at Waterloo and the start of the First World War in 1914. From the middle of the nineteenth century colonial rulers and missionaries became aware of major population declines in these small territories, giving rise to fears of extinction of the distinctive cultures of the Pacific. This was a widespread phenomenon, but became a particularly dramatic issue in Fiji, where British governors had early suggested that Fijian natives should be exempt from labour required to establish plantations needed for colonial revenue. Instead, they imported labour from India to plant sugar cane on land taken from the Fijians. Population numbers were prominent in the discussions over this and other government policies. In retrospect one might even argue that the course of Fiji's history was irrevocably and dramatically shaped by the population issue (see Hull and Hull, 1973 for a detailed study of this history).

Indigenous Fijians numbered 140,500 in 1874 when Britain assumed government of the islands. Over the next 30 years numbers fell steadily, going down to 94,000 at the time of the 1901 Census. In contrast to the pride in growth exhibited by the Dutch in Java, the British in Fiji worried about population decline, and encouraged the Fijian Chiefs to investigate the issue in the debates of their Great Council. The Chiefs first identified introduced European diseases, such as the measles epidemic of 1875, as the cause of diminishing numbers. Then they charged that Fijian women were inhibiting growth as they enforced traditional post-partum taboos on intercourse, and brought on barrenness through repeated attempts to procure abortions. The British Governors responded to the Chiefs that there might also be some problems associated with the unhygienic housing conditions, and the habit of forcing women back to subsistence tasks soon after the birth of a child. A commission in 1896 summarized these speculations, and concluded that the Fijian women had developed a 'weakness of maternal instinct'. Government put in place a number of measures designed to improve the lot of Fijians, but within a few years noted that while some of the initiatives were continuing, others had been found irrelevant. Strangely, though the policies were said to be of little apparent impact, a few years later the population began to grow. The five years after 1905 were a turning point, and after 1911 the number of Fijian births exceeded deaths in every year except for the influenza epidemic of 1918. The Fijians numbered 84,000 in 1921, and grew to 98,000 in 1936.

More than half the Indians indentured to work sugar cane between 1879 and 1916 decided to settle in Fiji, and their numbers grew quickly. By 1921 there were 60,000 Indians, making up nearly 40 per cent of the total population. While the Fijian population was recovering, it was not growing as fast as the Indian population, and the British government officers warned Fijians to grow faster or face being a minority on their own islands. That came to pass in 1944, at a time when Fijian growth rates exceeded 2 per cent, and numbers of both racial groups exceeded 100,000. Fiji was not alone in experiencing a rapid increase in population in the twentieth century.

Later colonial officers in Fiji would lecture the races on the need to control population growth rates or face economic disaster. What had been the sign of prosperity and stability now was seen as the greatest threat to long-term development. In the 1960s and 1970s a vigorous family planning campaign brought the rates of population growth of both groups down, but with a greater decline in Indian fertility. Subsequent political events – independence, two coups, and struggles to rewrite the constitution of the nation – have shown how the memories and spectres of population growth of different ethnic groups played a determinant role in setting political, social and cultural agendas in the islands, long after the last colonial servants had retired half a world away to Britain.

3.4 Demographic revolutions

The twentieth century produced both the phenomena and the understanding of a major form of population change we have come to call 'demographic transition'. What Java and Fiji had experienced in unique ways in their microcosm could be seen in the histories of all societies of the Asia-Pacific. In the simplest form of explanation the demographic transition occurs when high and stable levels of mortality and fertility fall dramatically and stabilize again at low rates. The period between the high and low levels of stable rates is a time of unprecedented growth, and in popular terminology is sometimes called a population explosion. The first transition of this type took place in Europe, North America began a similar transition somewhat later. Explanations for these changes pointed to the impact of industrialization, modernization, nationalism, and the growth of education as forces which changed the way health care and birth control were made available to the mass of society. Most importantly technology made health care and birth control much more efficient and effective.

The countries of the Pacific Rim have had a remarkably varied range of experiences of demographic transition from the basically *laissez faire* approaches of spontaneous adoption of fertility control practices and the spread of private family planning clinics in the USA and Australia, to the development of officially promoted authoritarian family planning campaigns in China, Vietnam, and Indonesia. The most dramatic of this latter group is the experience of China, which, after a period of political diffidence about population control in the early years after the Communist takeover, developed from about 1970 onwards one of the most intensive programmes of population control ever seen.

The Chinese planned demographic revolution

Economic planning is the heart of the centralized socialist system in China, and this means that the demographic experiences of this huge nation are qualitatively as well as quantitatively different from the experiences of change in the capitalist societies of Europe and America. Economic planning is a continuous process, framed by a regular cycle of five-year plans adopted at all levels of government. Planning involves both horizontal and vertical consultations, with the planning agency at each level of government conferring with other departments at the same level before sending suggestions or decisions to different levels. The rhetoric of the planning process in China stresses careful examination of the 'concrete realities' and seeking 'truth through facts' in the course of developing targets. Read through Western eyes these litanies seem particularly hollow since empirical investigations of 'the realities' are often bounded politics which serve to protect entrenched leaders and their positions. In the final analysis, though, the plan represents a complex consensus among the different components of government and the Communist Party. As such it is applied as 'orders' to all members of society on the premise that the 'people' are deemed to have agreed to the plan through the official representatives of their interests. Population plans are conceived as a specialized component of the total planning process, with the State Family Planning Commission responsible for setting 'reproduction targets' which extend in practice down to neighbourhood or work units.

The major forms of national family planning policy are contained in documents of the Central Committee of the Communist Party, the Five-Year Development Plan, and the directives of the State Family Planning Commission. The structure and function of the programme is also affected by the decisions of the Ministry of Health, the Ministry of Transport, and other agencies charged with service and logistic responsibilities for family planning. Central policies are expressed in terms of general principles, and long-term numerical targets. On their own they do not constitute a blueprint for action, and in fact the generality of expression leaves a fairly wide margin for interpretation by lower government levels which are responsible for the concrete planning and implementation of policies.

A typical scenario for the development of policy is illustrated by the One-Child Policy adopted at the central level in 1979. The first hints of such a policy came in 1977 and 1978 as various local and provincial governmental levels, grappling with leaders' demands for immediate reduction in fertility, faced the problem of how to ensure equitable compliance with the goals of drastically reducing the rate of population growth. Small scale innovations with a policy of setting a maximum family size were suggested and tested, and these were reported to higher levels of government and through the mass media. Demographers presented population projections which showed the implications of various family sizes for the size of the population at the turn of the century which indicated potential populations of 1.4, 1.2 and 1.1 billion people in the year 2000 if there were average family sizes of 3, 2 or 1, respectively.

A poster promoting the 'One child per couple' policy

In June, 1979, Premier Hua Guofeng called for measures to reward one-child families, and provide old-age security to childless people. This marked the start of the official national campaign for 'One child per couple'. It was acknowledged by some leaders that the 'One child' slogan was primarily an ideal, and early statements showed they anticipated at least 30 per cent of couples would have more than one child. Demographic calculations indicated that the policy would meet the target of holding population down to 1.2 billion in the year 2000. However, the simplified rhetoric of the campaign, overly enthusiastic calls from the leadership, and misunderstandings by local cadres, gave the impression that all couples could have only one child. Government acknowledged in 1984 that there were grave problems with the policy when the Central Committee of the Communist Party said that the rigid notion of a one-child limit had created a 'big hole' (of people defying the policy) because the policy was so obviously unenforceable on a large scale. As a result they called for the opening of a 'small hole' (through rules specifically allowing second births), but only on condition that there be no third or higher parity births allowed for members of the Han ethnic majority group.

What had been an inadvertently rigid guideline now became a bureaucratically rigid set of rules. Reactions varied around the nation, but in many regions it was reported that the use of contraception dropped substantially, and the range of 'exceptional' cases skyrocketed. In response to local pressures the Party issued a new directive in 1986 calling for a greater effort to reduce the range of 'exceptions' (Greenhalgh, 1986) but the local officials were still able to rationalize their implementation plans in terms of 'local concrete realities' and the national calls went largely unheeded.

The 'One-child policy' has been a matter of continuous struggle within China, and regular criticism from outside. Major fertility reductions had already registered before 1979, as shown in Table 3.2. It was not the concept of the 'One-child policy' *per se* which produced the decline, but rather the combined effect of millions of parents wanting to have smaller families and the pressure of government to encourage them and millions of others to have even fewer children than they might have preferred in terms of their personal needs. The justification for this action by government was that without drastic measures China would be unable to feed itself, much less develop a rich economy, and this message was strongly communicated to the entire populous. In the authoritarian setting of China this means that today it is difficult to obtain valid social survey information on the number of children women might 'prefer'. In recent years the government has found that it is also impossible to obtain reliable information on the number of children women are actually having, such is the widespread practice of refusing to report births to survey interviewers and registration officials. Thus while surveys in the 1990s have recorded fertility levels below 1.8 children on average, the official government statistics are adjusted to a level of 2.0 to account for undercounts.

Table 3.2 *The great fertility declines of East Asia as a whole, and the nations of China, Indonesia and Japan, 1950–2050 (total fertility rate[1])*

Year	East Asia	China	Indonesia	Japan
United Nations estimates of actual total fertility rate				
1950–55	5.86	6.11	5.49	2.75
1955–60	5.59	5.48	5.67	2.08
1960–65	5.58	5.61	5.42	2.01
1965–70	5.64	5.94	5.57	2.00
1970–75	5.06	4.76	5.10	2.07
1975–80	4.20	3.26	4.68	1.81
1980–85	3.70	2.50	4.06	1.76
1985–90	3.40	2.41	3.31	1.66
United Nations medium assumption for projections				
1990–95	3.03	1.95	2.90	1.50
1995–2000	2.89	1.95	2.63	1.50
2000–10	2.65	1.99	2.23	1.53
2010–20	2.34	2.10	2.10	1.66
2020–30	2.16	2.10	2.10	1.80
2030–40	2.11	2.10	2.10	1.93
2040–50	2.10	2.10	2.10	2.06

[1] Total fertility rate (TFR): hypothetical average number of births per woman if current fertility continued for the full reproductive life of women from age 15 to age 49.

Source: United Nations (1995, pp.482, 588, 674, 676)

3.5 Demographic tensions

If the social transformations which led to the major changes in fertility and mortality can be called revolutions, then it is perhaps appropriate to look at some of the demographic consequences of these changes as states of long-term demographic tension. The vast changes of social and cultural life which produce small family systems across East Asia leave in their wake a series of difficulties, often related to the conflict between the old systems of beliefs being out of synchronization with new patterns of behaviour. Instances of such skirmishes abound in the Asia-Pacific, and include such things as the rising sex ratios at birth in China, South Korea, and Taiwan, the conflicts over the appropriate roles of women and men in families and in the labour force, and the apprehension over the twin phenomena of rising expectations of life at birth and the rising proportions of old people in the population.

Sex ratios at birth

Around the world human populations have a remarkably stable sex ratio at birth. For every 100 girls born each year, there are between 104 and 106 boys born, and the ratio is so constant that demographers use the figure of 105 with confidence, whether they are studying urban Europeans, New Guinea tribals, Japanese farmers or Chinese labourers. The slight excess of boys reflected in this number is not maintained through life. In fact, biological studies posit that the number of boys conceived is much greater than the number of girls, but male foetuses are more prone to spontaneous abortion and stillbirth. In their first year of life, and for most ages thereafter male mortality is greater than female mortality until, at the end of the life span, surviving women greatly outnumber men. Thus under natural conditions it might be expected that females would demonstrate greater robustness than males, and there would be a slightly larger number of females in the population overall. It is thus a matter of great concern to see that in many East Asian societies the sex ratios at birth are rising to unprecedented levels, and the mortality rates of women exceed those of men.

Observers of these trends have long pointed to traditions of male domination in East Asian societies to explain the complex set of factors reducing the survivorship of females. In China, Taiwan and South Korea these traditional behaviours were disappearing and by the mid 1980s the sex ratios at birth were close to normal levels, indicating that the practice of female infanticide (and accompanying failure to report the birth of a girl child) had become very rare. Since then, though, data from these three countries have shown rising sex ratios at birth well above the level of 110, and in some regions reaching 115–120 overall. For births of higher birth order (like the third or fourth birth) the reported sex ratios went higher still, though the number of women having so many births has become very small in these low fertility countries. This was not so much the re-emergence of infanticide, but the application of modern technologies of gender determination to give some couples the option to abort unwanted pregnancies – and in these societies the desire for boys combined with the desire for small family sizes meant that the decision to abort led most often to the elimination of higher order female births.

For women in East Asia the issues of rising sex ratios at birth are thorny. On the one hand, mothers are avoiding female births because they prefer to have sons for all sorts of economic and cultural reasons. On the other hand, widespread sex discrimination exacerbates the already disadvantageous position of women in societies, reinforcing such decisions. Governments in China, South Korea and Taiwan have not been particularly successful in preventing sex-selective abortions, but Singapore and Malaysia have been able to discourage the practice through tight control of the medical professions, and strong public education campaigns. From a purely demographic viewpoint the sharp rise in sex ratios at birth in the 1990s foreshadows serious problems in the marriage markets of East Asia in the years 2010 and above, as the large cohorts of males compete for marriage partners from the small cohorts of females.

Women's roles in families and workplaces

While Asia-Pacific societies grapple with the conflicts arising from traditional gender patterns and modern small family systems, they are also confronting serious issues of gender in the organization of industrial societies which are now so widespread as to constitute chronic afflictions of globalization. These relate to the re-definition of roles for women and men in the work force, in the domestic sphere and in civil society. In Japan, China, Indonesia; in fact in most countries of East Asia, industrialization has been the engine of economic growth, and the work forces of both factories and offices have absorbed increasing numbers of young women. As women attain recognition for what they regard as just demands for equal standing in changing societies, they find problems are not confined to the formal structures of employment and government, but also relate to the home where they are expected to shoulder a large portion of the domestic duties of cooking, cleaning and childcare. For growing numbers of young East Asian women the conflicts between the demands of work and the demands of housework pose troublesome choices.

The first choices they face are whether to marry, and when to marry. In the past it was the decision of their father, and sometimes reflected negotiations to cement relations between two families with complemen-tary economic interests. Today the choice young women make is to marry, but at a much later age, and to a partner selected by themselves. In Japan, Thailand, and many cities of East Asia there is also a growing tendency for women to remain unmarried, preferring spinsterhood to domestic exploi-tation. It is too early to determine how widespread such a phenomenon will become in other countries of the Asia-Pacific, but various strategies to reduce dependence on men through the avoidance of marriage have been seen, both in the rising practice of cohabitation in societies like Australia, New Zealand and the USA, and substantial delays in the age at first marriage related to women's education and employment patterns throughout East Asia.

For the majority who marry, the key choices are whether, when and how often to have children. In the past this was determined by traditions, families and chance, but in a time of fertility control, women are better able to determine these questions themselves. In many countries of Europe the decisions they are making lead to family sizes of only just over one child on average, and this means that eventually populations will decline, sometimes at fairly rapid rates. In the Asia-Pacific, evidence of this pattern emerging is still restricted to developed nations, such as Japan, Australia, New Zealand, Canada, the USA, South Korea, Singapore and Taiwan and developed regions of relatively poor countries, like Shanghai and Jiangsu in China, Bali, Jakarta and North Sulawesi in Indonesia, and Bangkok in Thailand.

The determinants of the number and timing of childbearing are greatly influenced by the social institutions of work and child care which are available. It appears that industrial nations, like Italy, France and Spain, which make it difficult for women to care for children while maintaining job security and promotion possibilities are more likely to see fertility fall far below the levels needed for population replacement – the average fertility of slightly over two children over reproductive life (Chesnais, 1996, p.738). Where social supports for women's work are available, as in northern Europe and Australia, fertility tends to hover just below the two child average, but at levels of 1.8 or 1.9 children on average it takes a longer time for population decline to set in, and the pace of decline is moderated.

Ageing people and ageing populations

Demographic policy making in East Asia contains a strange contradiction. From the middle of the century governments increasingly accepted the notion that high fertility and the consequent high rates of population growth threatened the economic well-being of the nation. Classic Malthusian ideas about the race between population and food supply were elaborated with concepts of population pressures on capital formation and the quality of social services, and leaders called on people to have fewer children, often citing maximums of one or two children at most, for the good of the society as a whole. In the 1980s and 1990s, as it became clear that low fertility had been or would soon be reached, some policy makers hardly paused for self-congratulation before seeing problems in this policy success.

Their anxieties had two dimensions. First, they perceived the threat of labour shortage. Particularly in settings such as Japan, South Korea and Taiwan, the economic growth which lowered fertility was thought to need a continuous flow of new entrants into the labour force to keep the factories and construction going. For some policy makers this meant that fertility should be maintained – that the workers should be home-grown. Second, the inevitable consequence of fertility decline was that the balance of numbers between different age groups would change. The age distribution of the rapidly growing population was like a pyramid, with many more people at younger ages than at older ages. When fertility falls, the bottom of the pyramid gets smaller, and over time the numbers of people in each age group become more similar. The sides of the pyramid become more straight and perpendicular (Figures 3.2a, b and c). On average the population grows older, and as time goes on the proportion of the population in the oldest age groups increases. By and large, these are people who have left the formal labour force, and are assumed to make greater demands on society for health and other forms of care. What the policy makers of East Asia increasingly realized was that the very speed with which they reduced fertility meant that the shift in proportions of the population to the older age groups was also rapid. This is particularly true in China, but also haunts the policy makers of Japan and many developed countries in the West.

If the threat of human numbers to the ecosystem is real, and if the rate of growth population puts pressure on the creation and maintenance of social capital, then the response to problems of population ageing in the Pacific should presumably not be directed to a revival of growth rates, but rather a search for social mechanisms to ensure that the aged are healthy, productive, and in possession of a continuing livelihood.

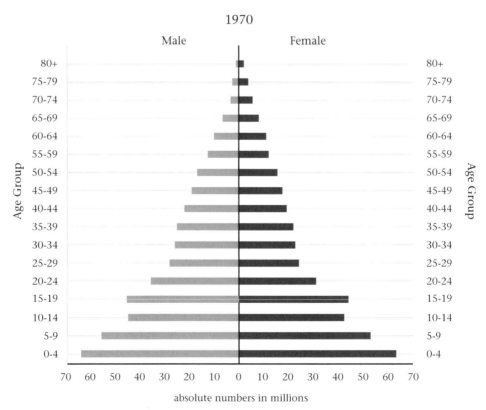

Figure 3.2(a) *Age structure diagram ('population pyramid') China, 1970*
Source: United Nations (1994, pp.266–7)

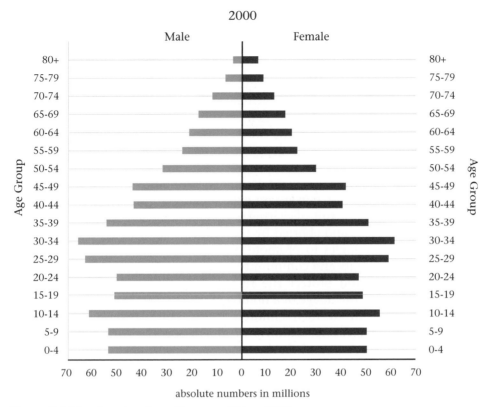

Figure 3.2(b) *Age structure diagram, China 2000*

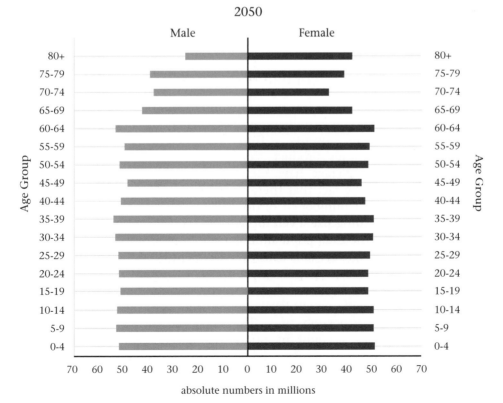

Figure 3.2(c) *Age structure diagram, China 2050*

3.6 The struggle for decent demographic futures

We can see that the populations of the Asia-Pacific are engrossed in the large-scale changes wrought by the demographic transition from high to low rates of fertility and mortality, and the pervasive social challenges to accommodate the quest for equitable treatment for women and the ageing. They thus share many of the basic demographic problems of European and other Western societies. But the ways these problems are manifest in different cultures and nations depends on the current commitments of societies.

East Asian nations are caught in many contradictions. So it is that China, South Korea and Taiwan are experiencing very high sex ratios at birth, while at the same time declaring policies of gender equity. The female foetuses are detected and aborted by the millions of parents who want to use medical technologies to promote old-fashioned preferences for sons, while the governments and community leaders sign international conventions to promote and protect the rights of women. Similarly Western countries marvel at the image of a homogenous Japanese nation where the elderly are cared for by their children at the same time that Japan is struggling with increasing numbers of elderly people with no familial support, and who increasingly look to the state to save them from penury.

While it is possible to see the end of the great demographic revolutions in East Asia which will slow the growth and age structure of populations in the next century, it appears that the demographic skirmishing will continue for the next few generations at least. This implies that the demographic issues of the twenty-first century will centre less on the question of how to reduce mortality and fertility, and more on how to have a stable low fertility society which provides a decent life for all members.

The inexorable rise of numbers

The end of the transition to low mortality and low fertility does not mean the end of population growth. Because the children born at the end of the era of high fertility take twenty or thirty years before they begin having their own families, they produce 'echoes' of that earlier baby boom. Though women on average have many fewer children than their own mothers produced, the fact that there are large numbers of new mothers means that the total number of births will go up in a series of regular boomlets of diminishing size. Even though the average family size is below replacement level, the total population continues to grow.

However, when fertility falls below replacement levels of an average of 2.1 births for each woman, population numbers eventually peak, and then begin to decline. The timing and pace of the decline depends on when fertility goes below replacement levels, and how far below replacement it is before it stabilizes (or possibly rises). The UN population projections take this uncertainty into account by offering different scenarios reflecting assumptions about future fertility. Table 3.2 showed the medium projections of fertility for East Asia and major countries, indicating what many would regard as an 'ideal' trajectory of fertility decline to 2.1, and then stabilization. In the very long term this would lead to a stationary population.

The future is unlikely to take such a path, and in fact there are strong indications that the countries of the Asia-Pacific have already set course in a different direction. Figure 3.3 shows population numbers under the high, medium and low fertility variants for East Asia and the three most populous East Asian nations. If the experience of many European countries is a guide, fertility will not stabilize at 2.1 children on average, but rather fall further to between 1.2 and 1.8. Thus the low projection assumptions may be closer to likely reality than the medium projections which are based more on stated government policies than any consideration of realism.

Looking back to Figure 3.1, it is possible to imagine what shape the Asian population curve could take in the next few hundred years. First, population growth will gradually stall and for a short time will plateau. Then, depending on the number of women who choose to have one, two, or no children, population numbers for nations will fall at different rates. Those able to maintain fertility close to replacement level will have gradual declines in numbers, while those with fertility rates closer to one child on average will have rapidly accelerating declines. The picture then might be the obverse of the massive increases in population between 1650 and 2000, with demographic momentum carrying population numbers down as it had once carried them up.

Of course this long-term scenario is totally dependent on assumptions which can only be validated as the future unfolds. It assumes that the different social structures determining fertility levels are not radically modified by major changes to the economy and systems of governance on a scale comparable to the industrial and post-industrial revolutions. If national and regional governments create social structures conducive to childbearing, it is possible that women might begin having over two children on average in the period following the demographic transition, but there is little evidence of such governmental intentions at the close of the 1990s. If anything many governments of the Asia-Pacific promote gender policies which disadvantage women in employment, and reinforce unequal domestic responsibilities, two major elements discouraging reproduction.

The scenario also assumes that mortality patterns remain relatively stable. At the moment the maximum expectation of life in the Asia-Pacific is around 80 years of age. If it was to rise well above 100, then population numbers would continue to grow for some time before sub-replacement fertility would bring them down. Again, trends do not indicate that it is likely for the huge populations of the Asia-Pacific to attain such improvements in survivorship. None the less, while we might be very sceptical about trends changing, we should also consider the demographic thinker of 1650 looking at the historical record of the middle ages to try to imagine what might happen by the year 2000. They could have dreamed most mightily, but never imagine the lives we live today.

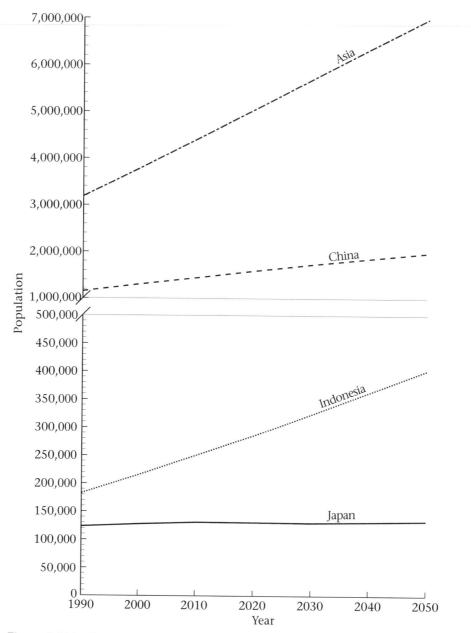

Figure 3.3(a) *Prospect of population numbers, 1990–2050: high fertility variant*
(Asia in these graphs refers to total continental Asia, including the subcontinent and West Asia.)
Source: United Nations (1995)

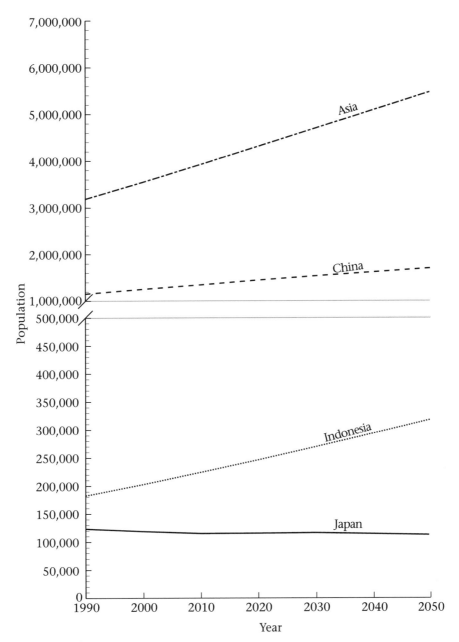

Figure 3.3(b) *Prospect of population numbers, 1990–2050: medium fertility variant*
Source: United Nations (1995)

In thinking about the future of populations, though, it will be more important than ever to consider not so much the populations of nations, but the welfare of national populations. This is not only or even primarily a question of affluence. It is much more concerned with the attainment of decent standards of living which are sustainable. In East Asia, as in the rest of the world, this presents a major challenge both in terms of balancing and optimizing the utilization of resources, and also balancing the distribution

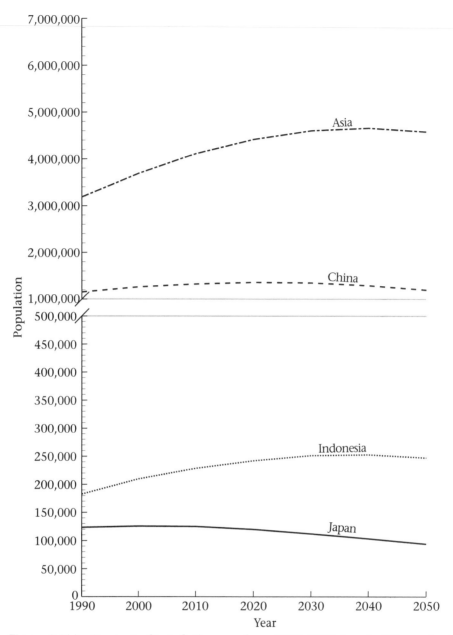

Figure 3.3(c) *Prospect of population numbers, 1990–2050: low fertility variant*
Source: United Nations (1995)

of resources within and between societies. This is the major reason why governments and peoples of the world have been concerned about the rates of population increase, and routinely call for efforts to reduce high levels of fertility in order to moderate the long-term rates of population growth.

From the purely demographic viewpoint the impact of controlling rates of population growth create new challenges in the ageing of populations and in the ways in which gender roles are reconstructed. The former challenge is an inevitable consequence of rapid fertility reductions in this century, and the latter is a critical element in ensuring that populations do not collapse in the next century. For many governments it will be difficult to re-orient thinking from seeing the manipulation of population growth as a tool to achieve welfare, to the guarantee of welfare as a means to avoid population collapse. These challenges are not unique to East Asia, but they are of greater magnitude in the Sinic cultures of East Asia where authoritarian governments and patriarchal traditions have accelerated the pace and impacts of demographic transition in comparison with the experiences of the nations of Europe, North America and South America. From the perspective of the Pacific Rim, the way the Chinese, Indonesians and North Americans respond to these challenges will determine the numbers and welfare of millions of communities and billions of individuals for centuries to come.

3.7   Conclusion

East Asia is the most populous major land mass, and it contains China, the most populous nation on earth. As the end of the twentieth century showed, assumptions about the continuity of nations cannot be taken for granted. China, the USA, and Indonesia are all large multicultural societies which have in the past and could in the future face disintegrative pressures. They could break into smaller nations which would fall much lower on the league tables of populousness, much as happened to the USSR. But ultimately the growing pressure of humanity is not measured in nation-states or cultures, but the reproduction of numbers. The Asia-Pacific region will inevitably see major growth of population before seeing any decline.

References

Asian Population and Development Association (1989) *Demographic Transition and Development in Asian Countries: Overview and Statistical Tables*, Tokyo, The Asian Population and Development Association.

Brown, L.R. (1995) *Who Will Feed China? Wake Up Call for a Small Planet*, New York, W.W. Norton and Co.

Carr-Saunders, A.M. (1936) *World Population: Past Growth and Present Trends*, London, Oxford University Press.

Chesnais, J.-C. (1996) 'Fertility, family, and social policy in contemporary Western Europe', *Population and Development Review*, vol.22, no.4, pp.729–39.

Dobbs-Higginson, M.S. (1994) *Asia-Pacific: its Role in the New World Disorder*, London, William Heinemann.

Greenhalgh, S. (1986) 'Shifts in China's population policy, 1984–86: views from central, provincial and local levels', *Population and Development Review*, vol.12, no.3, pp.491–515.

Hull, T.H. (1990) 'Recent trends in sex ratios at birth in China', *Population and Development Review*, vol.16, no.1, pp.63–83.

Hull, T.H. and Hull, V.J. (1973) 'Fiji: a study in ethnic plurality and family planning' in Smith, T.E., *The Politics of Family Planning in the Third World*, London, George Allen and Unwin.

Jones, G.W. (ed.) (1984) *Demographic Transition in Asia*, Singapore, Maruzen Asia.

Lutz, W. (ed.) (1996) *The Future Population of the World: What Can We Assume Today?*, Laxenburg, International Institute for Applied Systems Analysis.

McEvedy, C. and Jones, R. (1978) *Atlas of World Population History*, Harmondsworth, Penguin.

Ueda, K. (1980) *A Demographic Guide to Asian Populations*, Tokyo, Southeast Asian Medical Information Center.

United Nations (1994) *The Sex and Age Distributions of the World Populations: the 1994 Revision*, New York, Population Division, Department of Economic and Social Information and Policy Analysis.

United Nations (1995) *World Population Prospects: the 1994 Revision*, New York, Population Division, Department for Economic and Social Information and Policy Analysis.

Widjojo, N. (1970) *Population Trends in Indonesia*, Ithaca, New York, Cornell University Press.

CHAPTER 4

Migration and the diaspora communities

Lucie Cheng and Marian Katz

4.1 Introduction

Global economic restructuring and changing relations among nation-states of the Asia-Pacific has led to the expansion and acceleration of the movement of peoples in the region in the last quarter of the twentieth century. This has altered, as well as intensified, existing migration patterns and created the conditions for new patterns to emerge. This chapter will focus on continuity and change in the migration experiences and identities of three important diaspora peoples of the Asia-Pacific: the Chinese, Japanese, and Filipino. Our discussion will be organized around three main questions.

1 What kinds of variation do we see among the diaspora communities of these groups today?

2 To what extent are these patterns similar to those of the past?

3 What is new about contemporary migration patterns and diaspora communities?

We will pay special attention to the new patterns which we see emerging in the late twentieth century.

To address these questions, we will first present an analytical framework which organizes migration patterns, diasporas, and diaspora identities according to their important types. We identify three main patterns of migration and five types of diasporas. We will examine the various combinations of migration patterns and diaspora types and the identity orientations emerging from these various combinations. These types and patterns must be understood as 'ideal types' which means that the real cases lie on a continuum between these distinct 'ideal types' and various degrees of mixed and overlapping forms.

When we study the diaspora communities in the Asia-Pacific today, the most striking feature is their diversity. Diversity in terms of places of origin and destination, reasons for and modes of moving, age, gender and class composition, personal resources and skill levels, and cultural tastes and practices. Moreover, the diversity within groups is as notable as that between them.

Thus the USA has witnessed an increase in the number of illegal immigrants from mainland China working for slave-wages in Chinatown sweatshops at the same time as the number of mainland Chinese moving to the USA, and throughout the region, as investors in private enterprises has been on the rise. Nor are Chinese migrants only from the extremes of the class spectrum. Growing numbers of people in the middle range are moving as well, entering the middle ranks of managerial, administrative and professional occupations as well as operating small businesses.

The Filipino and Japanese diasporas exhibit striking heterogeneities as well. On the one hand there are Filipino construction workers and domestic workers dispersed throughout Asia, while on the other hand, members of the Filipino elite run businesses in Manila from their mansions on Long Island, New York. Among Japanese-Americans, although the dominant trend is toward assimilation into the mainstream of American life as evidenced by high rates of out-group marriage, there is still over-representation in certain occupations and locations, such as in gardening and nurseries on the West coast. Throughout the Asia-Pacific, in contrast, managers of Japanese transnational corporations are spending as many as 20–30 years living in countries outside of Japan, yet retaining their Japanese identities and life-styles.

We see this diversity in part because global restructuring has altered some and intensified other existing migration patterns. This includes changes in the size and direction of migration flows, a proliferation of migration channels, including the growing commoditization of residence rights, and the growing heterogeneity of migrant populations. In addition to these shifts and variations on *existing* migration patterns, *new* patterns have emerged as well. Notably, along with one-way and round-trip flows between countries of origin and destination, we now see an increasing amount of serial international migration (migration to one country, then on to another) – especially among certain occupations such as domestic servants and professionals – and gender differentiation is often a striking feature of these flows.

In order to explain the patterns and changing configurations that we observe, we will refer to the economic, political and cultural processes which construct membership and status boundaries and hierarchies, and are often based implicitly, if not explicitly, on group-level characterizations such as race and ethnicity. In the past migrant groups were seen as fitting neatly into such systems of classification and ranking because they were perceived as relatively homogeneous. With the increasing heterogeneity of migrant populations and the development of interracial/transnational class-based networks, however, it is increasingly difficult to support such oversimplified depictions.

Global economic restructuring since the 1960s has provided certain conditions for a new Asian diaspora. Faced with a crisis, precipitated by a downturn in the world economy, capital permanently cast aside many existing industries in favour of more competitive economic activities, and simultaneously sought to re-establish profits by investing in locations with cheap and limited labour and environmental regulation. Pervasive plant closures and relocations and the emergence of new industries through an emphasis on innovation joined to produce a profound realignment of capital and labour, a rise of new economic powers, as well as a shift in the relations of nation-states.

Perhaps nowhere is this restructuring more far-reaching than in the Asia-Pacific. As Japan and the four 'little dragons' of South Korea, Taiwan, Singapore and Hong Kong have emerged as the more powerful newly-industrialized countries the position of these once primarily labour-exporting countries supplying the cheap labour needs of the more advanced USA, Canada and Australia, has shifted to manufacturing and services aimed at the more competitive sectors of economies world-wide, and they are now importing cheap labour from their less fortunate neighbours.

4.2   Migration and the nation-state

Current concerns about migration are tightly linked to the rise of the nation-state system, and often have less to do with the actual experience of spatial mobility than with the problems migration poses for defining the boundaries of, and determining membership in, the nation-state. New migrants, however, smudge this neat picture because their memberships in families, nations and groups traverse the state boundaries of the host country. In the past, short of exclusion, the ideal means for eliminating these smudges was thought to be erasing them via assimilation – that is, by incorporating immigrants entirely into the host society. In practice, assimilation has never been as straightforward or complete as in theory, and the early version of assimilationism, which imagined incorporation as conformity to the dominant social group, has been challenged by ideas of multiculturalism and now multinationalism.

Despite their differences, all three of these approaches – assimilationism, multiculturalism and multinationalism – share a concern with facilitating the incorporation of minority groups into the polity of the state, and thus new immigration is seen as problematic by all of them. The difference between the first two approaches and the last lies in the nature of the state-building project. While assimilationism and multiculturalism presume the nation-state, the multinationalist approach argues for a state which not only tolerates the coexistence of multiple cultures but more importantly acknowledges ethnic differences by incorporating their political representation through autonomous local government. Most modern state-building projects have been that of the nation-state type, but the former Soviet Union and the People's Republic of China are closer to the multinational model, albeit with certain important qualifications.

Conventional histories treat relatively stable populations within nation-state boundaries as normative, and periods of migration are, by contrast, seen as aberrations which require explanations. For a long time explanations for migration consequently tended to focus on push and pull factors outside of the nation-state. Later scholarship paid increasing attention to forces within nation-states acting through government policies which have swung between encouraging and restricting migration both out of and into their borders. Consider the active recruitment of Chinese labourers by American business to the USA in the middle of the nineteenth century followed by their official exclusion beginning in 1882. Modern state-building processes in non-Western societies are a mixture of response to, and consequence of, Western expansion. Japan, for instance, carried on lively maritime trade throughout East Asia until it was perceived that Christian missionaries were asserting themselves too aggressively into Japanese life. In response, Japan closed her borders such that no foreigners could enter, nor could Japanese residing outside of the country return.

Even before the adoption of Western ideas about nationhood, the Japanese perceived Western cultural influence as a threat to the harmony and stability of the society and sought to prevent such problems by officially restricting migration. All modern nation-state building projects rest on the foundational assumption that members (i.e. citizens) share a common culture – especially values. It is on this basis that all can be expected to follow a common set of rules or laws. Thus, nation-building processes by definition problematize cultural differences, and nation-states try to solve this problem by excluding those who they perceive as 'unassimilable'. The modern nation-state asks of every new immigrant group: 'Are they assimilable?'

Nation-building projects differ, however, in the criteria they use to answer this question. Japan represents one end of the continuum where the criteria are clear cut: unless you are born in Japan and have Japanese parents, the answer is an unequivocal 'no' – immigrants are forever foreigners. In contrast, in countries like the USA, Canada and Australia the criteria allow for the legal inclusion of people of diverse origins, yet the application of these criteria has often been influenced by cultural notions of assimilability which have expressed – at times explicitly and at times implicitly – class, racial and ethnic biases.

In this section we have highlighted the importance of government policies of the nation-state in determining migration flows and the incorporation of minority groups. Even when migration has been severely restricted, the numbers of people trying to cross borders illegally attest to the persistence of migration as a permanent, rather than a temporary, feature of modern societies. For instance, with regard to the USA we find that, 'After nearly a century and a half of Asian-American history, the newly arrived immigrants in most cases still made up half or more of the Asian-American populations today' (Dirlik, 1993, p.313).

4.3 Diverse experiences or diverse narratives?

Conventional history is the history of nation-states and generally historical writing has served to provide legitimizing narratives for existing status hierarchies and power relations. This means that the history of migration has tended to be written from the perspective of nation-states. Even in countries supposedly proud of their immigrant history, nation-building narratives have shaped the ways these histories have been told.

The primarily anglophone countries of the Asia-Pacific are the 'migrant states' of Australia, New Zealand, Canada, and – the one with prototypical status – the USA. As movements of peoples have accelerated world-wide the US experience has become increasingly relevant to other parts of the world. In fact, many countries, especially in Europe, have turned their eyes to the study of migration in the Americas in attempts to better understand the changes immigration is bringing to their own societies.

They may not get much help from traditional US migration studies, however, which have for most of the twentieth century stuck to a single narrative, epitomized by Oscar Handlin's 1951 study, *The Uprooted*, which John Lie summarizes as follows:

> The sojourn of immigrants entails a radical, and in many cases a singular, break from the old country to the new nation; migration is *inter*-national across well-defined national territories and boundaries. In the process of unidirectional crossing, migrants are 'uprooted' and shorn of premigration networks, cultures, and belongings. At the shores of the new land, migrants enter the caldron of a new society. The melting pot 'assimilates' migrants; the huddled masses become Americans.
>
> (Lie, 1996, p.303)

The assumptions built into this narrative predetermine what will be 'heard' as legitimate descriptions of the migration experience. One consequence of this is that much immigration research is more prescriptive than descriptive. Since immigrants are seen as entering American society as a *tabula rasa* (blank surface) – or at least as blank 'slates'. What is of interest is not what they bring with them but rather the erasability of their pasts, in other words, how available they are for inscription with 'American' culture (language, habits, life-styles, etc.). We can see from this account that the image of the immigrant experience was not one of creative re-invention or mutual adaptation, but rather of the new arrivals rejecting their pasts and embracing the social world the earlier arrivals have made for them. Notably, this narrative helps to normalize locating immigrants at the bottom of the social ladder by re-imagining them without any previous social statuses that might conflict with such a location. It is often roots, in culture and social networks, which give individuals access to opportunities and power. The uprooted immigrant was by definition disempowered and thus less of a threat to national unity. Little resistance to this depiction was expected on the part of immigrants themselves, because giving up one's roots was seen as the first step towards becoming American – and becoming

American was celebrated as the only path to status, prosperity and happiness.

This does not mean that immigrants in fact cut off their connections with their home countries, but it does mean that this part of their lives was de-emphasized and hidden from the popular imagination. One way of understanding the recent popularity of the term 'multiculturalism' is that it serves as a key word for the shift in national perceptions of the value of roots. Under new conditions of global economic and political restructuring, having roots is increasingly coming to be seen as an asset rather than a flaw, and the works by migration scholars calling for a re-evaluation of the nature of immigrants' ongoing transnational connections may be seen as a response to these new conditions.

Understanding this narrative, which has dominated migration research for much of the twentieth century, helps us to understand why so much migration research has focused on measurements of 'assimilation' such as naturalization rates, and education and income levels. It, moreover, establishes the very categories used by researchers to study migration: clearly bounded nation-states and migrant groups, and unidirectional migration flows.

None the less, this model for a time was thought to describe fairly accurately the experiences of significant proportions of many immigrant groups to the English speaking countries of the Asia-Pacific in the late nineteenth and early twentieth centuries. Many European immigrants left their homelands under circumstances which made their return, or even ongoing links to the country of origin, very difficult. The Eastern European and Russian Jews are perhaps the most obvious case in point, but not the only one. Many Irish immigrants, for instance, while maintaining a strong emotional attachment to Ireland, still could not viably return and make a living there. Despite research, which revealed high levels of return migration even for European immigrants to America, this model has not been seriously challenged until recently.

Two main phenomena, among others, leading to this challenge are the tremendous increase in migration within and from the Asia-Pacific, and the increasing visibility of the works of scholars whose ancestries can be traced to this region. Figure 4.1 shows major migration flows in the Asia-Pacific in the 1990s (see **Eccleston *et al.*, 1998, pp.20–1**). Among all the receiving countries, the USA is clearly the largest. In terms of sending countries, between 1971 and 1992 China (including Taiwan), South Korea and the Philippines after Mexico contributed the most immigrants to the USA. Within the Asia-Pacific, intra-regional migration has also been on the rise. Take Japan for instance, alien resident registration figures show that intra-regional immigrants, mostly from South Korea, mainland China, Taiwan and the Philippines, have consistently exceeded extra-regional ones, and the numbers are rising rapidly. In 1994, of the total 1.35 million registered aliens, almost 73 per cent were from other Asian countries.

The breakdown of explicit racial discrimination in academia in the early 1970s in the USA opened the doors for an increasing number of

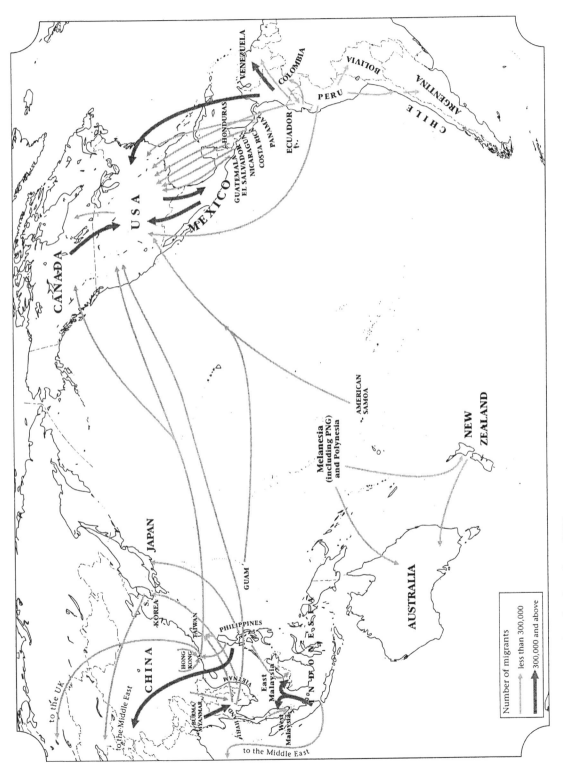

Figure 4.1 *International migration, 1990s*
Source: Segal (1993), Stahl (1996) and Silverman (1996)

minority scholars, including those of Asian descent. A distinctly Asian-American perspective on immigration which challenged the old narrative began to surface. As nations in the Asia-Pacific experienced differing transformations, some, such as China, lost a generation of bilingual scholars to North American and Australian universities, while others, such as South Korea and Taiwan, attracted the return of their highly-educated expatriates. This unprecedented two-way flow of Asian intellectuals provided both the material conditions and the wherewithal for a new narrative, one that would give voice to the diasporic characteristics of migration rather than the previously exclusive focus on ethnicity. The latter concern has led to the emergence of 'multiculturalism' within the nation-state, whereas the former seems to open up a space for the birth of multinational states.

4.4   Types of diasporas

The term 'diaspora' has its origins in Greek antiquity, but recently its usage has been expanded to include social formations which were not thought of as diasporic in the past. Khachig Tololyan (1996) has argued that this re-naming of various communities of dispersion formerly known as ethnic and racial minorities, refugee and exile groups, overseas communities, and so forth 'is the result of change in the politics of discursive regimes as well as the product of extra-discursive phenomena'. In the last section, we pointed out the rise of Asian scholars in the English-speaking states of North America and Australia and the accelerated multidirectional flows of people in this region as the most relevant discursive and extra-discursive phenomena leading to the application of 'diaspora' to dispersions of Asians, including Chinese, Koreans, Filipinos and Japanese.

At the core of the concept of diaspora is the notion of the involuntary scattering, usually by force, of a people to many different locations away from their homeland. Typically, diaspora also means the loss of that homeland leading to a condition of permanent exile. Further, to be a diaspora means to reproduce inter-generationally a sense of identification with this group, which also means in practice to find ways of reproducing at least some aspects of the common culture in the new environment, often part of this is the idea of return. Diaspora suggests a commitment to maintaining a sense of roots that lie outside of the country where one lives. It is this sense which has made it a useful concept for describing patterns of group resistance to the processes of political incorporation and cultural homogenization promoted by the increasing integration of local, regional and global economies. Recently, scholars have particularly used the term in two ways: to highlight the persistence or emergence of political formations excluded from the nation-state system; and to redefine cultural identities (ethnic and other) in modern multi-ethnic societies.

We will use the term diaspora broadly to mean any minority community within a multi-ethnic polity, e.g. nation-state, which takes common ancestry, actual or imaginary, as the basis for membership, and promotes a collective trans-local/trans-state identity. Thus we can examine variation in the type of diaspora both between different diaspora communities within the same 'host' country (such as the Chinese, Filipino and Japanese diasporas in the USA) and between communities of the same diaspora in different 'host' countries (such as Chinese in Malaysia, Thailand, Indonesia, Australia, Canada and the USA).

There are five main types of diasporas summarized in Table 4.1 and listed below.

1   Diasporas of imperial expansion.

2   Diasporas of forced expulsion (or removal) and exile.

3   Labour or proletarian diasporas, such as Italian workers, Filipino domestics and so forth, i.e. those who left their homeland to find work or to sell their labour; in contrast to the fourth type.

4   Trading/entrepreneurial/financial and managerial diasporas that refer to the movement of business people involved in trade or transnational and multinational corporations, such as the 'middleman minority', Japanese managers and Taiwanese entrepreneurs, and recent immigrant investors and financiers.

5   Intellectual/professional/scientific diasporas, referring to the multi-directional movement of the highly-educated peoples whose mobility created the discursive regimes of 'brain drain' and 'brain gain' in the mid twentieth century, and in the late twentieth century shifted to the more supranational perspective of 'brain flow'.

Table 4.1   *Five main types of diasporas*

Diaspora type	Cases
1 Imperial expansion	Greek, Roman, British, Spanish, Portuguese, Japanese
2 Forced expulsion and exile	Jewish, African, Armenian, South-East Asian, Salvadoran
3 Labour or proletariat	majority of Asian diasporas in the Asia-Pacific in the nineteenth and early twentieth centuries, including Chinese, Japanese and Filipino; also Mexican
4 Trading/entrepreneurial and managerial	Jewish, Lebanese and Chinese traders and entrepreneurs, Japanese managers
5 Professional/intellectual	Filipino nurses, Russian scientists, Chinese engineers, Korean professors, American English teachers

Note that while the first two types of diasporas emphasize the predominance of external forces and the individual migrants as total persons, the last three put the emphasis on the interaction between specific labour niches created by changes in the world political economy and individual circumstances. For this chapter the greater significance of the latter three types is highlighted. Note also that these are 'ideal types' and that real diasporas may exhibit mixed forms.

4.5   Migration patterns, types of diasporas and diasporic identities

This section introduces a framework under which the five types of diasporas discussed above can be organized. We treat the state-building project and the migrant-group orientation as two major dimensions. These dimensions are not static, but instead must be historicized. Thus a migrant group that once intended to reside in the host country temporarily may turn into permanent residents at another time; and a state which insisted on assimilating its diverse immigrant populations in the beginning may shift toward allowing cultural pluralism. We also want to emphasize that changes on both dimensions are not unidirectional. Just as sojourners can become settlers, settlers can also become sojourners and so on and so forth. All five types of diasporas are discussed, but we focus on the four types prominent in recent histories of the Asia-Pacific: refugee/exile, labour, entrepreneurial/managerial/financial, and professional/intellectual diasporas. The links between these diasporas and identity formation are also examined.

The imperial expansion diaspora is associated with only the settler migration pattern, that is a one-way flow from place of origin to place of destination. In this case, unique identities are formed as colonial migrants seek to distinguish themselves both from their country of origin and the indigenous people(s) of the country of destination. There may or may not be ongoing links between the colonizing diaspora and the country of origin, but a collective identification with the home country persists as long as the colonial status persists even though the majority of migrants see themselves as settlers and have no intention of return. In the Asia-Pacific the main representatives of this group are the British and other European diasporas in past centuries which are now the dominant groups in the Americas and Australia/New Zealand. The Japanese who settled in Manchuria, Korea and Taiwan during Japan's imperial days are another example.

The classic diaspora is a one-way flow resulting from forced expulsion or removal. This kind of diaspora is usually the result of colonization, war and persecution. The involuntary character of such migrations means that a large proportion of migrants may continue to desire to return to their country of origin. However, the other distinguishing characteristic of this kind of diaspora is the high barriers to return. It is this latter characteristic that creates the tendency of this group to orient toward settlement in the country of destination rather than toward return. Even when group members form organizations aimed at influencing affairs in the country of origin, they tend to draw on their status as members of the country of destination for their organizing strength. This diasporic strength is recognized by both countries of origin and destination, and historically has been the reason for their persecution and exploitation. In the Asia-Pacific today we see this type of diaspora illustrated by the dispersion of South-East Asian (Vietnamese, Kampuchean and Laotian) refugees throughout the region. This type of diaspora also highlights the import-ance of state–state relations and exposes the moral dimension of contemporary migration: what happens when people are forced out of their traditional homelands but are not welcomed to resettle in any other country? This predicament suggests an additional category of homeless diasporas. While some new migrant groups are welcomed everywhere, others find themselves welcomed nowhere.

The next two types of diaspora became prominent during the period of Euro-American hegemony in the region. Certain 'middleman' or 'service' diasporas, such as the Chinese who were already spread throughout South-East Asia, were particularly valued by colonial powers for their communi-cation and transportation networks. More important, however, were the labour migrations which created the first large-scale Asian diasporas in the Americas. Today, labour migrations are important sources of both continuity and change in the region. For example, the earliest Asian labour diaspora in the USA, the Chinese, continues to be one of the most important, accounting for the revival of the garment manufacturing industry in New York. As a regional phenomenon, the gender and occupational differentiation of the Filipino labour diaspora to Japan, South Korea, South-East Asia and the USA has been particularly striking.

The early Chinese labour diaspora was mostly young and male and of limited education. These migrants were sojourners in that they were expected to send a large portion of their earnings to their families in the home country as remittances and they were expected to return to the home country to settle and raise families. This pattern was also encouraged by labour recruiting countries which only wanted to welcome the migrants on a temporary basis. Exclusionary laws and racist practices, especially those which restricted family reunification and formation, created the conditions for a sojourning pattern and labour diaspora to be reproduced inter-generationally. Gradually the Chinese labour diaspora has shifted from a sojourner to a settler pattern for several reasons: (a) changing US laws and racial/ethnic relations; (b) changing gender composition (family forma-tion) – many labour migrants are now young and middle-aged women; and (c) the rise of an ethnic economy.

Filipino migration to the USA before independence was complicated by the fact that they were US nationals without citizenship. This unique political status together with a culture divergent from the Confucian-dominated societies of North-East Asia where Chinese, Japanese and

Koreans hailed, produced a self identity that seems more troubled than the other three Asian groups, and a separate discourse. Epifanio San Juan, Jr. argues that Filipino-Americans should not think of themselves as Asian-Americans but simply as Filipino-Americans. In contrast, contemporary Filipino labour migrants in East Asia may be categorized as sojourners, in that their stay is legally understood to be temporary and they generally tend to send home a major proportion of their wages as remittances and eventually to return to the Philippines.

The Jews in Europe, Chinese in South-East Asia, Asians in East Africa, Armenians in Turkey, Koreans in America and others have been labelled 'middleman minorities' by scholars because many among them have traditionally occupied an economic position in the social structure as traders and small business entrepreneurs playing the role of 'middleman' between producer and consumer, owner and renter, employer and employee. This is the fourth type of diaspora. Edna Bonacich argues that the intention to sojourn rather than to settle leads to a 'stranger' orientation to the host country which is manifested in certain economic and social behaviour, notably thrift, concentration in occupations that are portable and easily liquidated (such as trade) and communal solidarity. The racial or ethnic distinctiveness of the group, whether real or constructed, makes it a convenient target for hostility from both clients and dominant business groups. This hostility reinforces the communal solidarity and the desire to return. The collective orientation toward the homeland characterize them as diasporans.

A late twentieth-century twist on the 'middleman minority' might be seen in the diaspora communities of Japanese managers of Japan-owned firms world-wide. They live close by each other, establish Japanese schools for their children, give rise to neighbourhood markets that speak Japanese and stock Japanese food, and in general maintain a distinctively Japanese community within the host country.

Another late twentieth-century phenomenon is the flow of immigrant financiers, or those with capital. Although host-country requirement of a certain minimal amount of money deposits as a condition for immigration is not new, its function, operation and consequences are now quite different from the past. Whereas such monetary requirement was first designed to avoid immigrants from becoming dependants of the welfare state and thus was calculated to reflect living expenses of the potential immigrant, the requirement now is fairly high, and is intended to facilitate capital accumulation and creation of employment opportunities in the host country. Many states, whether rich or poor, have instituted policies to utilize this requirement as rights to permanent residence or even citizenship are sought. An obvious example is the USA.

The fifth type of diaspora, while resulting from all three migration patterns, is most highly correlated with the third migration pattern: serial transnational (i.e. trans-state) migration. This pattern is distinguished from the others in that it describes the situation where individuals move repeatedly across national borders depending on job opportunities, work conditions and cultural milieu. To the extent that different common origin groups specialize in different professions and types of intellectual labour (a kind of ethnic niche phenomenon) these diasporas may exhibit an ethnic character. None the less, the importance of their identification with their status as highly-educated workers occupying important roles in the capitalist world system means that these groups share a kind of universalistic, cosmopolitan or hybrid identity which is disconnected from any particular place of ancestry and makes them think of themselves primarily not as citizens of any nation-state but rather as global citizens for whom home is everywhere and everywhere can be home.

The most striking example of this type of diaspora may be found among Chinese professionals from the PRC, Taiwan and Hong Kong. It is also evident among Filipino doctors and nurses who have migrated widely, depending on the varying demands for their specialization combined with changing migration legislation in different countries. There are also signs that Americans of various ancestry are beginning to participate in such migration flows. For example, many English as a foreign language (EFL) teachers spend their careers moving from country to country in the Asia-Pacific, according to pay and working conditions, lengths of contracts and their individual preferences for experiencing living in different cultures.

4.6 Changing configurations

The restructuring of economic and political relations in the Asia-Pacific has had the greatest impact on the latter three types of diasporas (labour, entrepreneurial/managerial/financial, and professional/intellectual). These three types of diasporas exhibit greater diversity in their relation to patterns of migration and group orientation than do the first two. The most important overall feature of restructuring in the Asia-Pacific has been the declining importance of the Euro-American societies *relative to* Japan and the newly-industrialized economies of South Korea, Taiwan, Hong Kong and Singapore. In other words, the most striking characteristic of relations in the Asia-Pacific prior to the last quarter of the twentieth century was the economic, political, social and cultural dominance of the USA, and to a lesser extent the other industrialized Euro-American societies. This meant that most flows were unidirectional, with capital and culture flowing from West to East, and people and goods flowing from East to West. Accordingly, the most striking *change* in the region has been the emergence of multiple industrialized and post-industrial centres, and the consequent demotion of the USA, whilst still important, from prominence to being only one of several important 'core' areas. The evidence of this change lies in the differentiation of existing flows between the USA and East Asia, the increasing number and types of flows among regions within the Asia-Pacific (including Australia and New Zealand) and the emergence of new kinds of migration flows.

Background

The earliest Asian diasporas formed around the regional land–sea trading system linking India, South-East Asia, Central Asia and China. With the decline of this system and the rise of European hegemony in the region, the dominant pattern became one of the movement of Asian labour to meet the needs of the industrializing economies of the European settler societies of Canada, Australia and the USA, and to work in Euro-American industrial enterprises established in Asia. These mid-nineteenth to mid-twentieth century migrant populations – whether from China, Japan or the Philippines – were similar in their large proportions of young, single males with limited education and often from rural agricultural backgrounds. Despite these similarities in composition of the migrant groups, their migration patterns and diaspora communities differed in distinct ways.

Three diasporas in the USA

Looking at three cases within a single host country allows us to examine how the same processes of global restructuring are experienced differently by different groups, and result in different migration patterns and diaspora identities. For each diaspora we will consider how migration patterns and state-building projects interact with the variables of race/ethnicity, language, education, gender, state–state relations, and economic status/incorporation in the construction of actual local identities.

If we focus on the USA we note that by the middle of the twentieth century, before the Second World War, the following variations in diaspora communities had emerged. The Chinese had become a distinct, urban, ethnic group with its own residential and business districts known as 'Chinatowns'. In comparison, the Japanese and Filipino communities were much less visible in the urban centres. Japanese, who were allowed to bring their wives, settled largely in the rural west and were concentrated in agricultural occupations. The Filipinos exhibited a serious bifurcation. Some, initially brought by the US government to receive American education and serve in its colonial administration, stayed on as professionals, while others came as agricultural labourers.

Racism is often targeted as the cause of the formation of Chinatowns, but Japanese and Filipinos were equally the targets of American racist ideologies and practices. Anti-Asian sentiments led to both *de jure* and *de facto* exclusion or severe restriction of Asians from the country and the segregation of Asians from the white European population within the country. Racism alone cannot account for differences in diaspora communities.

The Chinese diaspora in the USA
The Chinese diaspora in the USA has been characterized by ethnic resilience. The development of distinct Chinese communities, called Chinatowns when they occupied inner-city neighbourhoods, is the most striking evidence of this. Even though the Chinese diaspora has undergone

tremendous differentiation, the persistence and reinvention of ethnic neighbourhoods and ethnic economies is the distinctive feature of this diaspora community.

The duality of recent Asian immigration to the USA is reflected in the Chinese ethnic communities. On the one hand, many old Chinatowns had been deteriorating as the younger generations moved up the occupational ladder and out of the inner city, assimilating in varying degrees. But since the 1960s the majority of Chinese in the USA, like many other Asian groups, are foreign born. This influx of new immigrants has had the effect of reinvigorating the Chinese ethnic economy by supplying capital as well as both new labour and new consumers. Many Chinatowns have been revived as commercial centres, and to a lesser extent as residential communities for poorer new immigrants. There has also been a new phenomenon, the emergence of suburban 'Chinatowns' where new middle- and upper-class immigrants are reshaping the landscape according to their interests and tastes. Changes in US immigration laws have been, perhaps, the most important reason for the changing proportions of native and foreign born in the Asian diasporas in the USA. The strong and continued importance of family and ethnic networks in the Chinese

Chinatown, San Francisco

community, however, plays an equally important role in recruiting new migrants, both legally through family unification and occupational preferences, and illegally through the transnational networks of smugglers. The large flows of new immigrants and the structure of Chinese business networks promotes the reproduction of communities with strong senses of ethnic identity. We will return to these points in a later section where Chinese diaspora communities in various countries are compared with each other.

The Japanese diaspora in the USA

The Japanese diaspora in the USA at present is characterized by its assimilationist tendencies. This was not always the case. Before the Second World War, Japanese on the west coast developed many forms of ethnically-based associations and a strong sense of ethnic identity. A concentration in agricultural occupations, more equal gender composition, and the role of the Japanese government in sponsoring and monitoring migration meant that the Japanese came more as settlers than as sojourners. The success of Japan's industrialization and imperialist expansion in Asia provided some, albeit limited, protection for Japanese immigrants before the Second World War. The strong assimilationist orientation that we see today can be largely explained by the discrimination experienced by Japanese-Americans during the war, when they were forced to leave their homes for relocation camps (**McGrew and Brook, 1998, p.24**). Many families lost their property and possessions, and when the camps were dismantled the Japanese-Americans were advised not to settle together or return to the west coast. Although some Japanese ethnic communities were revived, they were the exception rather than the rule. In addition to intergovernmental relations and their affects on the group, the Japanese diaspora has been distinctive in its lack of new flows in the post-war period. Japan's economic and political stability may be credited for this 'unusual' pattern. The small numbers of new immigrants to the USA from Japan generally do not have connections with the older Japanese-American community, and they are culturally distinct from them.

The Japanese diaspora, in contrast to the Chinese, is marked by assimilation and discontinuity. However, were it not for the large inflows of new immigrants, assimilation might be seen as a more important trend in the Chinese diaspora as well. While the Japanese diaspora is the least heterogeneous of the three Asian groups we examine, it none the less does exhibit a distinctive new diaspora phenomenon. This is the diaspora made up of managers of Japanese transnational corporations assigned to work in offices and plants outside of Japan. In some parts of the USA this has resulted in suburban enclaves similar in some respects to the new suburban 'Chinatowns' in that they have developed a degree of institutional completeness such that the Japanese managers and their families can approximate the life-style they were used to in Japan – including shopping for food and clothing in Japanese stores and supermarkets, going to Japanese movies and sending their children to Japanese schools. Because these communities are so much determined by the corporations, however, the identities of these Japanese managers, and to a large degree their families as well, remains strongly oriented toward Japan. Consequently, they are unlikely to get involved in local politics. These communities thus exhibit a kind of sojourner orientation, while in other ways, via the corporation, they inhabit what might be best described as Japanese 'colonies' within the broad 'host' society. We see this not only in the USA but throughout the Asia-Pacific.

The Filipino diaspora in the USA

Whereas the Chinese diaspora in the USA has always displayed a strong ethnic resilience and the Japanese diaspora shifted from ethnic resilience to assimilation, the Filipino diaspora in the USA has always demonstrated a strong assimilationist tendency. Notably, even when Filipinos were the largest Asian diaspora community in the USA, they were one of the least visible. Even though ties between Filipino migrants in the USA and their families in the Philippines have often remained strong, the colonial relationship between the USA and the Philippines played an important role in determining the orientation of Filipino migrants toward incorporation and membership in American society.

The institutions – especially educational ones – established during US colonial rule have legacies in subsequent diasporic communities. The earliest Filipino migrants to the USA were members of the elite brought to America to be educated and trained to serve in the colonial administration. Later, when unskilled Filipino males were recruited as agricultural labourers, their prior exposure to American culture and values made them feel that they belonged and inspired in them a strong sense of injustice when they encountered prejudice and discrimination on the mainland. In contrast to Chinese and Japanese – who brought with them a sense of difference and an ability to rationalize that as outsiders they would have to endure being treated differently, at least for a while – being colonial subjects made Filipinos see themselves as 'insiders' who deserved full equality with other citizens.

To a great degree, the colonial experience smoothed the way for assimilation of the Filipino diaspora into the American mainstream. At the same time, this assimilationist tendency made it difficult for a unified or visible social movement to emerge among Filipinos as an ethnic group to counter ethnic discrimination. Thus, Filipino ethnic organizations have tended to be class specific. In addition to the colonial experience, other features of culture and social organization (differences in language, religion and family structure) make it difficult for Filipinos to participate in pan-Asian organizations and activities.

In contrast to the Filipino diaspora in the Asia-Pacific, where large numbers of female immigrants have become a major source of cheap unskilled domestic and sexual labour and a major source of nurses and medical technicians, the predominant current trend of Filipino migration to the USA is of highly-educated professional labour. Although they do not tend to settle in ethnic communities but rather to disperse throughout the country according to job opportunities, many Filipino professional organizations have emerged and become increasingly involved in political, rather than simply professional and personal, issues. The lack of an ethnic economy has contributed to pushing Filipino immigrants to assimilate into the larger society.

Diasporas in the USA: summary
Within the same host society, diasporas vary greatly. This variation results from the initial migration patterns, as well as from the position of the diaspora group within the host society as determined by the interaction of group-level and system-level characteristics. At the system level, opportunities for economic and political incorporation, which are partly determined by relations between the sending and receiving societies, play an important role. But the characteristics of the migrants matter as well. Race, religion and language will affect the amount of social distance perceived between migrants and the host society. Gender composition, education and family structure will further affect the ways in which migrants organize themselves and make claims on the host society. Two of the most important factors affecting diaspora identities are the immigration and naturalization laws of the host country, and the size and composition of new immigrant flows. Sending countries, such as Japan and China, which hold a *jus sanguinis* (legal claim based on common blood) definition of citizenry, not only allow political participation of diasporan populations but also bind their identity and help to perpetuate a sense of peoplehood across sites of settlement.

The increasing duality and heterogeneity of diaspora communities in the context of global restructuring is a challenge to the sense of a coherent ethnic identity. It can be expected that the changing meaning of 'ethnic' identity will be a topic of growing interest among Asia-Pacific diaspora communities.

Examining several groups in a single host country highlights the interaction of group-level characteristics and system-level variables in shaping diaspora communities. Looking at a single diaspora group across a variety of host countries, in comparison, highlights the importance of the host government and society in shaping diaspora identities. It is helpful in distinguishing which group-level characteristics appear to have transnational relevance.

Cross-state variation within one diaspora: the overseas Chinese

The Chinese diaspora in the Asia-Pacific – including Malaysia, Thailand, Vietnam, Indonesia, the Philippines, Japan, Australia, Canada and the USA – is the oldest and most developed diasporan group in the region. Chinese in many countries, even after several generations outside of China, continued to be raised to see China as their home. In the words of one Chinese-American:

> I am Chinese, born in Vietnam. Now I am an American citizen ... In Vietnam, it was my birth place, but I never felt comfortable there, because we were treated as foreigners. It is my place of origin but not a home I feel close to. When we were growing up, we were taught to believe that China was our home. That's where your ancestors are, so one day you will go back to China.

> (Lee, 1991, p.127)

Thailand has often been pointed to as an interesting exception to this trend. The actively-assimilationist policies of the Thai government went further than any other country to incorporate Chinese fully into Thai society. In contrast, exclusionary policies in Malaysia resulted in the establishment of the separate Chinese state of Singapore.

The boundary maintenance effort of the Chinese diasporans has received continuous encouragement and support from both state and society of China. The *jus sanguinis* definition of citizenry provides for the participation of overseas Chinese in the Chinese polity. In fact, the Republic of China on the mainland and in Taiwan and the People's Republic of China have quotas in their legislative bodies and national assemblies reserved for overseas Chinese representatives. Both governments have also developed a terminology to refer to overseas Chinese and to distinguish among them according to citizenship, generation and birthplace. Chinese diasporans were recognized as a special category for privileged treatment and protection as well as for appeals to financial, political and social assistance. During the Cultural Revolution from the mid 1960s to the mid 1970s, dependants of overseas Chinese who remained in mainland China were singled out for invidious persecution and discrimination for their presumed subversive connections. The division of the Chinese state into different political regimes has created an ambivalence among the diasporans. Their identity is further complicated by the Taiwanese independence movement, the most vocal segment of which seeks to sever Taiwan and Taiwanese from both the state and nation of China. Changing and multiple meanings of being Chinese has become an important topic of discussion among members and scholars of the Chinese diaspora.

The first important modern change in diaspora identities for Chinese probably occurred just after the communist victory in 1949. While some Chinese were attracted to return to their 'homeland' to help in building the new nation, others, less sympathetic, reacted by deciding to break with their China-oriented identity and try to assimilate more fully into the societies where they had settled. Pressures on Chinese minorities throughout Asia who had developed extensive transnational, regional and even global business networks were exacerbated by anti-communist fervour. Malaysia, the Philippines and Indonesia waged series of anti-Chinese persecutions, the worst case being the murder of thousands of Chinese residents of Indonesia. Both rival states of Taiwan and the People's Republic of China developed programmes to resettle Chinese refugees and exiles from South-East Asia.

Two results of contemporary restructuring that appear to impact on Chinese diasporas in the Asia-Pacific are, first, the growing openness and economic development of mainland China and, second, the state-building projects of the host countries which have varying effects depending on whether they emphasize a single national culture, as in the case of Malaysia, or a multicultural society, as in the case of Australia. According to at least one author, Wei-ming Tu, there has been a recent trend of emigration of Chinese from the nationalizing states of South-East Asia to the states emphasizing multiculturalism as part of their national identities – Australia, New Zealand, Canada and the USA – reflecting a collective desire to retain their cultural identity as Chinese. However, this motivation to re-migrate may be misguided, as numerous scholars have pointed out that the current 'multicultural' state-building projects of these countries are only skin-deep; if not wholly illusory.

4.7   Emerging diasporas: a transnational professional/service class?

Because theories of international migration have been developed from the study of the early phase of capitalist restructuring and largely derived from the experience of European migrants, the migration experience has been characterized (as discussed above) as a one-way flow of labourers who enter the host society from the bottom of the social ladder and gradually become assimilated into the host society. Thus, when attention was drawn to the movement of highly-educated intellectuals and professionals from less developed to more developed societies – particularly from Asia to the USA – this phenomenon was labelled 'brain drain' reflecting the one-way flow process of assimilation. That this view has been slow to change is a tribute to the power of the discursive regime which has come to hold sway on the academic mind. There are two factors which make the experience of these migrants different from those in the past. The first factor, which makes professional migrants unique, is their relation to capital and the portability of their resources. The second factor is a general characteristic of international migration which may come to affect the movements of skilled and unskilled labour alike. That is the development and acceleration of communications and transportation networks which make continuity of relations with homeland society the norm rather than the exception, and part of everyday life rather than something cut off from it.

Asian migrants in the Asia-Pacific have probably always maintained more ongoing ties with their home societies than have European migrants. Hostile and exclusionary practices by the host societies, based on both racial and ethnic differences, reinforced the importance of maintaining these ties. But it is only in the current phase of development of global capitalism that the labour market conditions have existed for the emergence of a truly international, or transnational, labour force. And such a labour force seems to be emerging first among highly-skilled intellectual and professional labour. As developing economies become increasingly high-tech, national competition in the world state system leads nations to compete in attracting the best highly-skilled intellectuals (scientists, engineers, professors) and professionals. At the same time, educational systems (secondary and tertiary) in the less developed countries, under the influence of developed countries, especially the USA, have been redesigned to articulate with the educational systems in the more developed countries. This has greatly facilitated the flow of professional labour across national boundaries. The international flow of professional labour has also been facilitated by immigration legislation giving preferences to individuals with skills seen as important to the national economy.

For a long time debate focused on the degree of harm the loss of professional labour would do to the less developed countries, with many arguing that it would leave them even further behind. While the verdict is not yet in, it is clear that sending and receiving countries both gain and lose by this arrangement and, to the extent that the professional class is truly becoming internationalized, the questions as posed by this debate seem less and less relevant. For the more developed countries, reliance on highly-educated labour from abroad means a possible loss of hegemony due to rapid technology transfer which these professionals facilitate. The governments of many less developed countries encourage this technology transfer by their former nationals, even going so far as to establish data banks of their professionals abroad. These governments also periodically offer incentives to attract the return of these professional migrants, and many of them do return. Even a small number of such returnees can play a significant role in national modernization.

It is no longer the prospect of permanent return that concerns the governments of developing countries. In fact, the foreign ideas often adopted by such professionals in some ways makes them less than desirable candidates for repatriation. Instead, permanent cycles of short-term visits for work, teaching and research are encouraged. This new migration pattern, which is not only between countries of origin and settlement but often extends across multiple countries, in turn promotes the formation of international professional networks.

The conditions which contribute to the emergence of transnational professional diasporas can be summarized as follows. First, global economic restructuring, one part of which is the restructuring of the economy of the Asia-Pacific, creates an international division of labour on the one hand, and quicker and denser transnational communication and transportation networks on the other, which, hand-in-hand facilitate the growth of transnational migration patterns, networks, communities and identities. Transnational corporations and international professional organizations play a role here as well in facilitating the entrance of the less developed countries' professionals into the international job market. Second, new forms of immigration legislation and legal statuses – such as preferences for professional immigrants, dual citizenship, and non-citizen forms of legal residency for varying purposes and lengths of stay – are the other necessary condition for these transnational networks to be constructed and maintained. The third is variations in living and working conditions. Their actual decisions about where to move, however, will be further determined by the transferability of their credentials, by the pre-existence of personal and professional networks, and by the ability to reproduce in the new location the social and cultural life-styles they prefer. This latter criterion is facilitated by the emergence of a global, cosmopolitan and hybridized culture. Just as the flows of people are expanded and accelerated by globalization of communications and transportation networks, so are flows of consumer goods and services and other forms of cultural production. The expansion of education in less developed countries means the emergence of a middle class that is not guaranteed entry into the national elite. When education has been the mobility path of a group they tend to be strongly committed to individualistic and meritocratic criteria. These values and the actual content of education (e.g. English) further make such professionals particularly well-prepared to participate in the global economy and culture. Outflows of highly-educated migrants from Asian countries, however, are not necessarily detrimental to the home society; nearly all Asia-Pacific governments, with the notable exception of Japan, have called on 'their' diasporic communities to contribute money and technical skills to the state-building projects at 'home'. In the case of Japan, a new policy was implemented in 1990 to encourage the return of second- and third-generation Japanese emigrants to meet the needs for low-skilled labour in Japan.

4.8   Summary and conclusion

In this chapter we have first discussed the changing meanings of the concept of diaspora and reasons for its current popularity. A framework built on the two axes of state-building project and migrant-group orientation was developed to organize different types of diasporas in the Asia-Pacific. Using two comparative strategies, namely Chinese, Japanese and Filipinos in the USA, and Chinese in the USA and in South-East Asia, we have tried to relate sending- and receiving-country attitudes and policies, migration processes and ethnic identity to the different types of diasporas. We ended the chapter by pointing to the importance of emerging diasporas of professionals. With the acceleration of globalization in almost all areas of life, the heightened interest in diaspora studies seems to indicate a certain yearning for connection to one's origins. This is accompanied by an emphasis on community organization as the locus of political activity. This global/local configuration may be one of the most important modes of adaptation in the twenty-first century.

References

Dirlik, A. (ed.) (1993) *What is in a Rim? Critical Perspectives on the Pacific Region Idea*, Boulder, Westview Press.

Eccleston, B., Dawson, M. and McNamara, D. (eds) (1998) *The Asia-Pacific Profile*, London, Routledge in association with The Open University.

Lee, J.F.J. (1991) *Asian American Experiences in the United States: Oral Histories of First to Fourth Generation Americans from China, the Philippines, Japan, India, the Pacific Islands, Vietnam and Cambodia*, Jefferson, NC, McFarland.

Lie, J. (1996) 'From international migration to transnational diaspora', *Contemporary Sociology*, vol.25, no.3, pp.303–6.

McGrew, A. and Brook, C. (eds) (1998) *Asia-Pacific in the New World Order*, London, Routledge in association with The Open University.

Segal, A. (1993) *An Atlas of International Migration*, London, Hans Zell.

Silverman, G. (1996) 'Vital and vulnerable', *Far Eastern Economic Review*, 23 May, pp.60–4.

Stahl, C.W. (1996) 'International migration and the East Asia APEC/PECC economies', unpublished paper, PECC, Singapore.

Tololyan, K. (1996) 'Rethinking diaspora(s): stateless power in the transnational moment', *Diaspora*, vol.5, no.1, pp.65–97.

Further reading

Chan, Sucheng (1991) *Asian Americans: an Interpretive History*, Boston, Twayne.

Cohen, R. (1996) *Global Diasporas: an Introduction*, London, UCL Press.

Ong, P., Bonacich, E. and Cheng, L. (eds) (1994) *The New Asian Immigration in Los Angeles and Global Restructuring*, Philadelphia, Temple University Press.

CHAPTER 5

Race, ethnicity and language

Anthony van Fossen

5.1   Six degrees of separation

Racial, ethnic and linguistic discrimination across the Pacific has been closely connected with political and economic inequality. Race, ethnicity and language have often been most significant markers of class relations and they frequently provide the principles according to which conflicts over wealth and state power take place. In this way, race, ethnicity and language have been important in virtually all Pacific societies, but the levels of discrimination and inequality have varied considerably. This chapter examines why racial, ethnic and linguistic (REL) discrimination and inequality are so much higher in Japan, Fiji, and Malaysia than in New Zealand, Australia, and Hawaii in the late 1990s.

It is generally acknowledged that race, ethnicity, and language are very significant bases for organizing labour in these and other societies. Indeed, REL stereotypes frequently centre on the types of employment or unemployment of various groups and the degree to which their labour is or has been valued. Inequality and discrimination are associated with the jobs which various REL groups perform or are generally excluded from. Normally subordinate groups struggle for higher wages, better working conditions, or more job security and privileged groups often resist this. The opposition has been the strongest and most effective in Japan and it has been challenged the most successfully in Hawaii.

The general conclusion of this chapter is that REL discrimination will be lowest where workers have organized themselves to achieve common citizenship (Marshall, 1973) which subordinates REL differences – to gain civil rights, political power (in the form of a political party with a labourite orientation), and social rights to welfare and security. This has been the case in Hawaii in the post-Second World War period, primarily through developing strong trade unionism and a very powerful Democratic Party. This overcame a pre-war situation of REL discrimination which was much more similar to the one which exists in Japan in the late 1990s – where many workers are divided by employers on the basis of REL criteria, are unorganized by trade unions and frequently lack basic citizenship rights (e.g. being considered aliens in the country of their birth, being unable to vote, and having little access to health, education, or welfare facilities).

Extreme cases suggest several complicated aspects of racial discrimination. The Japanese have created a comprehensive system of ideologies and practices which subordinate the Korean minority to poorly remunerated, insecure, and dangerous occupations. Japanese emphasize Koreans' biological, intellectual, and emotional inferiority, although they are in fact so similar in physical appearance to the Japanese as to be indistinguishable in most contexts. Japanese parents often hire private detectives to investigate whether respective marriage partners for their children have Korean ancestry (Jo, 1987). At the other extreme, Hawaii represents almost a new type of society where most marriages today are between different REL groups and occupational segregation by race and ethnicity is weak compared to other Pacific societies.

5.2 Principal ethnic groups

Tables 5.1–5.6 show the principal ethnic groups in the countries examined in this chapter.

Table 5.1 *Japan (figures for 1994)*

Total population	125,034,000	
Total registered foreigners including those from:	1,354,011	(1.1%)
Koreas	676,793	(0.5%)
China	218,585	(0.2%)
Brazil	159,619	(0.1%)
Philippines	85,968	(0.1%)
USA	43,320	(< 0.1%)
Peru	35,382	(< 0.1%)
Thailand	13,997	(< 0.1%)
UK	12,453	(< 0.1%)
Vietnam	8,229	(< 0.1%)
Iran	8,207	(< 0.1%)
Canada	6,883	(< 0.1%)
Indonesia	6,282	(< 0.1%)
Australia	6,219	(< 0.1%)
Malaysia	5,356	(< 0.1%)
India	5,169	(< 0.1%)
Pakistan	4,507	(< 0.1%)
Bangladesh	3,955	(< 0.1%)
Estimated illegal immigrants	300,000	(0.2%)

Source: *Japan Statistical Yearbook 1996* (1995, pp.33, 53)

Table 5.2 *Fiji (estimates for 1991)*

Total population	747,000	
Indigenous Fijians	369,000	(49.4%)
Indians	341,000	(45.6%)
Part-Europeans	10,000	(1.3%)
Polynesian Rotumans	9,000	(1.2%)
Chinese/part-Chinese	6,000	(0.8%)
Europeans	4,000	(0.5%)
Other Islanders	7,000	(0.9%)
Others	1,000	(0.1%)

Source: author's synthesis from Douglas and Douglas (1994, p.163)

Table 5.3 *Malaysia (estimates for 1993)*

Total population	19,030,000	
Malays	10,655,000	(56%)
Chinese	6,470,000	(34%)
Indians	1,710,000	(9%)
Other	195,000	(1%)

Source: Valentine (1996, p.400)

Table 5.4 *New Zealand (census data for 1996)*

Total population	3,618,302	
New Zealand Europeans	2,496,552	(69.0%)
New Zealand Maori	523,374	(14.5%)
Pacific Islanders	202,233	(5.6%)
Chinese	82,320	(2.3%)
Indians	43,821	(1.2%)
Others	270,002	(7.5%)

Source: *New Zealand Official Yearbook* (1997)

Table 5.5 *Australia (figures for 1993)*

Total population	17,661,500		
of which overseas born	4,033,500	(22.8%)	
Grouped by some major regions of birth	*Number and percentage of total overseas*		*Percentage change 1984 to 1993*
UK and Ireland	1,224,200	(30.4%)	2.9%
Total Southern Europe	692,300	(17.2%)	–1.6%
South-East Asia	429,600	(10.7%)	97.1%
Western/Northern Europe	282,700	(7.0%)	0.5%
Northern Asia	235,400	(5.8%)	233.4%
Middle East	160,200	(4.0%)	63.3%
Southern Asia	131,100	(3.3%)	86.2%
Aborigines and Torres Strait Islanders	303,261 (in 1994)		

Source: *Year Book Australia* (1996); *Australian Immigration: Consolidated Statistics* (1995)

Table 5.6 *Hawaii (figures for 1990)*

Total population	1,108,229	
of which:		
White	369,616	(33.4%)
Japanese	247,486	(22.3%)
Filipino	168,682	(15.2%)
Hawaiian	138,742	(12.5%)
Chinese	68,804	(6.2%)
Black	27,195	(2.5%)
Korean	24,454	(2.2%)
Samoan	15,034	(1.4%)
Vietnamese	5,468	(0.5%)

Source: *State of Hawaii Data Book 1992*
(1993, p.44)

5.3 The case studies

Overview

The new society of Hawaii is particularly significant for studies of the Asia-Pacific, as it has, more than any other place, gathered together people from throughout the Pacific (Polynesians, Chinese, Japanese, Koreans, Filipinos, and white Americans, to mention only the most prominent groups). Systematic analysis of how they relate to one another as they become Hawaiians is likely to suggest some of the possibilities or limitations of a common Pacific identity. The blending or joining of these apparently discrete, initially exclusive and even antagonistic groups from the Pacific Islands, Asia and the US mainland has been remarkable in its tendency toward unity, rather than some Pacific version of *apartheid* or sustained segregation. Clearly this requires explanation.

Despite the relatively recent migration of most of the people of Asian and European ancestry, it is noteworthy that there is a strong sense of distinctive Hawaiian identity. Important distinctions are made between outsiders (*malihini*) and insiders (*kama'aina*) of whatever REL background. This may suggest the eventual possibility of a greater Pacific community which can, to a significant degree, transcend race, ethnicity, and language. It is not coincidental that Hawaii is the home for important institutions such as the East–West Centre, where the value of this greater Pacific identity is explored by people gathering there from throughout the region.

Hawaii, New Zealand, and Australia are places where settlers over the last two centuries have outnumbered and, to varying degrees, marginalized the indigenous inhabitants. By contrast, the original REL groups maintain political sway in Japan, Fiji, and Malaysia. In all six there has, historically, been considerable REL discrimination and even violence at various times. In the new settler societies, however, this has tended to recede and to be condemned in official policy and, to a lesser degree, practice.

Multiracialism and multiculturalism are often seen as objectives of these new societies. This has not been the case to a very significant degree in Japan, Fiji, and Malaysia. In these societies there has been a pronounced tendency for the political leaders of the dominant REL group to defend the unchangeable paramount position of the original inhabitants and see something subversive about requests (whether international or domestic) to grant full citizenship rights to REL minorities. In these societies there is an emphasis on the value of the original inhabitants' traditional culture and racial identity, their continuity into the present, and the essential foreignness of immigrant REL groups, even when they constitute (as in Fiji and Malaysia) well over 40 per cent of the country's population.

Most newcomers arrived as workers and the strength of the labour movements which they have formed, joined, or become marginalized from in all six places have had important, even decisive effects on REL relations. Migrants were admitted to provide cheap labour for capitalist enterprises. The tin miners of Malaya came under contract from China. Plantations brought indentured labourers from India to Fiji and Malaysia and from Japan, China, and the Philippines to Hawaii in the late nineteenth and early twentieth centuries. The expansion of factories after the Second World War brought southern and eastern Europeans to Australia and Polynesians to New Zealand. Koreans were forced to come from their conquered country to Japan as coerced factory and mine labour to support its imperial war effort in the late 1930s and early 1940s. To varying degrees, the attempts of the newcomers to shed REL stigma have involved opposition to poverty, inferior working conditions, and powerlessness. REL identity has been inseparable from class. In Japan most Koreans and other immigrant minorities have been denied effective union representation or proper citizenship (even in the elementary sense of being allowed Japanese nationality on acceptable terms). In Malaysia and Fiji, where migrant REL groups are much more significant than in Japan, the indigenous leadership of these governments has often been extremely antagonistic toward unionism (especially in its multiracial and political varieties) and demands for political equality.

On the other hand, class-conscious and inclusive multi-ethnic labour movements (such as emerged in Hawaii after the Second World War) have been the most successful in fighting REL discrimination, gaining influence over the state, and shaping the resulting new social forms. Even Hawaii's Republican Party, the ruling political organization for the dominant conservative plantation owners before statehood in 1959, became far more multiracial and centrist while it was being increasingly marginalized by the Asian-led and left-leaning Democratic Party, which was closely tied to the labour movement which had been at the vanguard of anti-racism. The plantation oligarchy of the 'Big Five' companies (Castle & Cooke, Alexander & Baldwin, American Factors, Theo H. Davies, and C. Brewer), which had relentlessly pursued divide-and-conquer strategies toward labour based on race, adjusted to the new realities. Even as its influence declined it made a kind of peace with a state government completely dominated by a Democratic Party organization whose leaders came close to proportionately representing Hawaii's REL balance.

In post-war Australia and New Zealand significant numbers of racially, ethnically, and linguistically distinct migrants have been admitted. Labour movements emphasize the value of making them full citizens, rather than as 'guest' workers who may remain temporarily or even permanently without ever being considered proper members of the national community or having any reason to expect that their children (born in the country) will be able to enjoy full citizenship.

The importance of the principle of citizenship in Hawaii, Australia and New Zealand becomes clearer in relation to the indigenous minorities of those places. Indigenous people are likely to define their rights in terms of their prior occupation or ownership of land, which is often seen as having been stolen or obtained from them on unfavourable terms. Land is a continuing focus of resentment and it is often felt that only its restitution will allow a proper restoration of the best values of the old society and allow rectification of the economic, political, and social marginality of the indigenous people.

The polities in these settler societies have extended full citizenship rights to the indigenous people and have institutionalized additional residual welfare programmes which are targeted at them. These settler societies are likely to define themselves more in terms of labour and progressive achievements. While there has been some recognition of the indigenous people's land rights, the results of this have not come close to satisfying a substantial proportion of the indigenous people. Most of the wider society's welfare provisions for them focus on the labour market – benefits to make up for the consequences of unemployment and programmes to increase their job qualifications and skills so that they are increasingly incorporated into the new settler-dominated society and political economy.

Nevertheless, many indigenous people continue to resist growing dependency and involvement in the institutions of the new society, and movements advocating indigenous sovereignty have emerged in all three places. The tendency of the new settler societies to include as many people as possible under comprehensive notions of citizenship can be seen in their attempts to co-opt these sovereignty movements and incorporate elements of them in official state institutions which claim to advance indigenous self-determination.

These new societies have also recently constructed laws and adminis- trative institutions opposing REL discrimination in general. Racists and even principles of REL classification have been placed on the defensive in ways which are unknown in Fiji, Malaysia and Japan. This denial of the legitimacy and even legality of REL discrimination somewhat paradoxically produces a strong critical consciousness of the nature and deeper meanings of REL distinctions which may not be as developed in those older societies where these are regarded as natural or taken for granted. In contemporary Hawaii, Australia, and New Zealand REL segregation is often seen as a problem for the social order. The legal system tends to subordinate REL distinctions to a larger common identity based to a significant degree on settler ideals of equality of opportunity and citizenship.

In Japan, Fiji, and Malaysia it is more frequent to see social order in terms of maintaining the distinctions between REL groups in a fashion which the dominant group sees as orderly and equitable. The differences between the REL groups in these types of societies may even be solidified by their laws and legal structures. By contrast, it is notable that much of the recent REL struggle of disadvantaged indigenous people in Australia, New Zealand, and Hawaii takes place in the courts or quasi-judicial tribunals (e.g. in relation to land rights). The juridical recourse of politically disadvantaged settler groups in Fiji, Malaysia, and Japan against REL discrimination is extremely limited.

In the settler societies of Hawaii, Australia, and New Zealand the largest of the most disadvantaged REL groups are indigenous and they define their rights as 'first nations' in far more ambitious territorial, political, cultural, and social terms. Since the early 1970s, there has been far greater appreciation of the collective REL rights of indigenous people and their separate legal personality. Aborigines in Australia, Maoris in New Zealand, and, to a lesser extent, the indigenous people of Hawaii have achieved a special category of citizenship rights. In this way they have made some progress in introducing principles of equity, rather than relying exclusively on equality of citizenship rights.

One of the reasons for 'glamour' associated with these indigenous nations has been the way in which their traditional ecological and medical knowledge and emphasis on cultural uniqueness has related to new social movements emphasizing environmentalism, alternative medicine and identity politics. Furthermore there is a general sense that the decolonization of the Third World should be followed by some internal decolonization. The Australian state has emphasized national 'reconcili- ation' with Aborigines and the New Zealand polity has focused on 'partnership' with Maoris – compromises which have involved granting back to these indigenous peoples title or rights to land and (in New Zealand also) territorial waters and marine resources. The processes of linguistic and cultural recognition and the extension of rights of political internal self- determination to indigenous people have not extended nearly as far in Hawaii, where the *Kanaka Maoli* are still seeking comparable collective rights over land and natural resources.

In all three settler societies the indigenous people have been defining their struggles in terms of 'sovereignty'. This concept (whatever its specific meaning) connotes the rights of indigenous people to control their legal status, institutions, territory, and development in ways which do not fit with conventional ideas of neutral, equal, and individualized citizenship in a common nation. This struggle for 'sovereignty' has focused on self- determination. The definition of this has ranged widely – from incremental legal or constitutional restructuring within existing polities to secession and the formation of new indigenous states. Generally the more pragmatic quest for autonomy within the existing state has been the principal goal of indigenous politics, at least in the short-to-medium term.

Hawaii, Australia, and New Zealand all have fairly extensive permanent governmental agencies or departments specifically concerned with indigenous issues. These define them within a larger context of a unified and stable polity and provide resources for moderate indigenous leaders. Nevertheless, the militancy of indigenous leaders in Hawaii, Australia, and New Zealand has been increasing. They equate their aspirations with the success of indigenous nationalists in eastern Europe and the collapse of Russian colonialism (for a Hawaiian example, see Trask, 1993). Nevertheless these same events have made leaders of most core states more resistant to indigenous and ethnic nationalism, which they increasingly equate with the violence and disorder in the Balkans and the economic and political disintegration of the former Soviet Union. In the post-Cold War world, primary arenas of REL debate in Hawaii, Australia, and New Zealand are likely to be defined by growing indigenous demands for self-determination and the insistence of most states that these requests be limited by their own supremacy.

New settler societies (particularly the USA) exert considerable power in setting international standards in REL, policy and ethics. These diverge substantially from the ruling REL morality in Japan, Malaysia, and Fiji. The smaller and weaker polities of Fiji and Malaysia have been much more prominent targets of international admonition than the powerful country of Japan, where the non-indigenous population is proportionately much smaller and not as visibly problematical. Recent Australian Labor governments have been critical of Malaysia and Fiji over issues relating to their REL policies, but the latter have replied by accusing Australia of hypocrisy in relation to the marginalization of its own Aboriginal people.

Particularly since the Fiji coups of 1987, which were justified primarily in terms of defending the paramountcy of the indigenous people (van Fossen, 1987), ties between the two countries have grown, as they see themselves as resisting inappropriate Western standards of REL morality. Malaysia lobbied strongly but unsuccessfully to prevent Fiji's expulsion from the Commonwealth in 1988 over REL discrimination in its policies. Business interests closely associated with the Malaysian government bought the largest Fiji conglomerate from its Australian owners in 1994 (van Fossen, 1995). Sovereignty in both countries has been defined in terms of the dominant religion of the indigenous leadership (Christianity in Fiji, Islam in Malaysia), which consigns the non-believers of minority REL groups to an inferior status and supplies a powerful legitimating ideology for their discriminatory policies and their opposition to world opinion on REL issues.

While Fiji and Malaysia are pluralist and foresee the more-or-less permanent coexistence of separate REL groups in a hierarchy, the Japanese enforce their ideal of a mono-REL society. The Japanese frequently portray themselves in terms of REL purity and uniqueness. Korean, Chinese and other minorities in Japan have been imprisoned within an ideology that they either assimilate totally, and lose their distinctive identities, or they remain in the limbo of being considered aliens, of foreign nationality, even though over 90 per cent of them were born in Japan. Although there have been some minor attempts to comply with the UN on human rights, minorities which affirm any significant degree of distinctiveness have not been naturalized and can legally be denied basic citizenship rights on the ground that they are aliens. Chinese and, particularly, Koreans were brought to Japan from their colonized countries to provide coerced labour and, after the Second World War, they have frequently been consigned to inferior status and despised occupations. Koreans in particular have often refused to request naturalization because the requirement of complete assimilation has generally been regarded as betrayal of their fellows and complicity in their own REL oppression. The Japanese have often agreed to repatriate the unassailable. Particularly prominent in their fears has been their association of Koreans (particularly those of North Korean ancestry) with radical politics. The policing of them and laws about their deportation have reflected concern about their leftist tendencies (Jo, 1987).

The subordination of new unskilled foreign workers in Japan indicates the persistence of REL discrimination and its basically repetitive structure within Japanese society and political economy. It is not a problem narrowly related to the Japanese conquest and subordination of Korea and China. The pattern has been repeated in recent years against Iranians, Malaysians, Bangladeshis, Filipinos, and Thais, who began to arrive in substantial numbers in the mid 1980s. By the late 1980s elements of the Japanese media and some conservative politicians had created a 'moral panic' about the threats of crime, disease and REL pollution which the growing number of foreign workers allegedly pose to Japanese purity. Although there have also been some stories about the exploitation and REL discrimination which these workers face, unsympathetic portrayals of them have been more prominent in the public consciousness.

The extent of Japan's power and prestige can be measured by its largely successful resistance to general global trends toward lower levels of REL discrimination. The Japanese debate on recent migrants from southern Asia and the Middle East has neglected resident Koreans and Chinese because they remind the Japanese of national disgrace in the Second World War. The Japanese prefer to forget about their ultimately unsuccessful colonial adventures in Korea and China. This is not because they are ashamed of the racism which these represented, but because they were defeated and this challenges the continuing Japanese sense of their REL superiority. The Japanese have never lost their pre-war sense of REL supremacy. This has, in fact, reasserted itself strongly in recent years as the country has become ever more powerful in international commerce (Lie, 1992).

Contemporary Hawaii represents, by contrast, a broader and freer society, a REL union. Its definition of Hawaiian-ness is seldom formulated in any permanent manner and its strength is in diversity. Its ideals of equal opportunity, citizenship, and diversity are constantly evolving. In this Pacific Islands melting pot many REL groups have come together to form a new society, but one which has given each REL group scope for developing its distinctiveness. Although Americans of Japanese ancestry in Hawaii, who constitute the largest single REL group there, have been less integrationist than others, their exclusiveness has been weakening considerably. The Americans of Japanese ancestry, like other groups in Hawaii, have largely been converted to a broader conception of their identity as Hawaiians and they have been important in promoting the distinctive multiracialism and multiculturalism of the state.

The case of contemporary Hawaii (where people of Asian and Polynesian background form a majority which has struggled to oppose REL discrimination and achieve full citizenship rights) appears to challenge suggestions that these ideas of equal citizenship are fundamentally 'Western' and therefore essentially foreign and inapplicable to societies such as Japan, Malaysia, and Fiji. The fact that these more universalistic relations have emerged in a society where so many different Asian, Polynesian, and European groups have converged indicates that there may be a tendency toward a more universalistic conception of universal citizenship or human rights independent of REL distinctions.

Japan, Fiji, and Malaysia tend to respond to the critics of their REL policies by claiming that they are matters of national sovereignty with which foreigners have no rights to interfere. Critics may be charged with cultural imperialism – attempting to impose Western notions of the rights of minorities in public life. There is a great deal of attention paid to maintaining cultural distinctiveness in Japan, Fiji, and Malaysia. The ruling elites of these societies see the indigenous people's cultural distinctiveness as their true essence, even though critics may see this idea as undermining a progressive human rights agenda. This institutionalization of localized experience and identity may not be capable of disabling effective domestic criticism of REL inequalities in the long run. However, for the time being there is considerable popular support among the indigenous peoples in Japan, Fiji, and Malaysia for the idea that other countries' criticisms of their REL relations are illegitimate attempts to deprive their national communities of the ability to fashion their own national standards. Yet, the constant challenging, renegotiating and complicating of cultural and REL identities appear to challenge static conceptions which are often articulated by political leaders of these three states. This is especially true when there are attempts to maintain these static REL relations by coercion within their societies.

Those in power in Japan, Malaysia, and Fiji often speak in terms of group rights which are often seen rather anachronistically in terms of small rural REL communities based on extended families of the same race, ethnicity, and language. Individualistic notions of REL equality are seen as jeopardizing this social model. In Japan the pressure is on minorities to resemble the majority (to assimilate or remain aliens), while in Malaysia and Fiji there are policies which emphasize the desirability and inevitability of REL pluralism, differentiation and uniqueness within a single governmental structure. In Australia and New Zealand there is a celebration of a multicultural ideal of harmony between REL groups which are entitled to maintain their distinctive identities in an atmosphere of tolerance, but which can melt into a core as they please. The actual amalgamation of REL groups has gone the furthest in Hawaii, where they have merged to form a new culture or society.

I will look now at the variety of REL formations in the six Asia-Pacific societies. I will pass from societies of Japan, Fiji, and Malaysia, where REL relations are clearly and even formally based on segregation and inequality, to societies of New Zealand, Australia, and Hawaii, where there is an ideal of voluntary integration and equality. This is a continuum, but the first three societies have parallels to each other, as do the second three. The distinctions between Malaysia and New Zealand are therefore greater than between any other two neighbouring societies on the continuum; for example, political rulers in Fiji and Malaysia defend REL relations in each other's country and develop some significant REL policies through copying the other (van Fossen, 1987), whilst New Zealand and Australia have somewhat parallel REL policies, but Malaysia and New Zealand have, at times, been in conflict over REL issues (not least, concerning how to treat Fiji's REL policies in international forums).

Japan

Defeat in the Second World War has not convinced the Japanese that their nation is not superior to all others. This superiority is seen as being produced by its REL homogeneity. A good example of this is the controversial comments in 1986 of Yasuhiro Nakasone, the Prime Minister of Japan at the time. He stated that Japan was on a 'higher level' than the USA because of its REL uniformity, as contrasted with the undesirable heterogeneity and mixtures of America. He saw this Japanese advantage as the result of a long tradition of REL purity. This valorization of isolation tends to colour Japanese perceptions of the outside world as well as aliens within their midst. REL purity is an important element of the self-image of the eternal Japan.

The question of foreign labour exploitation is never far way from REL relations in Japan. The Korean and Chinese are the largest migrant groups there because their ancestors were brought to the country as forced labour before and during the Second World War. Many in the new wave of migrants from across Asia (particularly, the Philippines, Pakistan, Korea, Bangladesh, Malaysia, and Thailand) are recruited by the *yakuza* organized crime gangs – women for prostitution and men for trucking, construction, and other businesses in which the *yakuza* are involved – either as owners, operators, or labour brokers (Spencer, 1992, p.764; Yamanaka, 1993, p.82).

The coercive and abusive conditions of immigrant labourers and the fact that they usually receive less than the minimum wage tend to consolidate the Japanese perception that other Asians within their midst are REL inferiors living in conditions which Japanese would not tolerate. The immigrants have little recourse against this brutality, as they may be expelled or (if working illegally) may even be imprisoned if they create trouble. Most second- and third-generation Koreans work in similar '3-K' jobs – *kitsui* (demanding), *kitanai* (dirty), and *kiken* (dangerous). They also suffer the legal disability of being aliens (since they usually refuse to eradicate their Korean *ethnicity*, which Japanese naturalization almost always requires of them). Like more recent immigrants, these 'permanent residents' do not have important citizenship rights (e.g. the right to vote).

The Japanese government has for a long time refused to ratify the UN International Convention on the Protection of the Rights of All Migrant Workers and Members of Their Families, claiming that it is in conflict with domestic law. Non-Japanese workers in Japan are the most likely to work in dangerous jobs, where health and safety laws are not enforced, where injuries are often not covered by workers' compensation, and where unemployment and other social welfare benefits are not available. They are increasingly prone to commit crimes reported to the police and to be regarded as a public danger. Japan has a growing underclass, which is perceived largely in REL terms.

Japanese labour organizations have tended to be the most strenuous local critics of the contemporary situation of REL discrimination. They have argued that migrant labourers should be included in a well-regulated immigration programme which guarantees that they be accorded fair and equal treatment in relation to Japanese workers. If this is not implemented, and the current system of super-exploitation is far from it, current levels of migration should be substantially lowered, as they serve to attack the wages and conditions of Japanese workers, as well as involving a host of associated problems (Spencer, 1992).

The unions have been ineffective in organizing most of these workers. The power of trade unionism in Japan – never very strong – has declined during recent years and the conditions under which migrant workers have come to Japan have tended to discourage or preclude union membership. Even long-resident groups such as the Koreans have not been active supporters of multi-REL unionism, partly because Koreans have tended to be segregated in sectors which are relatively difficult to organize and are similar to the Japanese in claiming REL superiority, homogeneity, and purity, as well as the virtues of exclusionism (Hoffman, 1992, p.487). The best prospects for reducing REL discrimination in Japan appear to come from international pressure, as there is considerable Japanese concern to avoid criticism. The Ministry of Foreign Affairs, which is the target of a great deal of it, has been rare among Japanese government ministries in favouring new non-discriminatory laws and policies (cf. Spencer, 1992, pp.774–5).

The past, present, and future of REL discrimination in Japan is closely connected with the incorporation of foreigners from the Third World into the labour market. With the ageing of the Japanese and the unwillingness of younger Japanese to perform necessary '3-K' jobs, there appears to be a structural, not merely a cyclical, demand for foreign workers. Small- and medium-sized enterprises may become so dependent on them as to demand that they be allowed to stay to do the work the Japanese increasingly refuse to accept.

This is likely to make the REL segmentation of the labour market even more rigid, as undesirable jobs become increasingly associated with non-

Japanese REL groups. It is improbable that they can be replaced to any significant degree by robotics or other technologically advanced equipment in which the Japanese excel, as some advocates of a homogenous Japan have hoped. The recent programme to attract the descendants of Japanese migrants from Brazil and Peru may have come close to reaching its limit, as almost 200,000 from these Latin American countries have taken up residence already, but they are reportedly disillusioned by their poor reception. It is more likely that there will be an increase in the demand for foreign workers. If the experience of northern Europe with 'guest workers' and the history of Koreans in Japan are any help, foreign workers may be unwilling to leave even if they cannot become citizens (Morita and Sassen, 1994; Spencer, 1992; Yamanaka, 1993). In this process REL inequalities may become even more intense, noticeable and conflictual.

Fiji

Internal opposition to REL discrimination has been considerably more organized in Fiji than in Japan, but so far attempts to create a democratic, multiracial nation have failed (Lawson, 1991). This is complex, because the beginning of such a society was being constructed by the Bavadra Labour government before it was overthrown by an indigenous Fijian (*taukei*) military coup in May 1987. Any hope for the restoration of his project was shattered by a second coup of September 1987 (van Fossen, 1987, 1991). Apologists for the coup makers suggest that any attempts to organize Fiji along lines other than REL discrimination are illusions, since differences based on race, ethnicity, and language are fundamental and cannot be displaced by quixotic unifying class politics. According to this view, REL inequality and separation are basic realities in Fiji. Dreams of overcoming them are dangerous and may even conceal hidden REL agendas, particularly those of Fiji Indians, who are accused of using egalitarian labourite politics to disguise their strategies to dominate the indigenous people (Scarr, 1988). On the other side, we find those who insist that REL tensions have been aggravated and even created by indigenous Fijian aristocratic politicians to preserve their feudal power. According to this view, they falsely pose as guarantors of indigenous land rights and identity when they are actually attempting to stifle legitimate challenges from progressive indigenous commoners (such as the deposed Prime Minister Bavadra), workers, and members of other REL groups who desire a more just and democratic national polity and common citizenship independent of REL criteria (Lawson, 1990; van Fossen, 1990). Regardless of the point of view, there is little doubt that in the decade after May 1987, there has been pressure against multiracial labourism, official government encouragement of the establishment of racially based unions, and a hardening of REL politics and discrimination in Fiji. The irony of this has been that the economic and political stagnation since the coups has been so great that even the coups' perpetrators have seen a new constitution (enacted on 25 July 1997) – which is less discriminatory toward non-indigenous citizens in the political realm – as being necessary to restore business confidence. It is too early to determine whether the current initiatives represent real reform of the basic structures of REL relations in Fiji or a series of largely symbolic gestures designed to alter an economic crisis without altering the fundamental structures.

Malaysia

REL discrimination in post-coup Fiji is only marginally higher than in contemporary Malaysia. Unlike Malaysia (where the Malays constitute 56 per cent of the population), indigenous nationalists in Fiji have been more apprehensive about one person–one vote democracy, since during a greater part of the twentieth century Fijians have been a minority. Most indigenous Fijian political leaders have therefore favoured the notion of specific entitlements based on REL criteria (e.g. reserving 82 per cent of the country's land for themselves and, for at least ten years after the 1987 coups, excluding all but the indigenous population from the highest governmental offices by either decree or constitutional provisions).

There is considerable division of labour by REL criteria in both Malaysia and Fiji. This has become slightly less pronounced in Malaysia. Here unions are generally more multiracial and most of the indigenous people (a rather heterogeneous group of non-Chinese and non-Indian lumped together by British and post-independence politicians as the Malays or *bumiputra*) have moved from rural peasant life and entered the most profitable commercial sectors to a greater degree than in Fiji. This is principally the result of affirmative action programmes which assumed their present strength more than fifteen years earlier in Malaysia. These were implemented after the Malay riots against other REL groups, which started on 3 May 1969 and lasted several days. These events still serve as a touchstone for comprehensive indigenous demands for preference, much as the May and September 1987 coups did in Fiji. In each of these years, most non-indigenous people of Malaysia and Fiji realized that their hopes of eventually being treated as full citizens were forlorn. The burden of this has been felt perhaps more acutely by the Indians, who have experienced higher levels of economic deprivation than the Chinese.

Although there is a debate between those scholars who think that REL discrimination in Malaysia is primordial (e.g. Esman, 1972; Milne, 1981) and those who see it as class-based (e.g. Brennan, 1982), the emphasis of constantly racializing situations is a preoccupation of the ruling Malay political elite to which workers seem far less committed as they attempt to deal with their situations pragmatically (Boulanger, 1991, 1992, 1996). The challenge which multiracialism appears to pose to the ruling elite is substantial, as evidenced by the government's arrest, detention, and imprisonment of over 100 Malay and non-Malay unionists, academics, journalists, politicians, and members of public interest groups in October 1987 on the grounds that they were creating a situation which endangered public order and might create a situation similar to May 1969 (Lee, 1990, pp.492–3). Similar arguments and tactics had been used in Fiji in 1987 against leaders of the Fiji Labour Party, trade unionists, academics, journalists, lawyers, and others suspected of left-wing sympathies. In both countries in late 1987 there was substantial regression into REL fundamentalism and separatism.

This is closely connected with the increasing political significance of religious fundamentalism among the indigenous people (Christianity in Fiji, Islam in Malaysia). This has somewhat paradoxical effects in giving divine legitimation to REL discrimination against unbelievers (most Chinese in Malaysia and most Indians in both countries), but also leaving an opening for the 'spiritually inferior' to elevate themselves through conversion (since both Christianity and Islam are universalistic).

This contributes to making the 'indigenous' category more porous (more open and harder to close) than other REL categories (e.g. Indian and Chinese, which are associated with distinctively ethnic and non-conversionist religions). In Malaysia considerable numbers of people with Indonesian and even Indian and Chinese backgrounds are classified as Malays (with Islamic religious affiliation contributing substantially to this redefinition). In Fiji strong affirmation of Christianity may help in enabling people with non-indigenous ancestry to 'pass' as Fijians. Since REL classification has become so crucially important in these two countries, intercalary cases may often be subject to debate. Paradoxically, a person's questionable claims to indigenous status may lead that person to associate with vehement indigenous nationalism to consolidate his or her claims. Malaysia's Prime Minister Dr Mahathir Mohamad may constantly racialize situations and pose as the chief defender of his Malay brethren, but in truth he has a substantially Indian background. James Ah Koy may be a Fiji Cabinet Minister proclaiming his loyalty to the coup makers and to the paramount goal of indigenous economic development, but he has a considerable Chinese heritage. Yet both have been classified as indigenous in official government race censuses. As in Japan, where Koreans often 'pass' as Japanese, some unlikely people have considerable ability to shape their REL identities for maximum opportunity or simply to avoid being disadvantaged.

Versatility in REL identification affects all six societies discussed in this chapter, to different degrees, and this may frustrate any attempt to clearly distinguish and enumerate REL groups in tight compartments. Ambivalent identification appears to have the greatest effect on the number of people identifying themselves as indigenous in the new societies – as witnessed by the rapid increase in their numbers in recent censuses in New Zealand, Australia, and Hawaii. There are far greater constraints on such changing self-identifications in jurisdictions where REL identities are far more legally structured and constrained – as in Japan, Fiji, and Malaysia.

It may become increasingly difficult for the Malay elite to continue to frame its fundamental opposition to organized labour in REL terms. While unions once had predominantly Chinese and Indian memberships (which outnumbered Malay membership by four to one as late as 1962), by 1980 most members were Malays and the proportion has grown steadily thereafter. The percentage of Malays in important union positions is even higher than their proportion in the rank-and-file membership. There is a tendency of unions generally to be among the most powerful (or least powerless) institutions encouraging REL equality and accommodation in the country (Boulanger, 1991, 1996; Jomo and Todd, 1994).

The response of the state has been to surround unions and other actively multiracial organizations with an ever larger number of laws attempting to restrict or even terminate their activities. It is not clear how effective this will be over the long term. The rapid economic development of the country increasingly converts Malays from rural yeoman peasants to urban proletarians. The escalation of REL-based rhetoric and actions from the Malay political leadership may not represent the strengthening of separate REL identities but their vulnerability in new circumstances. There is constant pressure on the Malay political elite to devise new ways of ethnicizing or racializing situations to give REL distinctions relevance, even if only in the chimerical world of Islamic revivalism (cf. Lee, 1990).

New Zealand

With New Zealand we begin to move away from societies such as Japan, Fiji, and Malaysia where full formal citizenship rights are denied to a large proportion of those who are not members of the politically dominant REL group. The definitions of the relative degrees and kinds of REL inequality thereby become more difficult to define in New Zealand than in Japan, Fiji, and Malaysia, where inequalities tend to be more codified and explicit. But it is also possible for REL relations to take place at two levels, of which one is the legalistic, formal, codified and idealized (often closely aligned with the 'political') while substantial actual inequality continues to exist at another level (usually characterized as 'economic'). In New Zealand, Australia, and Hawaii disadvantaged REL groups often strive for greater power and expansion in this 'political' sphere. Privileged groups are inclined to strive for 'small government' and greater reliance on the 'market' (not least in the sphere of labour, where contractual relations are greatly preferred over collective bargaining). In contemporary New Zealand, more than in Australia and Hawaii, it is easy to perceive the dramatic effect on REL relations of the victories of deregulation since the early 1980s.

The fundamental change in New Zealand's post-war REL relations began earlier than this. The 1973 oil shock and related processes and aftershocks altered the developmental trajectory of a country with virtually no petroleum resources. It had industrialized and employed large numbers of Maori and other Polynesian workers in manufacturing based on low energy costs, tariff barriers, and other features of the pre-1973 post-war world. The beginnings of indigenous Maori activism can be traced to approximately this year of crisis. For the previous period of post-war prosperity (during the 1950s and 1960s) there was an extremely low rate of unemployment by global standards. Maori male unemployment rates were only 2.3 per cent in 1961 and 3.5 per cent in 1971 (Haines, 1989, p.57). Maoris and Pacific Islanders who intended to stay in the country were working in a relatively unionized environment and generally had the goal of peaceful assimilation and common New Zealand nationality. During the long economic decline and polarization which have occurred since 1973, strong ethnic nationalist and sovereignty movements have grown among Maoris. They have tended to distinguish them from whites, Pacific Islanders (who were encouraged to come in the 1950s, 1960s, and early 1970s to fill the many vacant unskilled positions), and the more recent Asian migrants, who are much more likely to be business people or professionals.

During this period there has been an increase in laws prohibiting discrimination on REL criteria, but there has also been an escalating attack on industrial and social rights of full employment, collective bargaining, unemployment insurance, public ownership, state education, public housing, and general state welfare provision. All of this has hit Maoris very hard, as their unemployment rate has risen to extremely high levels. Increasing numbers have seen hope in pursuing unresolved land claims – relating to the Treaty of Waitangi of 1840 between Maori tribes and the British Crown (**Eccleston *et al.*, 1998, p.370**) – to gain more substantial territorial resources for self-determination or even separate nationhood in an independent Aotearoa/New Zealand. High, chronic unemployment reaching 12.4 per cent in 1981, 19.4 per cent in 1989, and 19.6 per cent in 1995 among Maori males (Haines, 1989, p.57; *New Zealand Official Yearbook*, 1996, p.292) and growing lumpenproletarianization have perhaps been most visible in the rise of large Maori (and, to a lesser extent) Pacific Islander gangs, which are sometimes associated with cultural revival as well as outlaw activities such as 'entrepreneurial' drug trafficking. In counterpoint to this, one should note that during the 1950s and 1960s Maoris (who were seldom unemployed in a highly unionized work-force) appeared to be integrating successfully into mainstream New Zealand society – reducing the still existing inequalities in such areas as income, education, and health.

Most New Zealanders continue to entertain the possibility of common nationhood. The descendants of British settlers (the vast majority of the *Pakeha* or non-Maori) derive a great deal of their sense of national identity from borrowed Maori themes and still feel some pride about the country's history of relatively humanitarian state policies toward the indigenous people, who gained relatively full citizenship rights earlier than in most other settler societies (Pearson, 1988, 1990). At the same time, in the early and mid 1980s, the most powerful *Pakeha* interests set off on one of the most radical deregulatory restructurings of the national polity and economy, followed by devastating increases in Maori unemployment and poverty.

This was aggravated as a cheaper reserve army of relatively non-unionized Pacific Islands labour (drawn principally from the Polynesian countries of Tonga, Western Samoa, and the Cook Islands) undercut Maori workers and tended to displace them from unskilled and semi-skilled jobs. This was particularly the case in the early stages of the restructuring in the mid 1980s, after which both Maoris and Pacific Islanders suffered growing immiseration together. Both groups have been increasingly seen as 'social problems' and used as 'explanations' for economic problems after 1973. Political and civil rights have even been denied to Pacific Islands migrants – as in the periodic early morning police raids on the houses of 'overstayers' (Loomis, 1990).

Not only have the rising number of unemployed people been effectively 'de-unionized', but over the years governments have discouraged and, more recently, legislated against union activities. A powerful institution promoting cross-REL solidarity has been considerably weakened. All this has occurred as the state has proclaimed an ideology of increasing Maori and *Pakeha* biculturalism, bilingualism, and equality of opportunity. Many Maoris' aspirations to assimilation are still strong. This was indicated by their strong support in the 1996 general election for the New Zealand First Party of the populist Maori lawyer and parliamentarian (and current Deputy Prime Minister) Winston Peters. He presents himself as a model of integration and a fervent exponent of a common New Zealand nationalism, which he defines as largely excluding Asian migrants. He has also criticized elements of the deregulatory agenda. He lost his position as Minister of Maori Affairs in 1990 after indicating that state intervention was necessary for Maori economic development, contradicting the position of the ruling National Party, which would later expel him. The kind of assimilation which Peters and many other New Zealanders favour is still viewed in largely bipolar terms (Maoris and Anglos forming the proper New Zealand nation). This can be illustrated by the support which Peters derived from Maoris and whites for his racialistic attacks on the 'excessive' levels of recent Asian immigration.

In Australia and Hawaii there has been a similar contest between indigenous assimilationists and nationalists. Indigenous nationalism has surfaced all over the world and has become more prominent with declining American hegemony and the crisis of accumulation since the early 1970s. In the long boom of the 1950s and 1960s indigenous people generally moved closer to the centre of their increasingly Americanized and 'modernized' national societies characterized by standardization, conformity, and mass production and consumption. Austerity and growing economic inequality began in the 1970s. The growing economic disadvantage of indigenous people has led to the increasing alienation of significant numbers of them from central national institutions and their quest for separation and self-determination. 'Difference' has been increasingly challenging assimilation in REL ideologies over the last 25 years (Friedman, 1994; Harvey, 1989). These processes are more visible among Maoris than among the indigenous people of Australia and Hawaii, although they are increasingly apparent there as well.

In the ever more bipolar Polynesian/non-Polynesian REL relations of New Zealand, the indigenous people are very important actors, although not as significant as in Japan, Fiji, and Malaysia, where they are politically dominant. In New Zealand we can also see the paradoxes of an indigenous minority's struggle focusing increasing control over the polity (or even sovereignty or political independence) at a time when world-wide the state and its resources are under attack. In New Zealand conservative politicians have become increasingly hostile toward Maoris since the late 1980s – sharply reducing resources for their agencies and organizations, under-funding the Waiting land claims tribunal, and employing the phrase 'institutional racism' to denote Maori 'privilege' and *Pakeha* 'disadvantage' (Spoonley, 1994). Thus the struggle in New Zealand illustrates, as clearly as any example we have, that actual REL inequality can grow substantially as the polity and economy are restructured, and even as the state outlaws, sanctions, and delegitimizes formal REL discrimination.

Australia

It would be difficult to find a place where REL relations have changed as rapidly as in Australia in the post-Second World War period. The country has moved from an Anglo-defined 'White Australia' to a multi-REL society where over one-third of the population consists of post-war migrants and their children. After the Second World War a large-scale immigration programme was launched which resulted in great numbers of people arriving from southern and eastern Europe – especially Greece, Italy, Malta, and the former Yugoslavia. 'White Australia' was abandoned and multiculturalism was introduced in 1973. The Commonwealth Racial Discrimination Act was passed in 1975. Beginning in the mid 1980s government policy was increasingly reoriented toward a recognition that Australia is a part of Asia, with a large proportion of immigrants being drawn from Asian countries.

All these post-war changes in the basic REL character of the country have been initiated by governments led by the Australian Labor Party, which is closely affiliated with the trade union movement. Indeed, it is not possible to understand these changes outside the context of Australian labour relations. The historical contingency of REL discrimination is clearly indicated by the extraordinary about-turn in the policies of the Australian labour movement. When unions were relatively small, weak and unorganized in the late nineteenth and early twentieth centuries, they were leading promoters of the 'White Australia' exclusion policy. This was regarded as providing some protection to local workers from cheap or coerced ('indentured') Asian and Melanesian labour. However, during most of the post-war period the labour movement has been the most powerful initiator and defender of the transition toward multi-REL immigration and a multicultural society. These are conceived as drawing immigrants into full membership in host unions and participation in the elaborate govern-mental institutions which the victories of the Australian labour movement have produced over the course of the twentieth century to ensure fair employment practices (Lever-Tracy and Quinlan, 1988; Quinlan and Lever-Tracy, 1990).

This transformation has been aligned with the metamorphosis of Australian society. Virtually every aspect of it has been modified by the large-scale post-war migration of people from diverse REL backgrounds. To a greater extent than in Japan, Fiji, Malaysia, and New Zealand, immigrants have been incorporated into the host society (not segregated) and there has been a considerable tendency toward class solidarity rather than divisions by REL criteria (Bertone and Griffin, 1992). The inclination in contemporary Australia has been toward guaranteeing full citizenship for immigrant and Aboriginal people (Jupp, 1991; Smolicz, 1995).

Although the Australian Labor Party initiated the post-war movement toward non-racialism, there has usually been an agreement between the major parties to avoid politicizing race, immigration, Aboriginal problems, or any other issues which might influence REL conflict. This consensus is currently under some strain at a time of high unemployment in the late 1990s. The first major politician to break the agreement had been John Howard, who was elected Prime Minister in 1996. In 1988 Howard had broken ranks with most of the shadow cabinet in his own Liberal (conservative) Party to attack multiculturalism and relatively high levels of Asian immigration. The backlash from this led to his being deposed as opposition leader in 1989. Although, when pressed, he continued to make rather general statements opposing racism, he refused to directly condemn the populist Independent MP Pauline Hanson after her much-publicized maiden speech in 1996 denouncing multiculturalism, Asian migration, and Aboriginal rights. Only after she had formed her own competing political party (albeit one which was supported by less than 10 per cent of the electorate) and daily negative accounts in the Asian media began to hurt Australia's image in the region of its major trading partners did Howard attack some of her proposals. This came a year after she had stated them in parliament and contained some ambiguity – 'The Hanson cure would be worse than the disease', Howard stated on 8 May 1997. Australia also appears to be more susceptible to REL conflict as the Howard government weakens union power and the elaborate systems of employment laws and arbitration which have guaranteed that immigrant labour has been incorporated on terms of relative equality with host labour, rather than being seen as tools of employers to reduce wages and conditions. The government has also attacked indigenous people's organizations, refused to commit itself to the, admittedly unrealistic, goal of previous (1983–96) Labor Party governments to produce Aboriginal equality by the year 2000; slashed funds for labour market programmes for Aborigines designed to reduce their high levels of unemployment (Jones, 1993); frustrated union efforts to reduce occupational segregation and discrimination against them (Altman and Hawke, 1993); and proposed laws to restrict their ability to make successful land claims pursuant to the High Court's historic Mabo decision of 1992 and the Labor Party's supportive legislation clarifying and extending it in 1993 (Brennan, 1995).

Nevertheless, many of the institutions and practices minimizing REL discrimination in Australia have become so established that only an upheaval could overturn them or even seriously reverse their direction. The new social order in Australia seems inimical to any retreat into the patterns of REL discrimination which prevailed before the introduction of multiculturalism in the 1970s.

Hawaii

Although there is considerable debate about the significance (Boylan, 1992) or insignificance (Wang, 1982) of ethnicity in Hawaii's politics, there is no doubt that multi-REL principles have become thoroughly institutionalized at all levels of the Hawaiian polity. This is closely connected with the fact that it is one of the most social democratic states in the USA. Multi-REL principles have been the basis of its strong labour movement and the unions' ally, the virtually unbeatable Democratic Party, holds all federal Senate and Congressional seats, all important state executive offices, and all but a few state legislative seats.

This has not always been the case. The Republican sugar plantation oligarchy (which owned the 'Big Five' companies) dominated the territory before the Second World War and created a system of REL discrimination which tended to favour members of its own heritage group. The elite had been formed by Caucasians and, to some extent, intermarriages with the indigenous Hawaiian aristocratic landowners. In the post-war regime Caucasians and indigenous Hawaiians formed the basis of support for the ruling Republican Party.

The planter elite imported contract labour (from China, then Japan, then the Philippines) for monocultural sugar production. The fact that the Asian workers soon became a majority left few opportunities for the independent white settlers who were so powerful in New Zealand and Australia and who tended, initially, to favour exclusion of non-white labour in these countries. The sentiment for exclusion was rarely encountered in Hawaii and it was almost always voiced among Asian workers who were already on the islands. The oligarchy attempted to divide the mostly Asian work-force by REL criteria and even by district or village of origin (with different wage rates and separate living areas). The elite could use Hawaii's territorial status to prevent many of Asian background from naturalizing and gaining citizenship. There was considerable worker resistance through-out the pre-Second World War period, but the effectiveness of this was significantly weakened by the ethnic character of unionism. Strikes encouraged planters to find new REL sources of labour overseas to further discourage unity and militancy. Political, economic and social life generally were filled with REL slurs and discrimination.

The labour movement rose dramatically after the Second World War on the basis of militantly multi-REL principles. One of the most radical American unions, the International Longshoremen's and Warehousemen's Union (ILWU), which had started organizing in the mid 1930s, was at the forefront – headed by the Australian Harry Bridges in San Francisco and

Jack Hall in Hawaii. It remains proportionately far more powerful in Hawaii than in any other American state. Its radical multi-REL unionism was attacked vehemently by the right for being communist. There were mass arrests of strikers and an attempt to rescind Bridges' naturalization on the basis of alleged communist affiliations, and Hall and six others were convicted of communist conspiracy under the Smith Act, Hall escaping prison only because his conviction was overturned by the US Supreme Court (Beechert, 1985; Holmes, 1994; Kent, 1990; Liu, 1984; Sharma, 1984a, b).

By the time of statehood in 1959 the ILWU, the broad union movement, and the Democratic Party had become a successful coalition for institutionalizing multi-REL principles in a multiracial struggle which has been called 'unions against colonialism'. Although unions in Hawaii have not achieved many of the early social democratic aims of the early ILWU, they have defied the general American trend in continuing to grow – with members constituting about 30 per cent of the work-force or about twice the average on the US mainland (McClain *et al.*, 1993).

Within the USA as a whole over a long period of time, REL discrimination and the disorganization of labour have been inseparable – both being the greatest in the South, which continues to have similarities to pre-Second World War Hawaii, where Asian-Americans were considered by whites to have very much the same roles as African-Americans in the South (Cheng and Bonacich, 1984). REL discrimination appears to be the lowest in *contemporary* Hawaii, which (out of the 50 states) today ranks first in the rate of employees covered by collective bargaining agreements and second in the rate of unionization (*State of Hawaii Data Book 1995*, 1996, p.340). Hawaii, the most heterogeneous of US states in REL terms, is even more notable because it is a clear exception to the general American tendency for REL heterogeneity to be used to weaken class solidarity, social democracy, the welfare state, and the ability of workers to negotiate successfully for better wages and conditions (Reich, 1981).

The Hawaiian unions' and Democratic Party's multi-REL struggle has been successful in removing REL baiting from the repertoire of successful public figures and dramatically lowering the level of REL discrimination in the state. This is especially the case of relations between whites (*haoles*) and Americans of Japanese and Chinese ancestry (who together form a majority of the state's population), but it has been less successful in combating discrimination against indigenous Hawaiians, Filipinos, Guamanians, Samoans, Puerto Ricans, Vietnamese (Haas, 1992) and African-Americans. Nevertheless, the level of REL discrimination is low compared to the other countries discussed in this chapter and other areas around the world. Even in a time of rising world-wide REL tension and violence, a new type of smoothly functioning, densely REL society is being born, as indicated, for example, by the fact that approximately 60 per cent of Hawaii's children born in 1992 were from interracial unions (Odo and Yim, 1993).

5.4 Summary

This chapter has related racial, ethnic and linguistic inequality and discrimination to labour markets and the ways in which they are organized by economic and political forces. It generally supports the view that REL inequality and discrimination are lowest in areas where labour union organization has been relatively powerful and militantly multiracial, multicultural, and multilinguistic. This has been the case in Hawaii, where unionism has been strong (especially by American standards) and where it has gained much of its strength by succeeding in breaking down the attempts of employers to encourage divisions of labour on the basis of REL criteria. At the other extreme, unions have been relatively weak in Japan and have not organized and integrated disadvantaged REL minorities such as the Koreans and recent immigrants.

In Fiji the attempt of the mid-1980s union movement and the new Labour Party to dissolve the old politics of REL conflict and replace it with a new politics of class was briefly successful, but the two military coups of 1987 overthrew and then further marginalized the elected Labour government. The coups were explicitly committed to restoring and intensifying the old politics of REL separation. Malaysia may be seen as in many respects similar to Fiji, but also as anticipating many of its efforts to organize and institutionalize REL discrimination, especially in attempts to limit any emergent class solidarity.

In New Zealand increasing class polarization and the disintegration of organized labour movements from the early 1980s have been accompanied by a considerable increase in REL inequality (particularly between whites, on the one hand, and Maoris and Pacific Islanders on the other), and mobilization around principles of REL discrimination (e.g. in highly politicized expressions of hostility to Asian migrants). Australia may be seen as a country where multiracial, multi-ethnic, and multilinguistic policies have received effective assistance from an organized labour movement and the Australian Labor Party. Policies have sought to include post-Second World War migrants as full citizens and to fight efforts to discriminate against them on REL grounds. Finally, in Hawaii labour organizations and the Democratic Party, which placed opposition to REL discrimination at the forefront of their agendas, have been largely successful. It is not too much to say that a new type of Pacific society is being born there.

References

Altman, J.C. and Hawke, A.E. (1993) *Indigenous Australians and the Labour Market: Issues for the Union Movement in the 1990s*, Canberra, Australian National University Centre for Aboriginal Economic Policy Research.

Australian Immigration: Consolidated Statistics (1995) Bureau of Immigration, Multicultural and Population Research, Canberra, Australian Government Publishing Service.

Beechert, E.D. (1985) *Working in Hawaii: a Labor History*, Honolulu, University of Hawaii Press.

Bertone, S. and Griffin, G. (1992) *Immigrant Workers and Trade Unions*, Canberra, Australian Government Publishing Service.

Boulanger, C.L. (1991) 'Workers are one race: constructive relations in the west Malaysian workforce', Ph.D. dissertation, Department of Anthropology, University of Minnesota.

Boulanger, C.L. (1992) 'Ethnic order and working class strategies in west Malaysia', *Journal of Contemporary Asia*, vol.22, no.3, pp.322–39.

Boulanger, C.L. (1996) 'Ethnicity and practice in Malaysian unions', *Ethnic and Racial Studies*, vol.19, no.3, pp.660–79.

Boylan, D. (1992) 'Blood runs thick: ethnicity as a factor in Hawaii's politics' in Smith, Z.A. and Pratt, R.C. (eds) *Politics and Public Policy in Hawaii*, Albany, State University of New York Press, pp.67–80.

Brennan, F. (1995) *One Land, One Nation–Mabo–Towards 2000*, St. Lucia, University of Queensland Press.

Brennan, M. (1982) 'Class, politics and race in modern Malaysia', *Journal of Contemporary Asia*, vol.12, no.2, pp.118–215.

Cheng, L. and Bonacich, E. (eds) (1984) *Labor Immigration Under Capitalism: Asian Workers in the United States Before World War II*, Berkeley, University of California Press.

Douglas, N. and Douglas, N. (1994) *Pacific Islands Yearbook*, Suva, Fiji Times.

Eccleston, B., Dawson, M. and McNamara, D. (eds) (1998) *The Asia-Pacific Profile*, London, Routledge in association with The Open University.

Esman, M.J. (1972) 'Malaysia: communal coexistence and mutual deterrence' in Campbell, E.Q. (ed.) *Racial Tensions and National Identity*, Nashville, Tenn., Vanderbilt University Press, pp.227–43.

Friedman, J. (1994) *Cultural Identity and Global Process*, London, Sage.

Haas, M. (1992) *Institutional Racism: the Case of Hawai'i*, New York, Praeger.

Haines, L. (1989) *Work Today: Employment Trends to 1989*, Wellington, New Zealand Planning Council.

Harvey, D. (1989) *The Condition of Post Modernity*, Oxford, Blackwell.

Hoffman, D.M. (1992) 'Changing faces, changing places: the new Koreans in Japan', *Japan Quarterly*, vol.39, pp.479–89.

Holmes, T.M. (1994) *The Specter of Communism in Hawaii*, Honolulu, University of Hawaii Press.

Japan Statistical Yearbook 1996 (1995) Tokyo, Statistics Bureau.

Jo, Y.-H. (1987) 'Japan' in Sigler, J.A. (ed.) *The International Handbook on Race and Race Relations*, New York, Greenwood, pp.129–53.

Jomo, K.S. and Todd, P. (1994) *Trade Unions and the State in Peninsular Malaysia*, Kuala Lumpur, Oxford University Press.

Jones, F.L. (1993) 'Unlucky Australians: labour market outcomes among Aboriginal Australians', *Ethnic and Racial Studies*, vol.16, no.3, pp.420–58.

Jupp, J. (1991) 'Managing ethnic diversity: how does Australia compare?' in Castles, F.G. (ed.) *Australia Compared: People, Policies and Politics*, North Sydney, New South Wales, Allen & Unwin, pp.38–55.

Kent, N.J. (1990) 'The development of trade unionism in Hawaii' in Moore, C., Leckie, J. and Munro, D. (eds) *Labour in the South Pacific*, Townsville, James Cook University of North Queensland Press, pp.226–31.

Lawson, S. (1990) 'The myth of cultural homogeneity and its implications for chiefly power and politics in Fiji', *Comparative Studies in Society and History*, vol.32, pp.795–821.

Lawson, S. (1991) *The Failure of Democratic Politics in Fiji*, Oxford, Clarendon Press.

Lee, R.L.M. (1990) 'The state, religious nationalism, and ethnic rationalization in Malaysia', *Ethnic and Racial Studies*, vol.13, no.4, pp.482–502.

Lever-Tracy, C. and Quinlan, M. (1988) *A Divided Working Class: Ethnic Segmentation and Industrial Conflict in Australia*, London, Routledge and Kegan Paul.

Lie, J. (1992) 'Foreign workers in Japan', *Monthly Review*, vol.44, pp.35–42.

Liu, J. (1984) 'Race, ethnicity, and the sugar plantation system: Asian labor in Hawaii 1850–1950' in Cheng and Bonacich (eds) pp.186–210.

Loomis, T. (1990) *Pacific Migrant Labour, Class and Racism in New Zealand: Fresh off the Boat*, Aldershot, Avebury.

McClain, D., Rees, R.M. and Turner, C.H. (1993) 'Labor unions' in Roth (ed.) pp.21–7.

Marshall, T.H. (1973) *Class, Citizenship, and Social Development*, Westport, Conn., Greenwood Press.

Milne, R.S. (1981) *Politics in Ethnically Bipolar States: Guyana, Malaysia, Fiji*, Vancouver, University of British Columbia Press.

Morita, K. and Sassen, S. (1994) 'The new illegal immigration in Japan, 1980–1992', *International Migration Review*, vol.28, pp.153–63.

New Zealand Official Yearbook (1996, 1997) Wellington, Statistics New Zealand.

Odo, F. and Yim, S. (1993) 'Ethnicity' in Roth (ed.) pp.224–9.

Pearson, D. (1988) 'From community to ethnicity: some theoretical considerations on the Maori ethnic revival', *Ethnic and Racial Studies*, vol.11, no.2, pp.168–91.

Pearson, D. (1990) *A Dream Deferred: the Origins of Ethnic Conflict in New Zealand*, Wellington, Allen & Unwin.

Quinlan, M. and Lever-Tracy, C. (1990) 'From labour market exclusion to industrial solidarity: Australian trade union responses to Asian workers, 1830–1988', *Cambridge Journal of Economics*, vol.14, pp.159–81.

Reich, M. (1981) *Racial Inequality: a Political-Economic Analysis*, Princeton, Princeton University Press.

Roth, R.W. (ed.) (1993) *The Prince of Paradise: Vol.II*, Honolulu, Mutual Publishing.

Scarr, D. (1988) *Fiji: the Politics of Illusion*, Kensington, University of New South Wales Press.

Sharma, M. (1984a) 'The Philippines: a case of migration to Hawaii' in Cheng and Bonacich (eds) pp.337–58.

Sharma, M. (1984b) 'Labor migration and class formation among the Filipinos in Hawaii, 1906–1946' in Cheng and Bonacich (eds) pp.579–611.

Smolicz, J.J. (1995) 'The emergence of Australia as a multicultural nation', *Journal of Intercultural Studies*, vol.16, pp.3–24.

Spencer, S.A. (1992) 'Illegal migrant laborers in Japan', *International Migration Review*, vol.26, pp.754–86.

Spoonley, P. (1994) 'Racism and ethnicity' in Spoonley, P., Pearson, D. and Shirley, I. (eds) *New Zealand Society*, Palmerston North, New Zealand, Dunmore Press, pp.81–97.

State of Hawaii Data Book 1992 (1993) Honolulu, Department of Business, Economic Development and Tourism.

State of Hawaii Data Book 1995 (1996) Honolulu, Department of Business Economic Development and Tourism.

Trask, H.-K. (1993) *From a Native Daughter: Colonialism and Sovereignty in Hawai'i*, Monroe, Maine, Common Courage Press.

Valentine, D. (ed.) (1996) *The International Year Book and Statesmen's Who's Who*, East Grinstead, West Sussex, Reed Information Services.

van Fossen, A.B. (1987) 'Two military coups in Fiji', *Bulletin of Concerned Asian Scholars*, vol.19, no.4, pp.19–31.

van Fossen, A.B. (1990) 'Politics and economics in Fiji', Review essay, *Bulletin of Concerned Asian Scholars*, vol.22, no.3, pp.68–73.

van Fossen, A.B. (1991) 'Australian and Canadian perspectives on class, ethnicity and geopolitics in Fiji', *Australian-Canadian Studies*, no.9, pp.151–6.

van Fossen, A.B. (1995) 'Corporate power in the Pacific Islands', *Current Sociology*, vol.41, no.1, pp.115–33.

Wang, J.C. (1982) *Hawai'i State and Local Politics*, Hilo, James C. Wang.

Yamanaka, K. (1993) 'New immigration policy and unskilled foreign workers in Japan', *Pacific Affairs*, vol.66, no.1, pp.72–90.

Year Book Australia (1996) Canberra, Australian Bureau of Statistics.

Further reading

For a general overview of racial, ethnic, and linguistic relations:

Rex, J. and Mason, D. (eds) (1986) *Theories of Race and Ethnic Relations*, Cambridge, Cambridge University Press.

CHAPTER 6

Religion

Julia Day Howell

6.1 Introduction

Westerners visiting East Asia as tourists or newcomers are often impressed by the colourful religious ceremonies they encounter there and are charmed that they can 'still find' so many people enthusiastically engaged in such activities. In fact, religions and spiritual movements are as much a part of East Asia's 'new look' as a part of its past – just as they are all over the world. At the end of the twentieth century there has been a global resurgence of religions, in both the East and the West. This resurgence is particularly evident in the former Eastern Bloc countries of Europe and in the newly industrializing countries of the Third World, including those of the Asia-Pacific.

If this comes as a surprise to casual visitors to East Asia, they are in good company. Until the 1970s, most Western social scientists expected that religions would die away as societies 'modernized'. This view was based on a limited understanding of twentieth century social changes in Western societies themselves and on the assumption that secular philosophies exported from the West would displace religious attitudes as East Asian societies industrialized. While secular philosophies, both of Asian and Western origin, are influential in many areas of East Asian life today, so are religious beliefs and values, and these religious beliefs and values are not just 'survivals' of old traditions held onto out of sentimentality. They also include religions new to the region and old traditions reworked in new forms. Nevertheless, the place of religions in East Asian social life and the way it is organized are changing.

In this chapter I discuss why the global phenomenon of religious revival has upset the expectations of social scientists and survey the new ways in which people in East Asia incorporate religious concerns into their lives. We also develop a familiarity with the variety of religious traditions in East Asia today and with leading trends in religious life in different parts of East Asia.

6.2   Which religions?

When we look at East Asia today, we find there not just what we might think of as 'Asian religions' (religions that originated there) but religions introduced from the West as well, like Christianity. Moreover, next to the well known 'universalistic' or 'world' religions (such as Hinduism, Buddhism, Christianity and Islam) we find many former tribal and peasant peoples still practising indigenous 'community' or 'primal' religions. In this section we introduce the major types of religions in East Asia as well as the somewhat anomalous Confucian tradition. We will also survey which religions are dominant in different parts of the Asia-Pacific region.

Universalistic and community religions

The 'universalistic' or 'world' religions are all products of similar historical circumstances that occurred in different parts of the world sometime between the sixth century BC and the seventh century AD. These circumstances or 'historical moments' were times when great agrarian civilizations had expanded and incorporated peoples of diverse ethnic backgrounds into powerful states. In such social environments on the eastern rim of the Mediterranean, in India and in China, spiritual leaders and philosophers developed teachings about the nature of the universe and humankind's place in it that could speak to all sorts of people, regardless of their race, social position or the place they might be living. Their messages, in short, were 'universal'. Moreover, as the great social historian Max Weber (1964) pointed out, the messages were in some way or another one of 'salvation': messages that escape is possible from what was viewed as the unsatisfactory nature of everyday life.

Weber also called attention to family resemblances amongst the universal or salvation religions that originated in the Near East on the one hand and, on the other, those that originated in South Asia and the Far East. Thus the Near Eastern religions Christianity and Islam each formed around a unique revelation from God and placed hope for salvation in a heavenly realm after a single, earthly life. In contrast, the South Asian religions (Hinduism and Buddhism) envision the individual human consciousness entering earthly life countless times until the prospect of enlightenment is understood and achieved during one final earthly life. Following the practices of enlightened or spiritually accomplished people in one's own time, and aided by the teachings of past masters (such as, in Buddhism, the Buddha Gautama born, in 563 BC) salvation from the suffering of repeated reincarnations can be achieved. Daoism, which originated in China around 300 BC, also has a tradition of learning through modelling on a master and transcending the unsatisfactoriness of life through transformed perception.

Confucianism, which is sometimes treated as a religion, is strictly speaking not a religion, but a moral philosophy advocated by the Chinese scholar Kong Fuzi (551–479 BC). Kong Fuzi ('Master Kong' or 'Confucius' as Westerners call him) advocated a system of social relations focusing on harmony through respect for hierarchy in the family and the state. He refused to comment on the supernatural. Nevertheless, his teachings eventually inspired ritual practices and veneration for the master that can reasonably be called religious. Furthermore, Confucius's teachings, which could be practised by anyone in a class-based society, did eventually spread widely, not just amongst Chinese people, but among North Vietnamese, Koreans and Japanese, giving the Confucian tradition a claim to a degree of universalism.

In contrast to these universalistic or partially universalistic traditions, 'community' or 'primal' religions are concerned only with the immediate world of particular villages whose heritage they are. Community religions consist of rituals, stories about the supernatural and often trance practices that relate living humans to their ancestors and to the non-human spirits who share their surroundings with them. Because of the way community religions focus on particular families' ancestors, on guardian spirits of local places and the like, these religions have great immediacy and vitality for locals, but are 'not for export'. They are not formulated so as to meet the needs of all people everywhere.

One well known set of community religious practices is Shinto. Shinto grew out of the folk religious traditions of Japan, but because it was seen to be useful to the Japanese state, it was formalized, somewhat like a universalistic religion. Thus the Meiji rulers, who came to power in 1868, sponsored Shinto as a state religion. They used Shinto rituals to reinforce the aura of the emperor, drew the many local shrines under bureaucratic control and taught a blend of Confucian and Shinto ideas to school children and soldiers. After the Allies defeated Japan in the Second World War, they forced the Japanese to dismember 'State Shinto'. Now Shinto exists only through local shrines and family rituals. (This is called 'Shrine Shinto'.) In any case, although Shinto was formalized at one point by the state, it was never unversalized. Whatever its form, past or present, it has remained a community religion; it addresses only the ancestors and local spirits of the Japanese people.

The South Asian and Near Eastern religions move east

Of the two major South Asian religions, Hinduism and Buddhism, Buddhism has had by far the greater impact on the countries of East Asia and the Pacific Islands. Except in Bali and in areas of Indian migrant enclaves (such as Fiji, the Malay peninsula and the major cities of South-East Asia), Hinduism is little seen there today. Only the practised eye will discern strong Hindu influences in court rituals of otherwise Buddhist Thailand and in court and village rituals of many Islamicized parts of Indonesia. This represents a curious inversion of the situation in India, the homeland of these two religions, where Hinduism outlasted its offshoot, Buddhism.

The origins of Hinduism are lost in India's past. Indeed until the time of the Muslim invasions, what we today call 'Hinduism' was simply the welter of religious philosophies, local rituals and sectarian practices in which people of the Indian subcontinent engaged. These various traditions and practices were not drawn together under a single standard nor united by uniform institutions. Those we now call 'Hindus' all revered holy books called the Vedas (compiled sometime between the mid-second and mid-first millennium BC) and shared a common pantheon (cast of deities). But they approached those deities through many different types of rituals and mystical practices, told different stories about them, and if speculative, reflected on those beings through many various philosophies. Buddhism, which can be seen as initially a sectarian movement within Hinduism, spread from its home in north-eastern India through former 'Hindu' areas of India and Sri Lanka. It was firmly established in the south by the first century BC. Legend has it that Buddhism was also active in Burma and Thailand by this time, however the first historical evidence of its presence in South-East Asia (in the form of stone inscriptions) dates from the time of the early Indianized kingdoms of that region, that is, from early in the first millennium AD. At this time Buddhism was also spreading into China.

The rise of Buddhism in East Asia, however, coincided with the beginning of its decline in India. By the twelfth century AD it had virtually disappeared from India, although it remains the dominant religion in Sri Lanka to this day. In South-East Asia Buddhism vied for influence with Hinduism, which spread through both mainland and island parts of the region at about the same time, and did not become clearly dominant in 'mainland' South-East Asia until the second millennium AD. Hindu sects remained important longer in the islands of South-East Asia, sharing court patronage with Buddhist monasteries and local cults until Islam overwhelmed both from the fourteenth century on.

Although long present in China, Buddhism did not enjoy great popularity there until a period of political disunity, banditry and famine in the third century AD. At that time, Confucian hopes for human happiness through respect for parental and state authority must have been embarrassed by circumstances. Buddhism, which took the problem of human suffering as its central issue and taught people more individualistic solutions to that problem, began to flourish. By the sixth century AD, Buddhism was strong enough to play a role in the foundation of the Sui Dynasty (AD 581–618) and reached its height of popularity and patronage during the Tang Dynasty (AD 618–907). It fell dramatically from favour in 'The Great Persecution' (AD 842–845) and thereafter persisted as but one (carefully monitored) of China's 'Three Traditions': Confucianism, Buddhism and Daoism. From China Buddhism, with Confucianism, spread to Northern Vietnam, Korea and Japan.

Both Christianity and Islam have close family connections to Judaism, an ancient Near Eastern religious tradition that originated in Israel. Christianity was inspired by Jesus of Nazareth, who was himself a Jew; historical records show that he was sentenced to death by the Roman overlords of Israel in about AD 33. Islam was based on revelations beginning in AD 610 to the Prophet Mohammed, an Arab merchant living in Mecca.

Top, the Wenshu yuan, an ancient Buddhist monastery in Chengdu, capital of Sichuan Province, China. Still visited by many pilgrims and tourists, the monastery had nearly 100 monks in residence in 1997. There is strong evidence of incense burning in the smoke to the left. Bottom, some of the stalls in the streets outside the monastery. The many sellers of Buddhist and other Chinese cultural objects show that Buddhism has a substantial commercial aspect in present day China

Like Christianity and Judaism, Islam recognizes a single God and the Prophet Mohammed is seen as the last in the line of Jewish prophets, including Jesus. However, followers of Islam (or 'Muslims') consider Jesus merely a human who reveals God's word, not, as Christians do, an aspect of God.

Today we associate Christianity in Asia and the Pacific with European culture, since Christian European missionaries, beginning in the sixteenth century AD, brought to the region the oldest churches still active there now. However, Nestorian Christianity, rooted in the ancient churches of the Eastern Mediterranean rather than in the Roman church, came to Asia much earlier, together with Islam and other now minor universalistic religions. The expansion of China's Tang dynasty west into Central Asia and the consequent revival of overland trade with India, Persia and lands beyond, created the opportunity for the spread of those religions to the Far East. In China's Great Persecution of 845, when 'foreign' religions like Buddhism were being suppressed, Christianity was made illegal. However it came to life again in China when Mongols invaded and conquered the Han Chinese, bringing Nestorian Christianity with them. This form of Christianity disappeared once again from China when the Mongols themselves were conquered in the mid-fourteenth century.

The new wave of European Christianity in North-East Asia began with Jesuit (Roman Catholic) missions to Japan in 1549 and China in 1583. In Japan, after a short period of tolerance, Christianity was outlawed and did not make a come-back until the opening of Japan to the West by the Meiji government in the nineteenth century. In China Christianity made little headway until the fall of the Qing dynasty in 1911 when disunity and greater openness to Western influences created more opportunities for its spread. In neither China nor Japan, however, did Christianity become more than a small minority religion.

The situation is different in Korea, where Christianity is now a mainline religion. The religion was brought to Korea in the seventeenth century by Korean intellectuals who met Jesuits in China. The religion faced periodic persecution there until the mid nineteenth century when Korea, like Japan, initiated an open door policy toward the West. The dramatic growth of Christianity in South Korea, however, has been quite recent, with a doubling of numbers in the 1970s.

In South-East Asia the major Christian areas are former Spanish and Portuguese colonies: the Philippines and the tiny former Portuguese outpost of East Timor (now claimed by Indonesia). Christianity made less impact on English and Dutch colonies in South-East Asia, in general attracting very few adherents in the Buddhist and Muslim kingdoms, but meeting some success in tribal areas where no universalistic religion was practised. In the Pacific Islands states, to which Muslim and Buddhist influences did not reach, Christianity has become the dominant tradition in the twentieth century.

In the lifetime of the Prophet Mohammed (c. 570–632) and the century following, Islam spread west around the Mediterranean and east through

Persia and India by conquest. However its spread to South-East Asia can be attributed mainly to trade. For centuries before the birth of the Prophet, Yemeni traders had sailed across the Indian Ocean to South-East Asia, trading and laying over there en route to and from China. When the West Asian traders converted to Islam, they brought that faith with them to the Far East. However it was not until the thirteenth century that rulers in the South-East Asian kingdoms started to convert to Islam, beginning with Pasai on the east coast of Sumatra. As Muslim rulers began to dominate maritime trade, the region quickly turned to Islam. By the fifteenth century, Islam had replaced Hinduism and Buddhism as the religion of state across the Malay peninsula and the islands of Indonesia, except for Bali, which remained Hindu-Buddhist. The southern Philippines, never the seat of Hindu or Buddhist kingdoms, was also Islamicized.

Today the native Malay population of Malaysia (nearly half the population of the country) are Muslims and around 87 per cent of Indonesia's population is Muslim. With over 200 million people, Indonesia is the largest Muslim country in the world. The southern Philippines remain strongly Muslim, only giving up a movement for independence from the Christian north in the mid 1990s. Christian communities in the southern Philippines today are the result of recent (post-war) migration from the Christian north and have aroused intense resentments among Muslims. Other Muslims in East Asia and the Pacific include surviving Chinese Muslim minorities in the People's Republic of China and Indian Muslim migrants to Malaysia, Fiji and numerous South-East Asian cities.

Community religions survived into the nineteenth and twentieth centuries in the Asia-Pacific in tribal areas and regions with small chiefdoms, like the hilly regions of southern China and mainland South-East Asia, eastern Malaysia (on the island of Borneo), the Outer Islands of Indonesia and the Pacific Islands. From this time, however, intense, mainly Protestant missionizing and the imposition of direct administrative control by British and Dutch authorities over remote regions of their colonies brought more and more small 'pagan' groups into Christianity. Muslim influence on tribal groups in Malaysia and Indonesia has also increased, especially after independence from colonial control raised the social value of Islam and brought pressures to convert to it as the dominant religion in those countries.

6.3 Religions: coming or going in modern East Asia?

Both radical and liberal social theorists of the 1950s and 1960s expected that as societies industrialized and became predominantly urban, religions would play a less and less important part in them. Marxists pointed to the role of religions in legitimizing (that is ideologically validating) the authority of kings and aristocracies in traditional states and took as a general rule that as the old agricultural economies changed to predominantly industrial economies and as representative governments replaced the old feudal regimes, people everywhere would recognize their religious beliefs as 'false consciousness'. Especially as communist societies built socialism, which was thought to enable the state to 'wither away', Marxists expected that religion too would become a thing of the past. Indeed Chairman Mao Zedong, leader of the Chinese Communist Revolution, considered it unnecessary to prohibit religions under the first constitution of the People's Republic of China because he expected that the Chinese people would abandon them anyway as they built a socialist society.

On the liberal (more conservative) side, Western 'modernization theorists' of the fifties and sixties sought to understand and predict the course of change in the many former European colonies of Asia and Africa that became independent after the Second World War. Modernization theorists predicted that these largely 'underdeveloped' societies (that is, societies with little modern industry) would 'evolve' along more or less the same lines as Western societies, once they started 'developing'. Unlike the Marxists, they considered pure forms of socialism unworkable and undesirable, but like them the modernization theorists read the history of industrialization in Western societies to imply that the 'New Nations' of the Asia-Pacific would become less religious as they became more industrialized and as scientific modes of thought became more widespread.

Sociologists of religion have devoted a great deal of attention to these theories and to evaluating them in light of the evidence of recent world history. While they clearly affirm that the place of religion in our lives has *changed* over the last two hundred or so years since industrialization started in the West, religions have *hardly disappeared*. The following sections present the main observations that have been made about the changing place of religions in 'developing' and 'developed' societies and provide examples of these trends in East Asian countries.

Secularization of government

The modern 'nation-state' form of government, that has replaced 'traditional states' in most countries, locates authority to govern in the citizenry rather than in hereditary and supposedly divinely appointed kings and queens. This affects a 'separation of church and state', as religious institutions once responsible for supporting the beliefs upon which the king's divine authority rested must not limit their sphere of concern to the moral and spiritual guidance of individual citizens. Government in the modern nation-state then becomes a 'secular' activity, that is, one that functions without explicit and necessary reference to religion (except insofar as politicians may consider this enhances their appeal to a portion of the electorate). In Western countries today governments are either secular or predominantly secular; in East Asian societies the secular state is but one of several forms.

In East Asia, Japan provides the clearest example of a modern nation-state whose constitution requires a separation of religion and the state, that is, forbids any religion from being made the state religion or from receiving support from the state and allows its citizenry free choice in matters of religion. Japan provides such a strong parallel to Western democracies in this matter because its present constitution was imposed on it by the Americans after the defeat of Japan in the Second World War. The Philippines and South Korea provide other examples of Asian societies with a full separation of religion and the state.

The People's Republic of China (PRC) illustrates a variation on the secular state model that has antecedents in the former Communist countries of eastern Europe and the Soviet Union. In those societies the official Marxist philosophy of the state casts religions as false beliefs and tools of oppression used by the defeated ruling classes. As such, religions were ideological rivals to the official state philosophy and the state supported various means, from education to confiscation of church properties, to encourage atheism. These eastern European states were thus not merely neutral secular states, but secular states hostile to religion. The communist PRC followed the atheistic secular state model although, as indicated above, its first constitution (of 1954) did not actually outlaw religions. Indeed in the early 1950s some effort was made to work with religious figures like the Buddhist Dalai Lama of Tibet, who was initially used as a channel of indirect rule, obviating the costly exercise of imposing direct control over that region. However leftist shifts in state policy, especially during China's Great Leap Forward (1958–60) and the Cultural Revolution (1966–69), brought thoroughly uncompromising attitudes to religions; religious activities were vigorously, even violently suppressed. The ousting of Buddhist theocracy from Tibet in 1959 and the ruin of its many monasteries was a dramatic example. Only since the fall of the Gang of Four in 1976 have religious groups been able once again to practice openly, but only if they are within the fold of organizations sanctioned and supervised by the state.

The secular state, whether modelled on western or eastern European antecedents, is by no means the only type of modern state in East Asia today. Several states, like Thailand and Indonesia, have 'established religions', that is, 'official' religions promoted and financially supported by the state. The official religion in Thailand, Buddhism, is closely bound-up with Thai identity and is one cultural factor which distinguishes the ethnic Thai majority (who are mostly lowland peasant farmers and city dwellers) from many of the hill tribes on the borders of the country. Buddhism is also associated with the still deeply honoured Thai royalty, who have historically supported the Buddhist monkhood and been legitimized by them. Today the Thai government has a parliamentary system with the king as titular head of state, but he is no longer recognized as a god. The government gives financial support to the Sangha (the bureaucratized monastic system) and the Sangha in turn has input into most levels of government. Thai law, however, is not Buddhist, but fully secular and there are no restrictions on proselytizing by other religions or official pressures on people to practice any religion.

The importance of religion to national identity also helps to explain the legal place of religions in Indonesia. There Islam played a crucial role in drawing together people from many different ethnic groups to oppose Dutch colonial control. Since then, however, some of the ethnic groups that joined in the independence struggle (1945–49) were Hindu-Buddhist (the Balinese) or largely Christian (like some Bataks clans), and since many Javanese Muslims did not want a state based on Islamic law, 'Belief in One God' was made the basis of the state rather than Islam. Now Indonesian law provides for state support of five religions (Islam, Protestantism and Catholicism [mentioned as separate religions], Hinduism and Buddhism) and citizens have the freedom to choose a religion – but not to opt out of religion! So-called 'new religions' (*agama baru*) are outlawed and there is official pressure to demonstrate active involvement in one of the five state sponsored religions.

While Indonesia, with around 87 per cent of its population Muslim, did not establish Islam as a state religion, Malaysia, when it became independent in 1957, did. In Malaysia not only is Islam the state religion, but as in Brunei, Islamic religious law is extensively used as the law of the land. This is so despite the fact that perhaps half the population are not Muslims, being unconverted indigenous tribal peoples, Hindu migrants from India (although there are also Muslim Indian migrants) and mostly Christian or 'Three Religions' (Buddhist, Daoist and Confucian) Chinese. The privileging of Islam as the state religion in Malaysia is actually part of a broader policy to legally advantage Malays 'in their own land' *vis-à-vis* immigrant groups whose numbers and economic strength were seen as a divisive legacy of colonialism. Being Muslim is part of the official definition of a 'Malay', a status which confers many advantages in education, business and civil service employment. Free expression of ideas and beliefs in Malaysia is restricted by severe penalties against proselytizing of Muslims by members of other religions and by laws against 'giving offence' to Islam.

When we look at the political sphere, then, the idea of the inevitability of secularization, which seemed to be so clearly demonstrated in the West, has not been uniformly upheld in East Asia. There are several states which have the American and western European type of secular, but not atheistic, state; and in East Asia we also find an atheistic secular state. Indeed China continues to vigorously restrict religious activity (albeit with limited success), when states in eastern Europe have given this up and have even enthusiastically reinstated the rights of religious groups. But in East Asia today we also find countries where people are required to practise some religion or where religious law even forms the basis of a good deal of state law. In understanding the continuing importance of religion in state affairs in East Asia it is helpful to appreciate the role religions often play in symbolizing a national identity and therefore in promoting national cohesion, as in Indonesia. We see a variation on this in Malaysia, where religion plays a key role in defining one ethnic identity (Malay) that has privileged status under national law. In some East Asian states, like

Thailand and Brunei, the continuing importance of royalty, with their historical ideological dependence on religion, also helps to explain the promotion of religion by the state.

Privatization of religion

When the authority of government leaders depends on the populace holding certain religious beliefs, religion is a public matter. A person's willingness to profess a certain religion is a sign of their loyalty to the state and reliability as a member of the community. In Western societies today, this notion seems strange. Older people remember when churchgoing was a mark of social respectability and even today 'networking' through one's fellow parishioners can be an employment asset in some circumstances. However, as long as the state is not founded upon a particular religion, an individual's choice of religion is a private matter and convention often makes it improper to press people we do not know well about such personal issues. In East Asia the situation is different in those countries founded upon a particular religion or religions, or where royalty remains symbolically important to the functioning of the state.

Where religion is a private matter it is not necessarily unimportant. Clearly in such cases it operates in a more limited social sphere than in societies where it is implicated in matters of loyalty to the state. However, even where religion is a private matter it may be intensely important personally to individuals. There is a parallel here to the shrinking role of the family in social life. In pre-industrial societies politics, production and reproduction were all organized through families; now in urban environments most families only perform reproductive and emotional support roles. As the scope of the family has shrunk, however, its emotional significance for many people has increased. Something similar may also be the case for religions but we need to look at this as a separate issue.

Religious affiliation and attendance

How religious *are* people in the West and in East Asia these days? In countries where there are substantial publicly conferred benefits for people who profess and demonstrate a religious affiliation (as in Malaysia for Malay people) or even penalties imposed on people who do not (as in Indonesia), we can be sure most people will engage in *some* religious observances. Still, there will be variations in how *much* religious activity people engage in; people may do the minimum necessary for their social purposes. Conversely, in societies where the state discourages people from being involved in religions, these policies are not necessarily successful. So, for example, in China, there has been a remarkable revival of religious activity in the 1990s, even outside the officially registered denominations. The Christian 'home church' movement in particular has experienced spectacular growth. So state policy is not a wholly reliable indicator of personal practice.

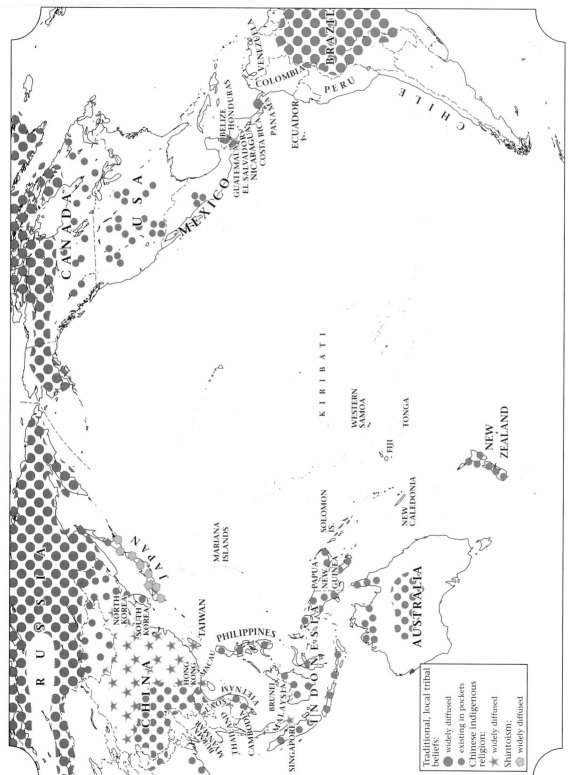

Figure 6.1 *Map showing areas in which traditional and local beliefs are held by significant numbers, 1993*

If we want to know what people actually believe and do, we have to ask them. We can ask them what religion they hold, if any (on census forms, for example). Even more revealing, we can look at scholarly surveys that ask people how often they actually attend religious services, pray, read religious materials and the like. Such surveys in Western countries show that from the 1950s to the 1970s attendances at mainstream Christian churches were dropping, just as the Marxists and modernization theorists expected. In fact these observations were part of the data that helped to form the picture of 'modern societies' which the modernization theorists expected to be copied elsewhere.

What the modernization theorists missed, however, was that from the 1960s spiritual activities *outside* the mainstream churches were on the rise in Western countries like the USA. These 'alternative' activities included participation in Christian sectarian movements and especially Pentecostalism. (Pentecostalism is a form of worship involving rhythmic singing and dancing. In many people this induces an ecstatic trance, interpreted as a descent of the Holy Spirit of God.) By the 1970s Pentecostalism had actually spread out of small sectarian churches into the established churches, helping to boost their flagging memberships. The spiritual revival of the sixties also included 'New Religious Movements' (NRMs), both of loosely Christian origins and of Asian and native American backgrounds. The relaxation of immigration laws restricting Asian immigration to the USA and Australia was one of the factors in the sudden prominence of Asian 'New Religions' in those countries. Similarly, the flow of migrants from Asian countries to the UK from its former colonies since the 1960s has been a factor in the increased prominence of Asian religions in the UK.

In the 1980s Christian groups in the USA and in eastern Europe became prominent in national politics, attracting increased involvement and support. In the 1990s both Christian sectarian groups and Asian 'New Religions' have expanded energetically into eastern Europe. Coming in the wake of Eastern Bloc independence movements and the break up of the Soviet Union, these 'alternative' religious groups have attracted enormous numbers of adherents, even alarming mainstream Christian groups like the Russian Orthodox Church.

Another form which religious revival took in Western countries in the 1980s and 1990s was the 'New Age' movement. This is not a single religion held together by one formal organization, but a label imposed on all kinds of individual and largely informal, group activities dealing with things 'spiritual'. It represents a further extension of the 'privatization of religion', where the individual becomes her or his own religious authority and takes inspiration from whatever sources appear to be valuable and attractive. Ideas and practices from Asian religions are important elements in the New Age movement everywhere.

In East Asia we do not have longitudinal data on religious attendances and beliefs comparable to those from Western countries. (That is, we do not have data from different time periods that enable us to infer trends.) However Japan has attracted much attention from modernization theorists as an East Asian society that has, for some time now, been highly industrialized and urbanized. What do studies of religious affiliation and belief there tell us?

On the one hand, official government statistics on religious affiliation in Japan from the 1970s show that religions there were literally unbelievably healthy: religious groups actually had more members than people who reside in the whole of Japan! Clearly something was wrong with those figures, but what? For one thing, like many proponents of Asian religions, Japanese people generally do not regard it as inconsistent to follow more than one religion at a time, so some people may have been counted twice, or even more often. Another problem with those government statistics was that they relied upon self-reporting by religious organizations, leaving open the possibility that their estimations were overly optimistic. Over counting could also be put down in part to the different ways groups attempted to estimate active members. Thus some Shinto shrines that saw themselves as serving an entire geographical area simply took the population of that area as their membership, even though the residents included Christians and others who would not or did not patronize those Shinto shrines. Similarly, national shrines visited by people from all over the country sometimes used the number of sales of amulets as the number of 'members'.

If government statistics actually tell us very little about how religious Japanese people are, scholarly surveys which have approached people individually show that fewer than half of the population actually belong to a denomination or sect. Such surveys show that only a very small percentage of the population have a high regard for religion or believe in supernatural entities. This suggests that irrespective of the story official government statistics on memberships show, the Japanese people are actually not highly religious. But does this mean that they are less religious now that the society has become industrialized and highly urbanized than in the past? We cannot reach this conclusion on the data available because we do not know how religious Japanese people really were. We know that in former times when most Japanese people lived in farming villages there were high rates of participation in village rituals, but because helping with these rituals was part of people's social obligations, we do not know what the range of people's personal beliefs was or how religiously active people would have been if they had not faced the same kinds of social pressures. This is a problem in comparing the religiosity of people in 'modern' societies everywhere with that of people in the distant past.

We can learn something about changes in patterns of religious activity in Japan, however, by looking at the history of religious organizations. Since Japan began industrializing we find that many 'New Religions' have been formed. Especially since the Second World War there has been an extremely high rate of formation of new sectarian groups. As in Indonesia, where there was a similar phenomenon after the war, commentators described the growth of 'New Religions' as being like the appearance of 'mushrooms after a rain storm'. In Japan these 'New Religions' are mostly

Buddhist-inspired. However others are eclectic, incorporating elements of several older religions including Shinto, Buddhism and even Christianity. They meet people's needs for a sense of community in largely impersonal urban environments and offer practical assistance with personal problems and illnesses through counselling and spiritual healing. In Indonesia the post-war 'New Religions' (now no longer legal) drew on Muslim, Hindu, Buddhist, Christian and indigenous traditions and have a heavy emphasis on the cultivation of a direct experience of God or the spirit world through meditation.

Box 6.1 'New Religions' in Japan: new truths meet new social needs

We can appreciate the appeal of 'New Religions' (*shin shukyo*) in Japan when we understand the role these groups play in people's lives. In contrast to the established (*kisei*) religions, Shinto and Buddhism, the New Religions (such as Reiyukai, Soka Gakkai, Tenrikyo, Mahikari, etc.) cater for the individual in an urban environment, loosed from ties of family and farming village.

Since times past Shinto and Buddhism have had a place in the social order of rural communities, each family (*ie*) making its regular contributions to Shinto festivals and having an enduring connection with a Buddhist priest. But less than 14 per cent of Japanese people now live in the countryside. In the city, these family obligations are difficult or impossible to maintain, being mobilized if at all only on the occasions of major 'life crisis rituals' (the Shinto priesthood for marriages and the Buddhist priests for funerals). Many people now regard those established religions as static, oppressively hierarchical and of little relevance to their lives in the city.

The 'New Religions', in contrast, recruit people as individuals and draw them into active social groups that provide a new sense of community in the urban environment. The common emphasis on attending regular neighbourhood meetings helps to create this sense of connectedness and the practice of new members quickly becoming recruiters themselves promotes heightened self-esteem.

The 'New Religions' also meet the needs of urbanites by offering counselling services for dealing with personal problems and life-style issues. This may be done through offering advice or by the use of ritual powers (for example, to be derived from recitation of a sacred text, placating an ancestor or ridding a person of an evil spirit). Members have a strong practical orientation to their groups, looking to them not only for 'liberation', but for ways to cope with misfortune and have a happy life. They often move from one group to another, trying out the techniques.

Because the 'New Religions' offer spiritual techniques for addressing practical problems of everyday life, they tend to be socially conservative. However, one of the largest of the 'New Religions', the Soka Gakkai (a variant of Nichiren Shoshu Buddhism) formed a political party, the Komeito ('Clean Government Party') as a vehicle for establishing a Buddhist state in Japan.

Cycles of religious invention, growth, decline and reinvention

Clearly religions (and religious-like activities) are not disappearing, either from Western or Asian countries. In light of this evidence the sociologist Rodney Stark offers an alternative to simple linear models of 'secularization'. The decline of the mainline Christian churches and their upstaging by sectarian Christian and other religious movements in the West he sees as merely a continuation of cycles of change that have been with us throughout history. Accordingly he rejects the 'steady decline' image of many secularization theorists and instead speaks of continuous processes of invention, growth decline and reinvention of religious forms, with new groups and sects maturing into substantial mainline (or church-like) institutions, only to decline in the face of competition from new forms.

We need to acknowledge, however, that Stark's model is based on experiences in Western societies where there is a 'free market' of religions, secular philosophies and other activities that might serve some of the same needs that religions serve. In Asia this is not the case everywhere. Both states like the People's Republic of China, which are hostile to religions, and those which seek to promote a certain religion or religions, like Indonesia, limit free 'competition' among religions by registering and regulating them. Also, such religiously non-neutral states restrict competition between the secular and religious spheres by rewarding either certain forms of religiosity or atheism. Stark's cycles of invention model is probably most readily applicable in East Asia to societies like Japan which have a neutral stance towards religion.

Formalization of religious organization

In tribal and peasant communities religion is normally interwoven with every aspect of life and the concern of both families and governments. The retreat of church influence over governments is only one aspect of the 'specialization' of institutions that characterizes modern life. More and more of our activities are carried out in the context of 'special purpose' institutions (schools, hospitals, business firms, voluntary organizations, etc.). Thus in the religious sphere we hear Christians lament that religion has become a thing that people only worry about once a week on Sunday, and even then, forget when they walk out the church door. Associated with this specialization of institutions (including religious ones) in modern life is the spread of formal organization and bureaucratic forms of association. Religion, like education, politics and just about everything else in modern life, has come to be organized through formal organizations to an unprecedented extent. This contributes part of the explanation for the proliferation of 'New Religions' in Indonesia, Japan, the Philippines and other parts of East Asia in the twentieth century: inspired leaders who in the past would simply have catered individually and informally to those whose attention they attracted, these days adopt principles of organization used by nineteenth and twentieth century Christian missionaries and secular political movements. Thus they acquire a formal written charter, statement of principles, and often a chairperson, secretary, treasurer and the rest of the bureaucratic equipment that enables organizations to effectively co-ordinate the activities of large groups of people. However, written charters and formal principles of association not only enable efficient incorporation of large groups of people, but also bring into focus differences of interpretation that stimulate factional disputes. The resulting splits contribute to the numbers of groups competing for public attention in the modern 'spiritual marketplace'.

The internationalization of religious organizations

Over the course of the twentieth century overseas missionizing has become very much a 'two way street', with religions of Asian origin moving West just as those from Western countries have moved East. In some cases Asian religions exported to the West and revitalized or reworked there through new formal organizations have been re-exported to the East. One of the earliest examples of this was the Theosophy Society's role in the revival of Buddhism among the intelligentsia of Sri Lanka. The USA has been the site of most of the 'hot housing' and re-export of Asian religions through new formal organizations. Recently, however, the vigorous New Industrial Countries (NICs) of Asia have been directly exporting their own organizations, whether 'New Religions', like the Korean Rev. Sun Myung Moon's Unification Church (a reformulation of Christianity with a strong Confucian imprint), or 'old' religions through new organizations, such as Taiwan's Buddhist Light mission, with its lavish overseas branches in the USA, Australia and Europe.

The internationalization of religions in this century has a distinctive cast, as formal organizations are used to maintain degrees of involvement and control amongst adherents that could not have been achieved in the past. New management techniques employed by multinational business firms are often adopted by internationalizing religious organizations and full use is made of modern electronic technologies like telephone, fax and e-mail to carefully co-ordinate worship and other activities across the globe.

6.4 Emergent patterns in East Asian religion and spirituality

In this section we examine some emergent patterns of religion and spiritual life in East Asian societies over the past few decades and enquire into the particular circumstances in which these patterns have developed. First we see that in East Asia, much as in other parts of the world, there has been a polarization in styles of religiosity. On the one hand, there has been a rapid rise in the strength and media prominence of fundamentalism, both among Muslims and Christians; on the other hand, there are signs of a countervailing liberalism emerging. Another pattern we see in several East

Asian countries is a revival of folk cults. Finally we note an age old theme in both East Asian and Western spirituality, millenarianism, is finding new expression in East Asia, even in its longest 'developed' society, Japan.

The rise of fundamentalisms

Both the overthrow of the government of the US-backed Shah of Iran in 1979 by militant conservative Muslims and the disturbing frequency in recent years of terrorism linked to Muslim extremists has drawn enormous media attention to so-called Muslim 'fundamentalists'. The vast majority of Muslims, who are not in any way linked to these events, lament the readiness of the Western media (with its Christian cultural roots) to fasten on such negative stories, continuing to fire Christian–Muslim antagonisms rooted in the medieval past. They rightly point out that the Shi'ite Muslims who have imposed a particularly conservative (and to Western eyes misogynous) government on Iran are globally a small minority denomination (even if the dominant denomination in Iran itself). Further, not all of Iranian Shi'ites were themselves supportive of the Islamic revolution in that country. Moderate Muslims also point out that only a very tiny minority of Muslims of any denomination support terrorist activities.

None the less, 'fundamentalism' is a live political issue in many Muslim countries, pushing moderate Muslim leaders alternately towards increased religious conservatism or outbursts of police actions to control threats to their leadership. Pakistan, Bangladesh and, to a lesser extent, Malaysia are caught in the act of balancing fundamentalist and more moderate Muslim interests. A mark of this in Malaysia is that Malays today are far more likely than at the time of Independence 40 years ago to follow Muslim regulations on the association of men and women and dress codes for women (though in Malaysia the code is taken not to require obscuring the face and bodily shape as in Saudi Arabia or Iran). This religious conservatism, however, is attributable as much to the influence of moderate Muslim movements championing Islam as a badge of Malay pride as to pressure from the few extreme fundamentalist groups. Indonesia, which in the early 1970s extirpated overt religious interests from politics and rigorously monitors all religious groups for potentially subversive activities, faces fewer problems with fundamentalists in the public arena. None the less, in the 1996–97 riots religious differences between Muslims and Christians struck the sparks that ignited complex social tensions.

Box 6.2 **Religion and social protest: the 1996–97 Indonesia riots**

Starting in October 1996 and continuing into 1997 a series of riots on the Indonesian island of Java caught the attention of the international media. All involved Muslim attacks on non-Muslims. In June of 1996 Muslim groups in Surabaya vandalized churches. In the following months there were more attacks on churches in Jakarta, the nation's capital. Then in October in Sitobondo in East Java, Muslim mobs angered that a convicted blasphemer received a sentence of only five year's imprisonment rather than death, ran amok. They damaged 25 churches and various public buildings and killed five people, including a Pentecostal preacher and three of his family. Just after the New Year of 1997 the West Java town of Tasikmalaya erupted in violence, followed by the town of Rengasdengklok. The rioting in Tasikmalaya started after local police beat up and tortured a Muslim teacher who had disciplined a policeman's son for stealing. In Rengasdengklok the trigger for the rioting seems to have been a Chinese (non-Muslim) woman shouting at Muslims for making too much noise during pre-dawn prayers at the mosque next door. Both Christian churches and Buddhist temples were ransacked and at least four people died. In Tasikmalaya at least six churches were burned and a Chinese woman was found dead in a ransacked shop.

Although there have been incidents of interreligious violence in the past on Java, most of the time Muslims, Christians, Buddhists and people of other religions get along with one another. Why did their differences explode into such terrible violence at those particular places and just at those times? Is 'religion' responsible for these distressing events? Most observers, including Indonesian academics, agree that religion has become a vehicle for other discontents for which there is no legitimate outlet in Indonesia's present political and legal systems.

Looking more closely at the riots in Tasikmalaya, for example, we find that a dispute was already brewing between land owners and developers who were planning to put up a shopping centre that would exclude local traders. As in so many cases, this dispute reinforced the perception of less

A resident 'nails his colours to the mast' during rioting in Tasikmalaya

well-off people that they are not getting their fair share of the country's increasing economic prosperity and there is nothing they can do about it. The involvement of people of Chinese descent in the development also played on the popular perception that that ethnic group is unfairly advantaged in the race for prosperity. As Indonesian Chinese, who make up a mere 5 per cent of the population, own by some estimates 80 per cent of the nation's wealth, they become an easy target for resentments. And because most Indonesian Chinese are Christians or Buddhists, whereas the vast majority of indigenous people are Muslims, ethnic resentments easily become religious antagonisms. This is especially likely in the lead up to elections (a national election was held in May 1997), when frustrations over lack of genuine freedom for political parties and the press contribute to social tensions.

In this situation, then, what is overtly a religious conflict can be seen on a deeper level to be ethnic and class conflict taking the particular form it does because other forms of political expression have been outlawed or rendered useless. Religion then serves to 'carry' essentially social and political movements.

East Asia has its Christian fundamentalists too. Although not associated with military terrorism, Christian fundamentalists have, as it were, struck terror into the hearts of other East Asian Christians because of the speed with which fundamentalist Christian groups have made converts, not just amongst the 'heathen', but amongst Roman Catholics and other Protestant denominations. This 'sheep stealing' has been of greatest concern in the predominantly Catholic Philippines, where richly funded fundamentalist American churches have been particularly successful – much as in many parts of Catholic Latin America. The rapid expansion of the American fundamentalist churches overseas coincides with the conservative Christian revival and push into politics in the USA beginning in the 1980s, when religious enthusiasm translated into greater resources available for mission activities. It also coincides, in part, with the growth of Pentecostalism in the churches, particularly (but not exclusively) in fundamentalist ones.

Although both Muslim and Christian fundamentalisms espouse many conservative family values and hark back to a better, if semi-mythical past, both are responses to the modern world. The term 'fundamentalism' is itself of quite recent origin, dating to a Bible congress of conservative Protestants in New York State (USA) in 1895. The congress agreed on five principles or 'five fundamentals' of Christianity, including the literal truth of the Bible. A publication in several volumes of *The Fundamentals* between 1910 and 1915 expanded on the agenda of the congress and attacked other Christian groups that attempted to interpret the Bible in its historical context and with due appreciation of its poetic and literary artistry. *The Fundamentals* also attacked scientific findings on human evolution and the role of science in undermining faith in miracles.

Christians who supported and developed such views have been called 'fundamentalists'. In the last few decades the term 'fundamentalist' has been extended to Muslims who seek to restore a mythic past through strict application of a particularly conservative and patriarchal interpretation of Islamic law.

Amongst fundamentalist Muslims there are also groups, called 'Islamicists', who have reformulated highly conservative readings of Islamic law and history as a basis for an Islamic state in the context of twentieth century societies. This term 'Islamicist' draws attention to the ways in which certain fundamentalist Muslim thinkers, such as Abu'l-A'la' Mawdudi in Pakistan and Al Banna in Egypt, have responded to the leading secular 'isms' of the twentieth century (liberalism, nationalism, socialism) in formulating their understandings of what it should mean to have an Islamic state.

Because the Muslim holy books contain highly specific directions on how the faithful should deal with one another in society, addressing areas of both civil and criminal law, and because the Prophet himself was both his people's spiritual leader and head of state, the relationship between religion and the state has always been a matter of intense concern to Muslims. Many have argued that their religion requires support from the state to be properly instituted; and for some this means they should have an Islamic state.

However, just how an Islamic state should be instituted in the context of twentieth century nation-states is not at all obvious, as can be seen from the great variety of political structures in countries with Muslim majorities today. The various forms of 'Islamism' developed by twentieth century Muslim thinkers represent attempts to formulate a basis for creating more rigorously Islamic states out of the societies in which the Islamist thinkers have found themselves. They have attempted to do this by reading into the practices of the Prophet Mohammed and his first successors forms of political association that answer the challenges of modern secular ideologies and yet are 'truly Islamic'. We see this, for example, in Islamicist writings that construe the Muslim community of the time of the Prophet as an 'Islamic republic'. Mawdudi also develops the concept of an Islamic 'theo-democracy' in which God is the 'sovereign', making each citizen a 'caliph' equally empowered to vote for the head of state; the head of state is to be restrained only by God and a Consultative Assembly, consisting of *ulamas* (scholars of Muslim law) appointed by the administration.

'Islamism' thus fashions Islam into an ideology, that is, a political programme explicitly justified by a comprehensive philosophy. In the last 20 years Islamist movements have become more revolutionary, increasingly working towards militant struggles for power and becoming less concerned with constitutional government. They have also become more sectarian (like many Christian fundamentalists), claiming other Muslims who do not share their ideological agendas are not true Muslims (Arjomand, 1989, p.119).

Looking for other parallels between Christian and Muslim fundamentalists, we see in both a rejection of the scientific world view (though not of scientifically developed technology), hostility to cultural and religious diversity in modern societies, and suspicion of women's activities outside the home. These similarities in Christian and Muslim fundamentalism probably have their roots in the common experience of overwhelming social and technological change that has affected people in so many parts of the world. Fundamentalists nonetheless use modern electronic media to spread their message and co-ordinate their activities, and use modern weapons technology when involved in terrorist and revolutionary activities.

Countervailing liberalisms

While Islamic and Christian fundamentalism attract a great deal of press coverage, there are also strong liberal currents in religion in East Asia. A case in point is the Indonesian Neo-Modernist Muslim movement. Most of the leaders of this movement were actually raised in a 'traditionalist' Islamic setting: in families and religious schools (*pesantren*) that followed the legal traditions established in Islam's medieval period. The 'Neo-Modernists', however, were among the first *pesantren*-educated Indonesians to have the opportunity, starting in the 1970s, to study abroad in Western universities. These combined experiences inspired them to read their holy books and legal traditions much as Christian historical-critical scholars have read the Bible: as documents which need to be understood in the context in which they were written, and as embodiments of general guidelines for society, rather than as specific injunctions that must at all times be applied literally. The Neo-Modernists have revived concerns of the so-called 'Modernist Muslims'. As early as a century ago in Indonesia, Muslim Modernists began urging Muslims to make their own interpretations of their holy books, rather than simply rely on medieval scholarship to determine lawful behaviour. The Neo-Modernists, however, have not adopted the anti-Western stance of the Modernists and see themselves as rescuing an ageing Modernism from narrow literalism. Neo-Modernism seeks to identify the essential meanings of God's revelations through the Prophet Mohammed that can then find appropriate expression in the many different social contexts people encounter. They also reject the idea that God's law requires a Muslim state to administer it, and so accept thoroughgoing religious pluralism (the co-existence of diverse religions in society with full equality under the law). Neo-Modernism has proved extremely attractive to Indonesia's increasing numbers of high school and university graduates and growing middle class.

Another example of liberal currents in East Asian religious life is the reconceptualization of Buddhism in Thailand and other 'Southern' Buddhist countries as 'rational' and 'scientific' because of the 'experimental' attitude developed towards the practice of meditation. Much as Western Christians in the nineteenth and twentieth centuries distanced themselves from folk beliefs in saints and miracles, so some South-East

Asian and Sri Lankan Buddhist intellectuals have tried to distance themselves from folk practices like making offerings to spirits and folk deities. In place of this kind of activity, they have put new emphasis on meditation. This is a practice enjoined on all Buddhists, but most postpone serious practice of meditation (which can be highly demanding) for 'another life'. Because Buddhist meditation can be used as a tool for spiritual exploration rather than simply as a way of affirming beliefs, intellectuals have been able to claim that their Buddhism is genuinely experimental. This kind of emphasis on meditation as an open-ended search for knowledge also enables its practitioners to readily identify 'kindred spirits' among other religions.

Revival of folk cults

Paradoxical as it may seem, just as Asians with an intellectual bent are drawn away from 'superstitious' folk practices towards religious activities involving universalized ethics and exploration of the mind through meditation, others are breathing new life into old folk rituals. In Taiwan and the People's Republic of China, for example, the calendar is bursting with celebrations of Daoist deities. In the Toraja area of the island of Sulawesi in Indonesia spectacular funerals that are the centre-pieces of ancestor cults are celebrated by Christians and non-Christians alike, despite government disapproval in the 1980s. In Korea, folk cults featuring the performances of shamans (trance specialists who mediate between the everyday world and the world of the spirits) have come back into vogue and even drawn official support from the government. Shamanism is also reviving in Mongolia, in the area whose practices gave the word 'shaman' to the world, but seemed for a time to be losing its traditions.

What accounts for this 'come back' of folk religion? There seem to be a variety of factors at work, differing from area to area. One important factor is actually the new prosperity in so many parts of East Asia. Thus former peasants, small-time merchants and city workers in Taiwan and mainland China who now enjoy business success find it appropriate to celebrate their good fortune not just by buying cars and bigger houses but by sponsoring religious ceremonies. To understand this it is well to remember that even in the modern world rational business practice does not entirely account for one's fate, so showing gratitude towards the supernatural, while simultaneously enjoying the prestige associated with sponsorship of a public ritual, is attractive to many people.

In the Toraja area (as in Bali, another island of Indonesia) the tourist boom since the 1970s has been another factor in encouraging folk ritual. Not only has tourism brought money into the local economy that enables people to afford their elaborate and costly funeral celebrations, but the respectful interest shown by foreign tourists in what they see as 'living religion' has helped to counter government attempts to eradicate community religions. In Mongolia the 'spiritual tourist' trade has brought Western 'growth movement' practitioners to the feet of native shamans and native shamans are adapting their teachings accordingly, presenting to both local and foreign audiences a new blend of East and West. In South Korea the government sponsorship of folk religion stems from a positive evaluation of indigenous tradition and decision to preserve it as part of the national heritage.

Millenarianism

A particularly dramatic form of religious activity is the millenarian movement. This is a social movement inspired by the belief that the world as we know it will very soon come to an end, and a new divine order will be imposed on earth, bringing complete happiness and fulfilment. There have been millenarian movements in Europe since the Middle Ages, especially since the growth of cities began to disrupt the old feudal order. In East Asia millenarian movements have become particularly widespread during the late colonial period, as Western domination and economic systems disrupted local ways of life. In Java in the nineteenth century hope in the coming of the 'Just King' (Ratu Adil) inspired uprisings; in the Philippines the Spanish faced numerous revolts led by people styling themselves as 'God', 'Jesus' or the pope; even China was racked by the Taiping Rebellion (1851–64) which hoped to establish on earth the 'Heavenly Kingdom of the Great Peace'.

Surprisingly to many people, millenarian movements are not entirely a thing of the past. They reappeared in the Philippines in the 1950s after a lull of 20 years or so, and also in Java in the 1960s, 1970s and 1980s. In the most widely publicized case there a former civil servant convicted in 1978 of plotting the overthrow of the President was widely understood to be a 'guru' whose followers considered him the Ratu Adil, or 'Just King'. Surely the most dramatic recent millenarian movement in East Asia, however, and one that vividly illustrates that such movements are not confined to peasantries disturbed by economic change, is the Japanese Aum Supreme Truth (Aum Shinrikyo) sect, established in 1980. This eclectic movement, incorporating elements of both Hinduism and Buddhism, was responsible for gassing people on five Tokyo subway trains in 1995, killing eleven people and injuring more than 5,000. The sect's membership included many well educated Japanese followers, including graduates from Japan's 'best' universities, and at the time of the leaders' arrest was spreading rapidly overseas, with the largest foreign branch in Russia.

6.5 Conclusion

Religions are very much a part of Asia-Pacific life today. In several Asia-Pacific countries, governments give official support to religion and there are considerable social pressures on people to have a religion. In other countries, governments are either neutral or actually hostile to religions, but nevertheless individuals still often involve themselves in some sort of religious activities. In such countries religion is a private matter and the variety of activities in which religion is important is typically not as great as in the past. Nonetheless, for some individuals, religion or spiritual activities are intensely important. Religions can be important in symbolizing a national or ethnic identity, in celebrating wealth and generating prestige, in providing a sense of community in faceless urban settings and in responding to rapid social change. In addition to lending themselves to these social uses, religions are also resources for those seeking to answer questions beyond the scope of science and technology and looking for a depth of experience that may be missing from everyday life. Thus regardless of patterns of social change in the wider society, religions are likely to continue to find new forms of expression in the Asia-Pacific.

References

Arjomand, S.A. (1989) 'The emergence of Islamic political ideologies' in Beckford, J. and Luckman, T. (eds) *The Changing Face of Religion*, London, Sage (pp. 109–23).

Weber, M. (1964) *The Sociology of Religion,* translated by Ephraim Fischoff, Boston, Beacon Press.

Further reading

Akbar, A. (1922) *Postmodernism and Islam, Predicament and Promise*, London, Routledge. An essay on the role of Islam in society in the late twentieth century.

Beyer, P. (1994) *Religion and Globalisation,* London, Sage.

Caldarola, C. (ed.) (1982) *Religion and Societies: Asia and the Middle East*, The Hague, Mouton. A country by country survey of relationships between religions and societies (including 'church-state' relations) in East and South Asia and the Middle East.

Dumoulin, H. (ed.) (1976) *Buddhism in the Modern World*, New York, Macmillan. Essays on the place of Buddhism in several contemporary societies.

Gilles, K. (1994) *The Revenge of God: The Resurgence of Islam, Christianity and Judiasm in the Modern World*, London, Polity Press. An attempt to account for the revival of the Near Eastern religions in the contemporary social and political environment.

Hardacre, H. (1989) *Shinto and the State, 1868–1988*, Princeton, Princeton University Press.

Keyes, C.F., Kendall, L. and Hardacre, H. (1994) *Asian Visions of Authority. Religion and the Modern States of East and South-East Asia*, Honolulu, University of Hawaii Press.

McFarland, N.H. (1997) *The Rush Hour of the Gods*, New York, Macmillan. On New Religious Movements in Japan.

McGuire, M. (1992) *Religion, The Social Context* (3rd edn) Belmont, CA, Wadsworth. Text on sociology of religion, focusing mainly on Western societies but providing concepts which can be useful in studying East Asian societies as well and some East Asian examples.

McInnes, D.E. (1972) *Religious Policy and Practice in Communist China, A Documentary History,* London, Hodder and Stoughton. A selection of published materials from the PRC on religious policy up to the early 1970s.

McVey, R. (1993) *Redesigning the Cosmos: Belief Systems and State Power in Indonesia,* Copenhagen, Nordick Institute of Asian Studies. On religion and power in Indonesia.

Marty, M.E. and Appleby, R.S. (eds) (1991) *Fundamentalism Observed,* Chicago, University of Chicago Press. A comprehensive survey of the phenomenon of fundamentalism in various religions across the world.

Matthews, A.W. (1995) *World Religions* (2nd edn) New York, West Publishing Company. An introductory text on comparative religion.

Murakami, S. (1980) *Japanese Religion in the Modern Century.* Translated by Earhart, H.B., Tokyo, University of Tokyo Press. Religion in Japan since the Meiji Restoration.

O'Brien, J. and Palmer, M. (1993) *The State of Religion Atlas,* New York, Simon & Schuster. Presentation in map form of data on the distribution and state of religions across the world. Some compromises in quality of data and nuance for the sake of visual presentation, but useful in forming a clear first impression.

Robertson, R. and Garret, W. (eds) (1991) *Religion and Global Order: Religion and the Political Order, Vol.4,* New York, Paragon House.

Sacks, J. (1991) *The Persistence of Faith: Religion, Morality and Society in a Secular Age,* London, Weidenfeld and Nicolson. On the diverse forms 'religion' takes in the post-modern world.

Sharma, A. (ed.) (1993) *Our Religions,* San Francisco, Harper. A collection of essays on the universalistic religions each done by a leading scholar on that tradition who is also an exponent of that tradition.

Spiro, M. (1982) *Buddhism and Society, A Great Tradition and its Burmese Vicissitudes,* Berkeley, University of California Press. A classic study of lived forms of Buddhism in a South-East Asian society.

Stark, R. (1985) *The Future of Religion: Secularization, Revival and Cult Formation,* Berkeley, University of California Press. Stark's modification of the secularization hypothesis.

Tambiah, S. (1976) *World Conqueror and World Renouncer, A Study of Buddhism and Polity in Thailand against a Historical Background,* Cambridge, Cambridge University Press. Study of Buddism in Thailand by a noted anthropologist.

Yang, C.K. (1967) *Religion in Chinese Society,* Berkeley, University of California Press. A classic sociological analysis of religion in Chinese society.

CHAPTER 7

Education

John Hawkins

7.1 Introduction

The dramatic economic and political developments in the Asia-Pacific region over the past decade have not gone unnoticed and have spawned a variety of books, articles and studies of various sorts seeking to provide some insight into this rapid rise to prominence. While the usual economic factors are generally cited as major conditions for this rise, what is most interesting to observe is the pre-eminent role that is assigned to both formal and non-formal education in explaining the rapid development of the Asia-Pacific region. As Rohwen (1995) argues in his popular book *Asia Rising,*

> Much of East Asia got an educational jump on other poor countries in the 1960s and sped ahead so fast that by the 1980s the Asian early birds were turning out children who were certainly more numerate than their counterparts in the rich world and often more capable of abstract thought of all kinds ... East Asia was well positioned for an educational triumph.
>
> (Rohwen, 1995, p.56)

He goes on to explain in detail how this investment in human capital led to rapid and sustained economic growth.

This picture is of course mixed when one looks at all of Asia, a vast and differentiated region of the world, but most nations in the region hold a high value of education, both for what it can do to spur the economy and as an end in itself. In this chapter I will examine education in the Asia-Pacific context, outlining the basic goals and objectives and sample statistics, looking at the elusive issue of 'motivation' and values in Asia-Pacific education, and exploring the relationship between education and development. Because of the breadth and depth of the region we will not be able to provide in-depth treatment of each and every nation but rather will paint in broad strokes some of the principal features of East Asian and Pacific education, with some specific examples from Japan and China.

North-East Asia

In North-East Asia, since the Second World War, Japan has emerged as the 'number one' nation in the region (although China is rapidly catching up) with remarkable economic growth rates reflected in a variety of educational indicators: educational physical plant, trained personnel, increasing enrolments at all levels, textbook production, audio-visual instructional aids, literacy rates and a variety of other indicators. Investment in education in Japan during the period from 1955 to 1980 grew 32-fold. Expansion occurred at all levels in the system, not always to the benefit of sound pedagogy (e.g. there has been a dramatic increase in the number of questionable private universities and colleges, complicated by a system dominated by national entrance exams for access to higher education).

Japanese students learning how to make a television programme

The Japanese educational system undoubtedly has produced remarkable results if measured only in achievement rates, and under certain assumptions, translated into productivity in the work place. Yet, Japan's educational leaders have not been satisfied even with this high level of accomplishment. Several major educational reform efforts have been pursued in the last decade, designed to restructure the educational system along several general lines. The reforms proposed focused on several important issues. First, was recognition that, because of Japan's wealth and leadership in the world, the educational system needed to be reassessed in order to prepare Japanese young people to maintain this position in the twenty-first century. Second, was recognition that lifelong learning must begin to replace the previous emphasis on credentials and the general educational background of individuals. Third, was the proposal to increase quality and creativity at the level of higher education, focusing more on the individual than in the past. Fourth, was recognition that Japan's technological pre-eminence ideally suited it to experiment with a variety of educational settings, including 'smart classrooms' or schools utilizing state-of-the-art educational technology. The central examination system was also challenged, and a credit system has been suggested for use in upper secondary schools.

How many of these reforms will actually be translated into action remains to be seen. Japan's educational system has gone through numerous reform movements (the most dramatic being the US occupation) only to re-emerge in traditional forms. Stresses and strains, however, are beginning to be felt throughout the system from school violence at the junior high level, bullying at all levels, to increasing cynicism and boredom at the collegiate level (with increasing numbers of Japanese high school graduates opting for foreign higher education). Japan's great wealth has permitted experimentation with various unusual efforts to address the perceived problem of the national system's rigidity. These efforts include setting up schools in other countries, outright purchase of foreign schools, and establishing branch campuses of foreign universities (often American) throughout Japan. Although much about Japanese education is impressive, a closer look makes the observer wonder about the degree to which it is a dynamic and creative force for change in Japan or, as van Wolfren (1989) suggests, simply another 'servant of the system' producing products in cookie cutter fashion.

Despite the differences between Taiwan and mainland China (size, political-economic system) the two countries hold several beliefs about education in common. Since the late 1940s both have proclaimed a strong faith in the power of education to transform the country and the people into a modern state. Both have invested relatively heavily in the educational enterprise, focused on literacy campaigns, expanded educational opportunities at all levels, instituted national and local entrance examination systems, and more recently, engaged in large-scale exchange programmes. Beyond those features, however, differences abound. Mainland China has been plagued by numerous, almost insurmountable problems: sheer size, a continuing population expansion despite sometimes draconian fertility control measures, sluggish economic growth during the 1970s and early 1980s, enduring political instability, shifting political attitudes toward education as an enterprise (resulting in teacher disaffection and student cynicism), and the loss of a generation of higher level trained personnel because of the Cultural Revolution (1966–76). Despite these obstacles, significant progress has been made in education in general: declining illiteracy, institution of a compulsory 9-year system, expanding higher education, an effective non-formal sector, significant advances in selected research areas, a growing privatization of education, and in the mid 1990s a rapidly growing economy that is fuelling social change efforts at many levels including education (Hawkins, 1997).

Taiwan has also moved steadily forward on many fronts. Economically, it is still one of the more advanced economies in the region. All levels of education have benefited from this economic progress, and Taiwan today boasts a highly developed educational system with high literacy rates, enrolment and completion rates, and access to higher education. Some major problems in planning for investment in education and a history of 'brain drain' to the West (particularly North America) remain. Yet, even these problems have declined in recent years because of Taiwan's rather phenomenal continued economic growth. Table 7.1 provides comparative demographic and financial data on East Asia and shows clearly the wide variation in scale and scope on these indicators.

Table 7.1 *North-East Asia*

	Population	*Education as % of gov. expenditures*	*Tertiary enrolment as % of age group*	*Literacy rate (%)*
China	1.2 billion	2.2	2	82
South Korea	44 million	16.8	42	98
Taiwan	21 million	20.0	26	86
Japan	124 million	16.2	32	99

Source: Far Eastern Economic Review (1996)

The two Koreas also represent great variation. So little is known about North Korea that no attempt is made here to summarize educational development in that country. Although both Koreas experienced similar historical and cultural influences in the past, the Republic of Korea (South Korea) has evidenced remarkable economic and educational growth since its almost total devastation during the Korean War. The Japanese colonial legacy of the pre-Korean War period left the Koreans with almost no educational administrative experience. Yet, a comprehensive educational system has emerged, complete with high literacy rates, large-scale access to higher education, and a fairly high correlation between investment in education and economic growth. Korea is often touted as another 'East Asian miracle' and evidence seems to suggest that this indeed is the case. The role of the state in the Korean economic and educational miracle has captured much attention in recent years. Fierce debates have waged over the positive and negative aspects of the syncretic merging of major institutions such as education and the formalized state structure. Two facts, however, emerge as central: there has been great success in almost all aspects of the educational enterprise; and there is great political instability and disaffection among Korean youth, particularly in higher education. Almost continual student-authority clashes at most major universities have evidenced the latter. The instability that these clashes have created appears at times to threaten the progress that has been achieved during the past two decades. The recent financial crisis in Korea illustrates the limits of excessive control.

South-East Asia

A diverse region, South-East Asia consists principally of two groups of nations: the former Indo-China States (Vietnam, Cambodia, Laos, Burma/Myanmar) and the Association of South-East Asian Nations (ASEAN): Brunei, Indonesia, Malaysia, Philippines, Thailand, and Singapore (which Vietnam has now joined). The period of protracted war and isolation that has characterized the former group make discussing educational development difficult. A substantial amount of rebuilding has taken place in Vietnam, but Cambodia is still emerging from the incredible internal and external turmoil that it has been through. Each of these states has been relatively isolated from international affairs although Vietnam is currently heavily engaged with building political and economic linkages with the rest of the world. Although emigration from those countries has had an impact on the educational systems of other nations (including the USA) little research has been conducted on educational developments in these countries.

By contrast, the ASEAN confederation has been closely linked economically and educationally to the West and the rest of Asia. ASEAN was formed in 1967 to promote regional development among the six nations that form the group. Education was recognized as a crucial element in the modernization process. A unique adjunct group called South-East Asia Ministers of Education was formed to co-ordinate and share information and strategies for development. Each of the nations in the association has accomplished much in furthering basic education, literacy and numeracy. The so-called back to basics education movement in the 1970s swept through the region, and great efforts were made to improve the quality and quantity of both elementary and secondary education. Emphasis was placed on reading, writing and numeracy, as well as citizenship education, principally focused at the primary level. This movement was later criticized for ignoring other important elements of the curriculum but did succeed in laying a strong educational foundation for each of the ASEAN nations. Common to the region also has been a concerted effort to develop and expand various non-formal and informal educational efforts aimed at literacy, women's education, agricultural education, vocational-technical skills and health education. This mix of formal and non-formal education has contributed to the overall economic and human resource base of the ASEAN group. Some selected indicators for South-East Asia appear in Table 7.2.

Although there have been collectively shared successes, there remain important differences and exceptions. Indonesia, the largest and most populated nation in ASEAN, is resource rich (as is Brunei) in oil. This wealth has allowed greater investment in educational physical plant and training. Malaysia has focused much energy in education on 'Malayanization' by attempting to shift resources to the Malay population and to promote Malay culture among the other two central ethnic groups: the Chinese and Indians. This effort has resulted in some disaffection, particularly in the area of higher education. Thailand had emerged as the new 'little tiger' as

Table 7.2 *South-East Asia*

	Population	Education as % of gov. expenditures	Tertiary enrolment as % of age group	Literacy rate (%)
Malaysia	19 million	20.3	7	84
Philippines	65 million	15.9	28	95
Singapore	3 million	22.3	NA	91
Thailand	58 million	21.0	19	94
Vietnam	71 million	NA	2	94

Source: Far Eastern Economic Review (1996)

its economy had begun to lead others in the region and its educational system at all levels continued to expand and improve. Thailand began to exert leadership not only among the ASEAN group but among the former Indochina states as well. Like Korea, Thailand has now had to reassess its role, as a rapidly expanding economy and is seeking to reform its financial and other national institutions. Finally, the Philippines, once the leading nation in the group on almost all educational indicators, has fallen behind because of various political and economic problems associated with overall leadership and internal dissension, although recent reform efforts promise to move the Philippines once again forward. The literacy rate remains high – as does investment in education – but overall economic growth has declined and poverty has increased dramatically. The Philippines is also noted for large-scale 'brain drain' to the West of highly skilled professionals, as well as large numbers of students seeking degrees outside the Philippines.

Overall the ASEAN region of Asia has a well-developed, articulated system of precollegiate and collegiate education. The region is rich in both material and human resources and, although large pockets of poverty exist, the investment in education thus far has paid dividends in the general development of each nation. Continued economic and technical assistance from the international community accompanied by stable economic growth will likely contribute to the further development of an already substantial educational foundation.

7.2 Motivation and values in East Asian education

Motivation in individuals, let alone cultures, is a complicated characteristic to measure or account for. Yet it appears to be considered an important variable by those seeking to understand East Asia and its economic success. In the case of motivation among East Asians the stereotypes are becoming increasingly common. 'East Asians', as the region has been defined above, work hard, are disciplined, quiet, over-achievers, excel in mathematics and science, and so on. Furthermore, much of the data on these groups supports the stereotypical views mentioned above (White 1987; Cummings, 1986).

In this section a brief presentation of motivation factors attributed primarily to North-East Asians (Chinese, Japanese and Koreans) will be presented. As was noted above the region is too complex and varied to treat each group. However, that part of the East Asian region also referred to as the nations influenced by Confucianism (China, Japan, Korea, Hong Kong, Singapore, Vietnam and all overseas Chinese in other Asian nations) represents a large and interesting educational population and one that has emigrated to other non-Asian nations and is influencing the educational systems of those countries. By 'motivation' I mean 'the most important determinant of the difference between what a person can do and what he or she will do' (Amabile, 1983).

What must first be noted is that there are multiple explanations for high motivation and, therefore, achievement of East Asians. These explanations have, for example, been characterized as being defined by either a 'cultural' approach, or what some scholars call 'relative functionalism', or what others call the 'folk theory of success', or finally the 'need to achieve' which is more predominant among some cultures than others. All of these explanations are somewhat explanatory of the East Asian grouping. Other less documented explanations have to do with the role of Confucian thought, the influence of an ideographic language, a tradition of rote memorization and so on.

East Asia and Confucianism

In many nations, the role of the family is often seen as one important motivating factor for success in education. For example, how do ordinary, uneducated Chinese come to share common Confucian values? Willingness to work hard and defer rewards is often explained in reference to family organization. Authority relations, the success that China has had in re-establishing educational institutions, a new state and so on can be traced in some respects to the structure of the family and the values that it promotes. One major term that came to be associated with this phenomenon is filial piety; this was stressed throughout Chinese society, in schools, in textbooks, in magistrate's lectures, plays, local religion and so on. Gradually these values came to be shared throughout the population with a degree of homogeneity not found in other cultures and certainly not in Europe. Indeed, the cultural arguments and the role of the family in accounting for high motivation seem to be strong throughout all of East Asia leading to the question: why has East Asia emerged as a model of motivation and achievement?

As one of the three regions of the world competing for world superiority (the others being Western and North-East Europe including the newly developing Russian confederation, and North America), East Asia has Confucianism as a principal source of dynamism contained within a rich culture and history. On the other hand, the region has been insular and not very outward looking. Now many Westerners are taking notice of the region, not only because of its economic powers but family stability, low crime rates, high life expectancies, and superior educational motivation and performance. At the same time, there is some perception that with this level of achievement has come a cost: namely, individual personality. While there are obvious differences between nations in the region (Korea, Japan, China) Confucianism is the glue that holds them together (Rozman, 1991).

Although it is risky to utilize stereotypes based on culture and history, they are nevertheless often useful in setting the tone of the discussion. Rozman and associates found many of the following stereotypes regarding East Asians to be 'relatively true: individuals are characterized by self-denial, frugality, patience, fortitude, self-discipline, dedication, rote learning and an aptitude for applied sciences and mathematics' (Rozman, 1991, pp.28–9).

Some educational implications for these statements are that individuals from the region excel in efforts that require patience and unstinting effort over long periods of time, with delayed gratification: memorization and repetition are rewarded; individualism is downplayed both at home and in the school. In the school, motivation and achievement are highlighted by student diligence, rote learning, memorization (often reinformed by chanting in unison), emphasis on test-taking at an early age, and moral education. While all of this may suggest uniformity, in fact the opportunity structure (merit based competition) has been quite open in all three countries.

Other group stereotypes that help frame the discussion have to do with 'group orientation, acceptance of authority, deference, dependence, conflict avoidance, interest in harmony, seniority consciousness, and dutifulness' (Rozman, 1991, p.30). If one would look for the social unit that best encompasses these traits then probably the family and its extension, familism, would be a good place to start. Group organizations in East Asia, whether they are the family proper, or an enterprise (e.g. a school) are more strict in the degree of commitment required to join or be admitted and their exclusivity, than is the case in other societies. While there is certainly intra-regional variations in East Asia, the similarities outweigh the differences.

The educational implications of the practice of filial piety are not often discussed. In brief, the hierarchy of family relations (obedience, rites, responsibilities, etc.), polite language toward superiors, and a variety of behaviours associated with superiors and inferiors found their way into the school environment once education became more widespread. Just as there was a high degree of uniformity in the Chinese family, by the end of the Qing dynasty (1911) there was a parallel high degree of uniformity of belief and behaviour regarding learning which resulted in uniformly high motivation among students in the Chinese societies.

In Japan and Korea this was less the case and the spread of Confucian values came more through the spread of formal education than through the family. In Japan it can be found in the modern period in Motoda's Imperial Rescript on Education, drafted in 1890 and memorized by millions of teachers and students of the time. Within it are contained a blend of

Western notions of utility and practicality and Confucian notions of moral value, particularly loyalty and filial piety. While many would argue that there has been a post-war rejection of Confucianism in Japan (following its transformation into nationalism in the 1930s) it can equally be argued that it has survived in a modified form particularly in education. If it were argued that Japan's current success had something to do with Confucianism most Japanese would reject it out of hand. If on the other hand it were argued that certain values were critical to Japan's success – stability, order, belief in the family, harmony, hierarchy in the work-force, loyalty to employers and superiors, importance of diligence, self-cultivation and so on – then there would generally be a lot of agreement. In fact, these values can be characterized as 'Confucian' and all contribute to a structure supporting high motivation and achievement.

The motivating rituals and values found in the workplace can also be found in the schools. As Rohlen (1983, p.167) notes: 'Although schools in both cultures (Japan and the USA) have formulas for events, less depends on convention in the United States. School events and ceremonies are readily changed, and most are abandoned if student support lags. Japanese school events, on the other hand, appear uniform and constant. They depend on tradition and teachers. The Confucian appreciation for formality in ritual as expressive of the moral order lingers in Japan, just as our democratic and Protestant heritage inclines us to events with grass roots spontaneity that is informal and emotionally expressive'. Schools thus become a kind of Confucian moral community expressing values, order and discipline, transmitted by moral example, usually with the teacher in the lead. High motivation is far easier to sustain if there is a common sense of purpose, ritually reinforced and backed up by teacher behaviour.

Korea, on the other hand, had little resemblance to a Confucian society until the eighteenth century when it began to exhibit many of the Confucian characteristics generally associated with Japan and China. In some ways, Koreans became more Confucian than the Chinese from whom they borrowed many of the forms. Despite the fact that it was an alien creed and in many ways in conflict with more indigenous beliefs it nevertheless took root and spread throughout Korean society, especially the lower classes, through the educational system and the innovation of the Korean alphabet (Hangul). Behavioural assumptions regarding the value of hard work, meritocratic rewards, and the significance of formal education became deeply imbedded in Korean society, much more rigidly than in either Japan or China. It has not been difficult for Korean educators and parents to reinforce the already high levels of motivation among Korean students given the commonly held convictions regarding the reward structure. Koreans carried the notion of the power of education to transmit values to an extreme. Education was seen as being the central force in transforming society and it was not long after the Confucian tradition became imbedded in Korean society that a comprehensive, nation-wide state-run school system emerged (early 1400s). The formal study of officially approved texts (*Elementary Learning, Classic of Filial Piety, The*

Four Books, and the *Five Classics*) rote memorization of critical passages, and a powerful belief in the value of learning and education, characterized this early approach to formal education. The successful passing of crucial examinations led automatically to respectable official positions; one's future was assured. All of these early predilections toward education carried forward into the modern period. As Robinson notes:

> The Confucian tradition has shaped other modern sectors of Korean life. In the 1950s and 1960s government service continued to be a prime goal for educated elites. The expansion of higher education (from 60,000 college students in 1960 to over one million in 1985) in the postwar era was matched by an increase in the size of the state bureaucracy. Based on its ability to attract the best and brightest students, the relative efficiency of the South Korean bureaucracy, in spite of its many flaws, has been signalled out as a major contributor to economic growth.
>
> (Robinson, 1991, p.222)

The very strong links between formal learning and education, guaranteed employment, and nation building, were powerful links indeed forming the web supporting high motivation at the individual level.

Overall, scholars of East Asian societies, and particularly those focusing on the philosophical traditions of this region, agree that assumptions about human nature gave great credence to the power and role of formal education and mental training. This expressed itself in family rituals, work attitudes, study habits, the structure and organization of schooling, and finally, served as the foundation upon which individual motivation could be nurtured (Rozman, 1991, p.168). As Rozman states:

> It is particularly noteworthy that these societies channelled expectations towards schooling. In Korea the yanban (ruler) status was associated with education; it was widely sought and, once attained, led to higher aspirations to pass exams. In Japan literacy rates climbed steeply during the two and half centuries of the Tokugawa period. In China, the prestige of scholar-officials continued to draw vast numbers to the district-level examinations that might lead to higher-level examinations and elite social standing. Education to serve one's family, to help it rise in status within one's community, and, for some, to earn government recognition and office was a powerful magnet for the ambitious.
>
> (Rozman, 1991, pp.168–9)

One might also say that education served as a powerful motivator not only for the ambitious but for the ordinary as well, since it was the single societal sector where hard work paid off. Obviously, the system did not work flawlessly in any of these nations, and exceptions existed in all cases. However, the very powerful Confucian notion that successfully pursuing education leads to individual and social progress was deeply imbedded by the mid-twentieth century. As we begin to examine the modern period, more empirical forms of evidence become available and provide us with additional sources of information regarding the issue of motivation in the East Asia region. Here we will look principally at Japan although much of what is argued here holds true for the Chinese cultures and Korea as well.

Japan: achievement and motivation

The culture arguments seem to be the most pervasive and in some respects, the most persuasive. In most studies, the authors convey a subtle sense that Japan's educational successes accompanied by high motivation are, perhaps, culturally specific and flow from regional and cultural experiences.

In a comparison of the Japanese and American experience, three aspects of considerable difference have been noted. The first is the historical and cultural tendency toward educational centralization, in contrast to the vigorous role of local boards and the private sector in the USA.

A second major sociocultural difference relates to the varying sex roles for females with respect to higher education. In Japan, females tended to be primarily enrolled in junior colleges whereas in the USA females have started exceeding males in the enrolment rate in four-year institutions.

Finally, Japan has experienced a dramatic increase in the numbers of institutions of higher education since 1950. While this represents an increased role for the private sector the domination of educational standards and regulations by the Ministry of Education has continued.

The increase in students in higher education is reflected in the larger numbers of graduates

Against this more or less factual description of Japanese and US education, other studies provide an interesting 'perceptual' profile of the two systems. William Cummings in *Japanese Images of American Education* notes that 'Japan has been looking at American education much longer than America has been looking at Japanese education, and Japan has far more information' (1984, p.1). He discusses four classes of observers of US education in Japan and their approach in conveying to the Japanese public their perceptions of US education: 'Ministry of Education observers focus on aspects of finance, enrolments, and administration. Professors comment on the quality of academic life in the United States. Parents and students focus on events in the classroom and community. And Politicians seem most aware of the American disease of drugs, violence, and sex' (Cummings, 1984, p.11). The view is invariably one-dimensional depending on the interest group doing the viewing.

What emerges from Cummings' study is the cultural difference in interpreting a complex phenomenon such as 'education'. On the one hand, 'American education was seen as expressive, individualist, opulent, and creative, on the other as undisciplined, wasteful and hedonistic' (Cummings, 1984, p.11). These views, expressed through the Japanese media and other sources, reinforce the notion among Japanese students and parents that their system is superior and thus, in a circuitous way, contributes to a higher sense of motivation and need to achieve even more.

Many Western observers of Asian education have counterpoised tradition with modernity and suggested that only those nations that modernized (e.g. Japan, China and South Korea) and set aside their traditions made progress and accomplished high levels of achievement, thereby suggesting that such achievement was associated with high motivation. Asian researchers, however, argue the opposite. Kobayashi (1984) in particular debunks many of the stereotypes held by most writers who seek to explain Japan's success economically and educationally. He acknowledges the many successes that the Japanese have achieved and the creative ways they have maintained aspects of their traditional culture in the face of rapid modernization. But he introduces an ecological, theoretical construct against which to discuss differences in US and Japanese pedagogy. What is perceived as rote learning (and therefore Confucian) by US observers in fact is part of a complex, group interaction process inherent in Japanese culture: 'This rote is not really repetition since, from the practitioner's point of view, each "repetition" is regarded as always containing learning something new, such as miniscule modifications in writing *kanji* (Chinese characters) each time one does it ...' (Kobayashi, 1984, p.110).

The thrust of Kobayashi's argument is that contrary to many thinkers in the West, tradition and modernity are not mutually exclusive. In fact, aspects of Japanese tradition may contribute to their success in education:

> Thus, rote and imitation practices deemed outmoded by new scientific theories of teaching-learning which entered education in Europe and America during the time of the industrial revolution, are still maintained in the teaching–learning of traditional arts in a nation considered the most modern and industrial in Asia. Planners in developing countries sometimes argue that 'tradition' prevents modernization but this doctrine is too simplistic, as the case of contemporary Japan illustrates.
>
> (Kobayashi, 1984, p.113)

It might further be argued that maintaining high levels of motivation is an easier task when traditional practices can be called upon both for justification of the educational effort and for group support.

Given this rather brief overview of possible cultural and traditional sources influencing motivation what is there in the way of information regarding specific motivational attributes that applies to the Japanese case? The literature is generally weak in this regard, however some important generalizations can be generated, based on the studies currently available.

One area often examined in this context is 'self concept'. Despite the substantial body of US literature involving judgements of one's value and abilities along a number of dimensions (primarily called self-concept or self-esteem), data on the self-concept of Japanese students is limited. Fetters *et al.* (1983) reports the percentage of high school seniors that agreed with three statements on self-esteem:

I'm a person of worth
I'm satisfied with myself
At times, I think I'm no good

and another question about ability to enter (in Japan)/complete (in the USA) college.

Japanese responses to the questions about worth and self-satisfaction were much less positive than that of Americans; less than a third of the Japanese students agree with these statements while more than 80 per cent of the US students responded positively. The third statement elicited a higher percentage of negative response from Japanese students, especially from females (71 per cent agreeing with the statement that they felt they were no good at times in contrast to 49 per cent of Japanese males and 51 per cent and 41 per cent of US females and males respectively). The question about college showed a similar Japan–USA pattern with over 80 per cent of the US seniors judging themselves able to complete college while less than 40 per cent of Japanese stated that they had the ability to enter college (since the dropout rate from college is negligible in Japan, entering is essentially tantamount to completing college).

It is possible to attribute the patterns of responses above to distinctive cultural tendencies in socialization regarding appropriate expressions about self-judgement. Within Japanese society humility is valued as an essential ingredient of interpersonal harmony while overconfidence and public expression of beliefs that will reflect negatively on others are discouraged. US society, on the other hand, places a higher premium on self-confidence and self-assurance, and its competitive tendencies afford greater tolerance for and encouragement of public expression of one's capabilities.

What this means in terms of 'true' differences in distribution of self-concept between Japanese and American students is unclear. Japanese students, as a group, may be overly self-critical, professing greater concerns about their worth and abilities than they truly believe and thus be more 'realistically' motivated toward their personal educational goals. On the other hand, their self-opinions might also reflect realistic reactions to the tightly connected system of secondary and post-secondary educational stratification. In contrast, the responses of US students are more likely to reflect overconfidence and weaker societal linkages between school performance, opportunities, and self-esteem.

Another category of studies related to motivational attributes can be termed 'locus of control'. This category of attributes deals with the tendency to judge whether the factors responsible for individual actions and performances are under one's personal control (internal) or not (external). Current emphasis in applications of the locus of control is on an individual's causal attributions for their success or failure. Attributions to personal ability and effort are viewed as internal, while those focused on task difficulty; luck and fate are considered to be external factors beyond the control of the individual. Among the internal factors, effort is considered to be a changeable behaviour while ability (or aptitude) is seen as a more stable personal characteristic.

The evidence from the Japanese–USA comparisons with respect to locus of control and causal attributions for success and failure is mixed, seemingly varying across time and age group considered. The First International Mathematics Study included an 18-item scale intended to measure 'the extent to which man is perceived as having effective control of and mastery over his environment' (Husen, 1976, p.19). At all three population levels considered (thirteen year old, terminal year mathematics students, terminal year non-mathematics students), Japan exhibited high means (ranked First or Second among the countries) and low standard deviations while US means were much lower (close to bottom ranking) and the scores more variable. This meant that on the whole, Japanese students were more likely than students from other countries to feel that people have control over their own fate while American students were more likely to view people as helpless in the face of forces at work in the world. This finding runs counter to some popular stereotypes about 'Asian fatalism' suggesting that Japanese students, at least, feel they can succeed and achieve given the effort, time and energy aimed at a task and rarely reach the conclusion that 'I just can't get it'.

Other studies focus on the relative prevalence of ability, effort, luck and task difficulty in causal attributions regarding success and achievement. For example, in the Hess and Azuma study (1985) (the Japanese students were in the fifth grade while the Americans were in the sixth grade), both students and their parents were asked about their attributions for low performance in mathematics. Both Japanese children and their mothers were less likely to attribute poor performance to lack of ability and training in school and more likely to attribute it to lack of effort than US children and their mothers. US children were also more likely than Japanese children to blame poor performance on bad luck. At an earlier phase of the study (when children were four) Japanese mothers were more likely to emphasize children's natural abilities (effort and ability were not separated in this part of the study) and less likely to emphasize parental encourage-ment as reasons for their children's future success in school. The report authors interpret their results as supportive of a Japanese belief in individual control over success; i.e., internal changeable factors such as effort are more important than either internal stable factors (ability) or external factors (luck, task difficulty, quality of teaching, etc.).

Other macro factors may shed more light on what accounts for high motivation among East Asians but are clearly less easy to measure. The link between education and economic development as a factor in individual student motivation has been the subject of a few studies, although not specifically focused on Asia. Studies such as those by Allen (1978) and Ushiogi (1984) reveal that early on the notion that education was closely related to economic development was imbedded in the thinking of individuals in both government and business in Japan. As Allen (1978, p.33) notes: 'In neither sector (government and business), however, was educational policy fashioned by men committed to the belief in the sufficiency of liberal education; it seemed essential to them that adequate provision should also be made for professional and vocational training, directed towards producing experts'. Similar statements could be made about China and South Korea. It was with this early beginning that education became the route to a successful career in Japan. From that point on, most aspects of Japan's formal educational system were imbued with the concept that one studied, in preferred schools, in order to have a successful career. This 'career' orientation lays the base for the manner in which schooling is viewed by all sectors in Japanese society down to and including students and their parents. While most studies do not link student achievement and motivation it does not take a quantum leap to conclude that this rather direct relationship between education and economics is a powerful motivator. Ushiogi (1984) further elaborated on this argument with his study of the transition from school to work in Japan. In this study he traces the rapid expansion of higher education in Japan since the Second World War and the impact this has had on the Japanese labour market. He convincingly demonstrates that the educational experience that one has in Japan directly determines career paths and that students are motivated primarily by this knowledge. The motivation to study and choices on what to study comes from the knowledge that large business enterprises prefer to recruit students from faculties of law, economics, business management, commerce and engineering (highly maths and science dependent fields) rather than from the liberal arts (Ushiogi, 1984, p.10). Thus, students in Japan (and China and South Korea as well) are socialized from an early age to focus their studies and efforts on science and mathematics, in an attempt to enter the more prestigious universities, secure in the knowledge that if they are successful in this they will be recruited for the larger, more stable and lucrative Japanese businesses.

Moving further away from individual student effects and toward a more management theory approach at least two studies state that Japan's student successes are the direct result of the manner in which the schools are managed. Schiller and Walberg (1982) call Japan a 'Learning Society' and state that schools are organized in such a way as to enhance what they identify as seven productive forces in school learning: (1) ability; (2)

development level; (3) *motivation*; (4) home learning environment; (5) quantity of instruction; (6) quality of instruction; (7) classroom social environment (Schiller and Walberg, 1982, pp.411–12). The authors conclude that the Japanese educational system has incentives enhancing each of these factors thus providing the institutional context in which high achievement and motivation can be fostered.

Japanese educational television has also been singled out as a factor in promoting high levels of motivation among Japanese youth. In two articles (Tiene, 1983; Tiene and Urakawa, 1983) the authors note the national effort being made in Japan to provide, nationwide, a first-rate educational television system. The Japanese have what is termed 'massive TV penetration in (the) schools' (Tiene, 1983, p.20), excellent facilities (Tiene and Urakawa, 1983, p.19), high quality research to back up the programming (Tiene and Urakawa, 1983, p.20), 'ingenious production techniques' (Tiene and Urakawa, 1983, p.22). The authors contend that the national and local management of educational television of such high quality is a major factor in educational achievement and high motivation especially at the elementary levels (Tiene and Urakawa, 1983, p.21).

Although many scholars have pointed to the Japanese curriculum as a major element in Japanese successes in mathematics and science, Torrance (1982) makes a provocative argument that one unintended outcome of the curriculum is to create learning situations that stimulate high levels of motivation among Japanese students.

In his article on 'Education for quality circles in Japanese schools' he documents how both the formal and informal school curriculum allow 'Japanese children to receive practice and training in group or team creativity' (Torrance, 1982, p.13). In discussing some elementary classes he visited he noted that groups of Japanese children were doing research on health habits and problems of other students (for which they had constructed a questionnaire, administered it, and were tabulating statistics), working on problems of improving the playing fields and playground and improving the care and nurturing of the school animals (Torrance, 1982, p.13). He concludes: 'As I observed their behaviour, I had little doubt but that as adults they would be effective members of Quality Circle groups. Already they had mastered and were practising many of the requisite skills' (Torrance, 1982, p.14). His further observations revealed that by tackling 'real' life problems in their own schools they were more enthusiastic (motivated) when it came to the more structured, learning portion of the classes as well as doing homework and following through on assignments to say nothing of the fact that they were being well prepared for life as members of Japan's industrial society.

This is not to say that Japan's educational system is without problems. Some have already been alluded to above. Despite its relative success rate at the elementary and secondary levels major debates have raged in Japan, among the public, between the educational community and the administration, and among politicians and policy makers. One major issue, particularly at the elementary level, focuses on the fact that while

A young Japanese girl learns written characters

Japan has a national administrative environment (the *Mombusho*, or Ministry of Education) national curricular guidelines are not developed or written in such a way as to allow easy measurement or accountability. Officials at the national level get feedback in a variety of ways (from teachers, local prefectures, an annual sampling that the National Institute of Educational Research conducts, and so on) the overall notion of a system of accountability does not exist as it does in the USA for example. In general, because of the national system that is in place reform is slow and ponderous and the system lacks variation and is therefore less adaptable to change.

This is most evident at the High School level where several major reform efforts have been attempted since the *rinkyoshin* effort of 1984. Public interest in High School reforms is high but the actual implementation of policy recommendations from the various reports is low to non existent. The principal issue at the high school level is the need to diversify. There is an increasing lack of fit between the uniform curriculum and student's changing interests and needs. This is compounded by the all-prevailing college entrance examination that tends to drive much that happens in the Japanese high school, thereby stifling what reforms might be suggested.

At the local school level these pressures express themselves in a variety of socially deviant ways. The number of adolescents with behaviour problems, cases of juvenile delinquency and crime levels among young people have all been on the rise. Specific practices, more present in Japan than elsewhere, have also been on the increase. These include *ijime* or bullying (which has resulted in death and attempted suicide), and *tokokyohi* or school refusal syndrome. The rate of increase of these practices has been sufficiently high to cause alarm among both officials and parents.

7.3   Conclusion

East Asia is a highly differentiated region of the world with great disparities as well as unique similarities. As we have seen from the foregoing a common belief in the power and value of education seems to be held throughout the region. In short:

- investment in education is seen as a critical part of national planning
- the educational infrastructure is well developed in most nations
- the relationship between education and economic development is well recognized
- achievement rates are high by world standards
- motivational factors are an important part of East Asia's educational successes and stand in contrast to those of other nations.

There are several common features of educational development in the East Asian region that have contributed to a model that is somewhat unique by world standards. First, while the state is strong in each of the nations we have looked at, government expenditures in education as a whole are quite lean, particularly in comparison to Western standards (about 4–5 per cent of GNP compared to 6–8 per cent in leading Western nations, see Cummings and Altbach, 1997, p.290). Second, state involvement in establishing and maintaining a basic framework for educational goals and objectives is strong while avoiding micro management of that framework; thus principals and teachers are expected to do their job and know fairly well what that job is. Third, while most Asian nations have not been inhibited from borrowing and adapting educational forms from the West they nevertheless have done so within a context of what might be called 'Asian values'. This distinction between Western knowledge and Asian values is closely linked to the issues of motivation and achievement we have discussed above. Fourth, investment has been focused and phased to concentrate on the public primary school foundation, a timely expansion of secondary education and priority driven tertiary sector. And finally, where demand has exceeded the state's capacity or willingness to expand there has been a permissive policy toward the private sector filling the gap (so that, for example, in Japan, Taiwan, South Korea, Indonesia and the Philippines, the private sector accounts for over 75 per cent of all enrolment at the tertiary level).

As dynamic and forward looking as the region appears to be and as successful as the educational systems seem, a variety of questions nevertheless can be posed. High on most lists is the question of sustainability. Recent crises in the banking industries of most East Asian nations, and particularly in Japan, Korea and Thailand, have sent shudders through the region and revealed, among other things, that the region has difficulty working jointly to solve major economic problems. What were once local issues have become regional and even global and this raises questions for training of future generations. Another critical issue has to do with what many have referred to as Asian values. While this debate has centred on the difference between Western and Asian values (generally viewing Asian values as more traditional and in some ways superior in the face of declining values in Western education) many scholars and practitioners both in the region and without are now questioning the appropriateness of so-called Asian values in light of the more global reach of their economies and societies in general. This in turn raises questions about the ability of many East Asian educational systems to adapt to change, to develop new teaching methodologies, curricular approaches and measures of effectiveness. What worked so well in an earlier stage of economic growth and development may not be pertinent in the more global conditions of the late twentieth century. And finally, many are questioning the highly centralized nature of most Asian educational systems. To what degree will increased political liberalization demand a more locally involved and controlled educational superstructure and to what degree will central authorities allow such changes?

There does not seem to be, nevertheless, any slowing down of investment in education and rising levels of achievement. Asia's political and educational leaders seem committed to building on the strong educational foundation already in existence and taking advantage as well of opportunities to study overseas. Acquiring the necessary technological skills to face the twenty-first century is a priority of most nations in the region. There are great opportunities for both east and west to interact and learn from one another and to this end more exchanges will be a key factor for the enhancement of educational systems in Asia and elsewhere.

References

Allen, G.C. (1978) 'Education, science and the economic development of Japan', *Oxford Review of Education*, vol.4, no.1, pp.27–36.

Amabile, T. (1983) 'The social psychology of creativity: a componential conceptualization', *Journal of Personality and Social Psychology*, vol.45, pp.357–76.

Cummings, W. (1984) *Japanese Images of American Education,* paper presented at the East-West Center Conference in Learning from Each Other, Honolulu.

Cummings, W. (1986) *Educational Policies in Crisis: Japanese and American Perspectives*, New York, Praeger.

Cummings, W. and Altbach, P. (eds) (1997) *The Challenge of Eastern Asian Education*, Albany, State University of New York Press.

Far Eastern Economic Review (1996) *Asia 1996 Year Book*, Hong Kong, Far Eastern Economic Review.

Fetters, W.B. *et al.* (1983) *Schooling experiences in Japan and the US: A Cross-national Comparison of High School Students*, paper presented at the 1983 annual meeting of the American Educational Research Association, Montreal, Canada.

Hawkins, J.N. (1997) 'Science, technology and higher educational reform in China' in McGinn, N. *International Education Handbook*, New York, Praeger Press.

Hess, R.D. and Azuma, H. *et al.* (1985) 'Family influences on school readiness and achievement in Japan and the United States: an overview of a longitudinal study' in Stevenson, H., Azuma, H. and Hakuta, K. (eds) *Child Development and Education in Japan*, New York, Freeman Publishers.

Husen, T. (ed.) (1976) *International Study of Achievement in Mathematics: A Comparison of Twelve Countries, vols. 1 & 2*, New York, John Wiley.

Kobayashi, V.N. (1984) 'Tradition, modernization and education: the case of Japan', *Journal of Ethnic Studies,* vol.12, no.3, pp.95–118.

LeTendre, G.K. (1997) 'Disruption and reconnection: counselling young adolescents in Japanese schools' in Cummings, W.K. and Altbach, P.G. (eds) pp.101–15.

Robinson, M. (1991) 'Perceptions of Confucianism in twentieth-century Korea' in Rozman, G. (ed.).

Rohlen, T.P. (1983) *Japan's High Schools*, Berkeley, CA, University of California Press.

Rohlen, T.P. (1997) 'Differences that make a difference: explaining Japan's success' in Cummings, W.K. and Altbach, P.G. (eds) pp.223–49.

Rohwen, J. (1995) *Asia Rising,* New York, Simon & Schuster.

Rozman, G. (ed.) (1991) *The East Asian Region: Confucian Heritage and its Modern Adaptation*, Princeton, NJ, Princeton University Press.

Schiller, D. and Walberg, H.J. (1982) 'Japan: the learning society', *Educational Leadership*, vol.39, no.6, pp.411–12.

Shimahara, N.K. (1997) 'Restructuring Japanese High Schools: reforms for diversity' in Cummings, W.K. and Altbach, P.G. (eds) pp.87–100.

Tiene, D. (1983) 'Japan sets the pace in educational television', *Educational Technology*, vol.23, no.5, pp.18–22.

Tiene, D. and Urakawa, T. (1983) 'Japan's elementary science series: the chemistry of successful ETV', *Educational Technology*, vol.23, no.11, pp.19–24.

Torrance, E.P. (1982) 'Education for "quality circles" in Japanese schools', *Journal of Research and Development in Education*, vol.15, no.2, pp.11–15.

Ushiogi, M. (1984) *Transition from School to Work: Japanese case*, paper presented at the East-West Center Conference on Learning from Each Other, Honolulu.

van Wolfren, K. (1989) *The enigma of Japanese power*, New York, Alfred A. Knopf.

White, M.W. (1987) *The Japanese Educational Challenge: A commitment to children*, New York, The Free Press.

Further reading

Asian Development Outlook: 1997–98, Oxford, Oxford University Press.

Emerging Asia: Changes and Challenges (1997) Manila, Philippines, Asian Development Bank.

Hawkins, J.N. and Cummings, W. (eds) (1997) *Towards Transnational Competence: A US-Japan Case Study*, New York, Institute of International Education.

Hayhoe, R. (1996) *China's Universities: 1895–1995*, New York, Garland Publishing.

Masuyama, K. (1997) *Foreign Language Education at High School Level in the United States and Japan*, New York, SUNY Press.

CHAPTER 8

Women's movements in the Asia-Pacific

Chilla Bulbeck

8.1 Introduction

What possible connections or similarities can there be between the unmarried corporate manager in Manhattan, the teenage farm wife in rural China, the nurse working in a New Guinea highland village and the worker on a micro-electronics assembly line in Seoul? A decade ago Western feminists, and indeed feminists elsewhere in the world, may well have answered:

> They are all women and as such they receive less of their nation's economic, political and cultural resources than do their menfolk. Furthermore, they suffer particular additional controls and burdens which men do not face. In particular women often lack bodily autonomy and are exposed to rape and other sexual violence or do not have control over their reproductive powers.

Since the United Nations Decade for Women (1975–85 with a further meeting in 1995), however, the sense that women share common oppression has been placed alongside more comprehensive analysis of their differences. Some of these differences are historically based, arising out of pre-colonial societies as well as colonization and decolonization through which unequal economic exchanges have been produced in the contemporary global economic order. The terms First and Third Worlds capture this history in which white women were often part of the colonizing and civilizing mission, bringing religion and hygiene to the heathens. Today, the terms refer to the gap between rich and poor nations, developed and developing nations. For some commentators the wealth of countries like the USA, Australia and Canada is at least partially due to the poverty in countries like the Philippines and Papua New Guinea.

This chapter explores women's political activism in the Asia-Pacific as a reflection of this history of colonialism and imperialism. Despite their differences, women have forged international connections, common goals and co-operative projects, particularly as a result of the UN Decade for Women. These include responses to the Korean comfort women used by Japanese soldiers, attempts to alleviate unequal trading relations,

Australian government intervention to protect brides and sex workers and local activism against wife-beating. I explore the economic and cultural differences which have impeded these co-operative actions and how women have responded to their differences. Section 8.2 explores the limitations of the opposition 'First' and 'Third' World women, particularly in relation to the emergence of the 'Asian tigers' and through a critique of development as the self-evident goal for women in so-called developing nations. The next section explores the impact of international feminist discussions in reinterpreting the customs and practices of other cultures. While women from beyond the West use notions of 'women's rights' in their political campaigns, they inflect this Western idea with other claims derived from their own histories and values. Section 8.4 explores how women have responded internationally to the economic inequalities which divide them. Activism in relation to cheap factory labour in free-trade zones, domestic workers and sex tourism is discussed.

8.2   Comparing the status of women

Third and First Worlds?

The world is often divided into developing and developed nations, or variants of this opposition – Third World and First World, east and west, south and north, periphery and core. It is often claimed or assumed that women in the latter category are better off and that all women therefore strive to achieve 'development', to increase their paid labour, to improve their education, to throw off their 'atavistic' traditions like veiling, child marriage and polygamy and become equal political citizens with men in their nations.

Some Third World commentators identify such notions as akin to the role of many white women in the colonization process. Under colonization, too, white women were often experienced as part of the process which sought to 'civilize' and 'educate' 'backward' or 'heathen' women in Asia and the Pacific Islands, often in their roles as missionaries, teachers and so on. In Vanuatu, for example, missionary women tried to redirect women from raising taros to raising children, from outside to domestic work. However, colonized women did learn the language and culture of the colonizer which gave them access to a more prominent role in the newly independent nation. It must also be remembered, however, that in some countries the process of colonization meant women's traditional control of land or productive labour was often abolished or ignored.

Table 8.1 below suggests that women's political activism, measured in terms of suffrage, arose earlier in the Western nations and has led to greater political representation in parliament, except in the case of the communist nations like North Korea and China. Nevertheless, struggles for women's political involvement in a number of Asian countries arose at about the same time as they did in Western nations. Colonized women of all classes demonstrated on the streets for national independence. They also demanded an education, the right to vote, the right to enter professions, the abolition of practices like polygamy, child marriage, dowry, or women's inability to speak in public (Jayawardena, 1986). They learned not only from European feminists but also from each other. Pandita Ramabai of India influenced Kartini in Indonesia (see Box 8.1), who, encountering Ramabai as a school girl, thought 'not alone for the white women is it possible to attain an independent position, the brown Indian too can make herself free' (Jayawardena, 1986, pp.21, 137, 141–6).

Box 8.1 Raden Adjeng Kartini

Some of the contradictory strands in the liberation struggles of Asian women are revealed in Kartini's story. Raden Adjeng Kartini (1879–1904), the daughter of the Regent of Jepara in North Java, received a primary education along with her brothers, an unusual experience for Indonesian women at the time. However, her father denied her dream of studying in Holland. Instead, Kartini was introduced to Dutch philosophers and feminists through a Dutch colonial official and the wife of another Dutch colonial official. She reflected some of the desires of upper-class Indonesian women for emancipation through education, their revulsion against polygamy and their ambition for personal freedom through entry into the professions. In her writings, she drew on Dutch liberal humanism, radical socialism, the *noblesse oblige* of her father and the mystical spiritualism of her mother. But she also rebelled against the crassness and condescension of some of the Dutch and the sexism of her Javanese culture. She envied the 'free independent European woman', but she also noted 'the time has long gone by when we believed that the European is the only true civilization, supreme and unsurpassed'. Despite her opposition to polygamy, she was married to the Regent of Rembang in 1903 who already had several wives. However, he encouraged her to establish a school for the daughters of Javanese officials which had 120 enrolments by 1904. Kartini died in childbirth at the age of 25, attended by an incompetent Dutch doctor. Through the Kartini Foundation, schools were established in her memory while Kartini was officially declared a national heroine by the first Indonesian President Sukarno.

There are two days in the Indonesian calendar which highlight women's roles – Kartini Day and Mother's Day. Mother's Day celebrates the first Indonesian women's congress held in 1928, attended by nearly 30 women's associations. The conference led to the foundation of Prekatan Perempuan Indonesia, a federation which set out to improve the position of women and the family. Today Mother's Day reminds women of their double role, in which they are always a mother first, whatever their career or working situation. Indonesian marriage laws state that women must keep house for the family, although women are also encouraged to work and participate in national development. On both of 'their' national days, women may be reminded to be compliant wives and dutiful daughters, selflessly pursuing the interests of husbands and fathers (Pakpahan, 1996, pp.9–10). No wonder, then, that some women in Asian and Pacific nations yearn to be housewives, to be free of the double burden of household maintenance and other productive work, although Mies (1986) criticizes the impact of Western values in promoting the idea of the 'good housewife'.

Table 8.1 *Indices of women's well-being for 'developed' and 'developing' nations in the Asia-Pacific*

Indicator	'Developed' nations	'Developing' nations
Maternal mortality rate (per 100,000 live births)	Canada: 4 Australia: 5 USA: 8 New Zealand, Japan: 14	Hong Kong: 3 N. Korea, China: 41–44 Indonesia: 450 PNG: 900 for South-East Asia: 420
Women's life expectancy (years)	New Zealand: 78 Australia, Canada, USA: 80 Japan: 81	PNG: 55 Vietnam, Philippines: 64–65 Malaysia, China, N. and S. Korea: 71–73 Singapore, Hong Kong: 76–79 for East Asia and Oceania: 64
Women's fertility (births per woman)	New Zealand, Australia, Canada, USA, Japan: 1.7–1.9	Singapore, Hong Kong: 1.7 Malaysia, Indonesia: 3.3–3.5 Pacific Islands: 5.7
Labour-force participation of women	Japan, Australia, New Zealand, N. America: 46–50%	Fiji: 22% Indonesia, Philippines: 36% Hong Kong: 48% PNG: 58% Vietnam, China, Thailand: 68–70%
Female (aged 15–24 years) illiteracy	almost zero	Hong Kong, Singapore, Thailand: 4% Fiji, Philippines: 9% China, Malaysia, Indonesia: 17–18% Vanuatu: 32% adult female illiteracy for East Asia and Pacific Islands urban: 25% rural: over 40%
Percentage of women desiring university education for male and female children	USA: M-69%; F-66% Japan: M-73%; F-28%	Philippines: M-87%; F-85%
Females aged 20 and over who favour bringing up boys and girls the same	Japan: 34% USA: 62%	Philippines: 67%

Table 8.1 *Indices of women's well-being for 'developed' and 'developing' nations in the Asia-Pacific (continued)*

Indicator	'Developed' nations	'Developing' nations
Ratio of mothers who prefer next child to be male compared to female	(in Japan, between 1982 and 1992, the preference for a daughter if only one child was to be born rose from 48.5 to 75.7%; male preference is prevalent in the USA)	Philippines: 0.9 Indonesia: 1.1 Malaysia: 1.2 Fiji: 1.3 Thailand: 1.4 S. Korea: 3.3
Year of (at least some) women's suffrage	New Zealand: 1893 Australia: 1901 Canada: 1918 USA: 1920 Japan: 1945	Thailand: 1932 Philippines: 1939 N. and S. Korea, China, Singapore, Solomon Islands, Vietnam: 1945–49 Vanuatu: 1980
Percentage of national parliamentary seats occupied by women (1995)	Japan: 2% USA, Australia: 5–6% Canada: 10% New Zealand: 14%	Singapore: 0% Thailand: 1% S. Korea: 6% N. Korea, China: 21%
Percentage of ministerial positions held by women (4% world-wide)	Japan: 0% Australia: 9% USA: 10% Canada: 14% New Zealand: 15%	PNG, Samoa, Solomon Islands, Tonga, Tuvalu, Vanuatu, Vietnam: 0% Indonesia: 5% China: 7% Thailand: 8% Philippines: 14%
Status of the Convention on Elimination of all Forms of Discrimination Against Women	ratified: Japan ratified with reservations: Australia, Canada, New Zealand not ratified: USA	ratified: Philippines ratified with reservations: China, Indonesia, S. Korea, Thailand, Vietnam not ratified: Fiji, N. Korea, Malaysia, Marshall Islands, Micronesia, PNG, Samoa, Singapore, Soloman Islands, Vanuatu

Source: UN (1991); Kameda (1995, p.109); Tomasevski (1995, pp.10, 88, 116–17)

Consider the data in Table 8.1. You may have noticed that in general the East Asian nations record better figures than the South Pacific nations. Within the East Asian nations, the so-called 'Asian tigers' like Hong Kong and Singapore, share more similarities with the 'developed' nations than with many of the 'developing' nations, and should really be in the first column, although they are not thus identified by the UN. You might like to move the countries from column to column so that they are grouped according to similarities on each variable. Are there some countries which are always in the first column, the column which suggests higher status for women? Or is it the case that countries, whether developed or developing, reveal a higher status for women in some respects but not all respects?

Interrogating the measures of women's well-being

The second question we need to address is why these data have been chosen to indicate women's well-being and status. Are the figures in Table 8.1 applicable equally to women around the world or do they tend to suggest that women will automatically benefit from the outcomes of development – more formal education, a higher work-force participation, higher representation in the national government? Might this not be an imposition of Western feminism's ideas of what constitutes liberation and a failure to also measure aspects of women's autonomy and well-being which fall outside a developmental framework? For example, access to paid labour may denote industrialization in ways which reduce women's traditional control of production and its products. Development might involve a reduction in subsistence farming for cash-cropping; the former often controlled by women for the benefit of their families, the latter often placed in the hands of men by colonial governments, national governments and development agencies. Paid work may impose a double burden on women. Lower birth rates may reflect either women's greater access to family planning or the imposition of state population control policies. Are there other issues which may be of more relevance to women in some East Asian and Pacific Island nations, for example land ownership and inheritance rights, the capacity to bear a son and so become a mother-in-law, the ability to work less unpaid and paid hours of labour and become a housewife with free time? Does measuring women's political representation in terms of their numbers in national parliaments perhaps neglect the greater importance of women's groups at the village level in the lives of many women?

In response to these questions, it should be noted that many women in the so-called Third World endorse at least some of the goals of development – for example, a better education for women, better health (including reproductive health and freedom), a wider choice of well remunerated labour. But they also ask questions about 'development'. For example, 'Does everyone benefit equally?', 'Should we ask questions about environmentally sustainable growth?', 'Is working in the commodity sector necessarily better for women and men than labouring in the subsistence or non-commoditized sector?'

Before Ester Boserup's (1970) path-breaking analysis, *Women's Role in Economic Development*, international aid agencies duplicated colonial administrations in their assumption that women performed no productive labour. If women were considered at all, it was usually as the recipients of population policies, health and nutritional assistance in their roles as mothers. A decade later, thanks to the UN Decade for Women, it was established that women are one-third of the world's formal labour force and do four-fifths of all 'informal' work, but receive only 10 per cent of the world's income and own less than 1 per cent of the world's property. Thus the slogan 'women need development' was translated into 'development needs women'. But either way, women were seen as 'agents' in increasing economic activity so Third World nations could tread the same path to economic wealth which the industrial nations had shown them.

By the late 1980s, some of the costs of development had become more apparent. Deforestation meant that firewood, fruits and other products were no longer available. Shifting to cash-cropping meant that households no longer survived on food produced for their own needs but relied on the vagaries of international commodity prices. In her sustained critique of national accounting systems, Marilyn Waring (1988) noted that national accounts value:

- destruction above preservation (thus warfare contributes to gross national product but peace does not)
- processing the environment above preserving the environment (thus a tree has no value until chopped down, a river no value until dammed)
- production above reproduction (women's work in raising children is not counted)
- male activity above female activity (in many cases the handicrafts and food products women produce is not counted).

According to this analysis, 'development' means valuing those things which are counted in the national accounts and ignoring those things which are excluded. Thus the world spends enough money on arms every three weeks to pay for primary health care for everyone on the planet; the world spends enough every three days to purchase the agricultural equipment which will allow the developing world to approach self-sufficiency in food production. As a result of this misrepresentation of national well-being, countries are told by international agencies like the World Bank and the International Monetary Fund that they must balance their budgets and pay their foreign debts, and they must do this by reducing welfare programmes and encouraging even more commodity production. Thus many countries have now joined the 'economic miracle' nations of Taiwan, South Korea, Hong Kong and Singapore, by introducing free-trade exporting zones with generous tax incentives and the promise of a non-unionized labour force. I will return to an assessment of these programmes in Section 8.4.

Conclusion: peace, equality, development

The UN Decade for Women was held under the banner of 'peace, equality, development'. While few would argue with the goal of peace, it is interesting to note that women are far more likely to be the refugees displaced by both internal and external wars. Furthermore, women's bodies are often treated as the spoils of war, as well as a way of telling the vanquished men that they have 'lost' the battle (see Box 8.2). The foregoing suggests that development may not always meet the needs of rural women, dislocated by cash-cropping and perhaps forced to find work in free-trade zones.

Box 8.2   The rape of women in war: comfort women

During the Second World War the Japanese 'deceived or disappeared' from 200,000 to 400,000 women into 'comfort stations' (also referred to as 'sanitary public toilets'). 80 per cent of these 'comfort women' were Koreans, although some were Japanese (for example the daughters of poor families sold into prostitution), Chinese, Taiwanese, Filipino, Indonesian and Dutch-Indonesian women. Each woman was forced to service an average of 30 to 40 soldiers per day. Those who refused were beaten and tortured. An estimated 70–90 per cent died and none of the surviving women who have been traced have been able to bear children. Shamed by their experiences, Korean women remained silent. However, in the mid 1970s, Japanese women in the Asian Women's Association who were protesting against Japanese sex tourism discovered the 'comfort women'. Korean and Japanese women worked together and in 1991 South Korean women filed a lawsuit against the Japanese government demanding an official apology, compensatory payment, a thorough investigation of their cases, a revision of Japanese school text books identifying this aspect of colonial oppression of the Korean people, and the construction of a memorial museum. In 1992 the Japanese government made a formal apology to the Korean 'comfort women' (see Watanabe, 1994; Hicks, 1995).

Kang Soon-ae, one of the former 'comfort women', shouts anti-Japanese slogans during a protest in Cheju Island, South Korea, June 1996

The issue of equality raises the question of equality with whom? Should all women everywhere be equal? Or should equality be measured by a comparison with men in each nation? In terms of the latter, the female human development index compares the status of women with men in each of 33 countries for which it is available, using a combined measure of life expectancy, education, employment and wages. This reveals that women do not have the same status as men in any nation, although they are close in the Scandinavian countries (women's status as a percentage of men's is 93–96 per cent in Sweden, Finland, and Norway). Second are a group of largely Western countries, including Australia and New Zealand at 90 per cent, and the USA at 86 per cent. East Asian countries are at lower ratios, for example Japan at 78 per cent, Hong Kong and Singapore at 71 per cent, and South Korea at 65 per cent. To some extent this ranking parallels the non-gender specific human development index, which places Canada, the USA and Japan at the top; Hong Kong, South Korea and Singapore in rankings between 20 and 35; Samoa at 88th rank (out of a total of 174). Thus in the developing nations many women are worse off than *both* the men in their nations and the women in the developed nations. This issue will be addressed in the last section when I explore how women make connections across national borders, despite these economic disparities.

The next section explores the UN Decade for Women as a dialogue between women of different nations through which women from beyond the West interpreted feminism – forged out of Western women's experiences – to respond to their own cultural contexts.

8.3 Women's movement activism

The UN Decade for Women

The meeting in Mexico City in 1975 was the first time that a majority of UN conference delegates (73%) were women; additionally 113 delegations were headed by women. Women met again in Copenhagen in 1980 and in Nairobi in 1985. During the Decade (1975–85), many governments were encouraged to address and publicize issues concerning women. In the UN itself a number of organs expressly dedicated to the needs and experiences of women were spawned, including the Commission on the Status of Women, which feeds policies into the General Assembly; the Division for the Advancement of Women, with its various committees such as the Committee for the Elimination of Discrimination Against Women; the Division for Women and Development; and the UN Development Fund for Women (Unifem). Even so, women are still not well represented in the upper reaches of the United Nations.

Mexico to Nairobi
The Mexico meeting revealed the chasm of difference which separated women of the north and south. Domitila Barrios de Chungara, leader of the

Housewives' Committee in Peru, remembers being 'confounded' by the concerns she heard expressed: the problems of prostitutes, the lesbian experience, the need for equal rights, the idea that men were responsible for war, that men abused women. 'We spoke very different languages, no?' She rejected the idea of fighting against one's menfolk, instead endorsing the socialist goal of common struggle. As opposed to access to abortion, a concern of Western feminists at the forum, she felt that strength of numbers was the principal weapon of the oppressed (see Miller, 1991, p.200ff. for a discussion of the Decade). Where women from Western capitalist market economies stressed equality between the sexes, women from the developing countries argued for the acceleration of overall development. The World Plan of Action which emerged from the Mexico meeting recognized the impact of colonialism and neo-colonialism as 'among the greatest obstacles to the full emancipation of and progress of developing countries and all the peoples concerned'. It did not specify women or include sexism as an obstacle, despite hours of debate.

At the Copenhagen meeting in 1980, infibulation or female genital surgery became the major divisive issue, with Western women attacking it as 'barbaric' and 'backward'. In this climate, many Islamic women from countries practising female circumcision refused to condemn it, caught in conflicting loyalties between 'sisterhood' and the men of their nations. By Nairobi, more Western feminists were aware of the centrality of issues like drinking water or daily bread to many women. Some had become more circumspect in decrying foreign customs as signs of rampant and barbaric patriarchy. It is important to remember the colonial legacy when considering the responses of ex-colonized women to Western feminists' condemnation of so-called 'barbaric' practices. After Nairobi, concerned activist women in Africa campaigned more vigorously against female genital mutilation, but they framed the activism in terms of women's health and education or that this was not a practice advocated by the Koran, some people having wrongly associated it with Islam. They did not, on the whole, campaign against it as a patriarchal practice which sought to control women. Thus Third World activists question whether Western feminists should speak out against practices in other cultures, particularly when they do not understand their complicated cultural contexts and meanings (see Box 8.3). As a result of the Decade, more women from the developing nations saw the need for women-specific organization around certain issues – for example, domestic violence, rape, women's health – rather than assuming women's needs would automatically be met within political organizations dominated by men. The parallel non-governmental organization forums gained more significance in the exchange of infor- mation as the Decade progressed. Official delegates numbered 1,200 in Mexico and Copenhagen, while NGO delegates numbered 4,000 and 7,000. Since 1985 there have been other UN conferences of concern to women, for example women's rights in relation to violence (Vienna, 1993), the population and reproduction policies conference (Cairo, 1994), the summit on environment and development (Rio de Janeiro, 1992) and on social development (Copenhagen, 1995).

Box 8.3 The shifting meanings of social practices: veiling

When Western women demonstrated they were 'civilized' Victorians because they did not expose their flesh, exposure of breasts was deemed a sign of backwardness. In an ironic reversal, Western women today demonstrate their sexual liberation through bodily exposure and many have described veiled Muslim women as 'oppressed' by Islam and tradition. This reading is exemplified in the contrasting Gulf War images of the female American tank driver and the veiled Saudi woman who is forbidden by law from acquiring a drivers' licence. The image ignores Saudi women who are university educated, who have founded women-only banks or who practise medicine in women-only hospitals, and Kuwaiti women who have organized neighbourhood-level protests against the occupying Iraqi army. In these Gulf states, governments commend (and some enforce with punishments like stoning) veiling as an expression of independent Islamic identity in opposition to Western 'decadence'. In Malaysia, however, the government opposed a veiling movement which emerged among university students in 1970 and peaked in the mid 1980s. Full *purdah* is forbidden in many government and private offices and all Malaysian universities. This has been interpreted as a battle between the state and the Muslim religious leaders, not only over veiling but also family planning and the appropriate role for women in an expanding market economy. Older women and rural women did not adopt veiling, suggesting that even within Malaysia women responded differently to the religious invocations. Perhaps, young female university students were responding to the anxiety of their new roles, afraid they would be priced out of the marriage market by their education. Islam seemed to offer sure rules in an uncertain world characterized by the excesses of Western feminism, economic development and decadent secularism (Ong in Ong and Peletz, 1995).

Beijing: the conference of commitments

By 1989 data on women's increased poverty, a rise in female-headed households, increases in maternal and infant mortality, and slowing growth rates for education and entry into the labour force, showed that the gains of the UN Decade were being reversed. As a result, the UN agreed to hold a conference in 1995, the Fourth World Conference of Women, in Beijing.

The Australian delegation argued that Beijing should be a 'conference of commitments' in which countries nominated measurable targets for improving the status of women rather than merely endorsing vague 'motherhood' statements. These ideas were included in the Platform of Action, suggesting that governments 'should' develop implementation strategies, 'preferably' by the end of 1996. Strategies should have 'time-bound targets and benchmarks for monitoring' and include proposals for the allocation and reallocation of resources (Paragraphs 293 and 297). Even so, the language of the Platform gives little guidance on the development of such targets. In a document of 362 paragraphs, covering twelve areas, specific targets were identified in only three areas. These were universal primary education by the year 2015 and closing the gender gap in secondary education by the year 2005; reducing maternal, infant and child mortality and malnutrition rates; and to 'Ensure that clean water is available and accessible to all by the year 2000'.

Questioning the universal meaning of 'rights'

Although women found some common ground during the Decade, tensions remain, particularly between women in the developed and developing countries. Feminism has, on the whole, been a white Western movement and it reflects the cultures in which it operates. For example, in the USA and Australia the largest political campaigns of post-Second World War feminism have concerned the right to abortion. Some women in both the north and the south who are not of European background have countered that they have been forced to have sterilizations and abortions they did not want. For them, reproductive freedom is to have and raise in health and prosperity as many children as they desire to have. I will explore this issue of reproductive rights in relation to China's one-child policy. Another issue which has increasingly preoccupied women at the UN is sexual violence against women. In Vanuatu women use and adapt Western feminists' notions of rights to bodily autonomy to their own specific cultural situation. I return to the issue of economic inequalities between women around the Asia-Pacific in Section 8.4 on the international traffic in women.

Population policies and reproductive rights
To some outsiders, Anglo-Saxon cultures appear child-rejecting. The mother alone is expected to raise her child with little support from male or female kin. Thus, it is not so much married women, but mothers who have lower incomes than men, and so bear the cost of child-rearing. Women in the West lose status as they age, and lose their youth, looks and desirability to men. In such a climate, and when combined with increased sexual permissiveness, Western feminists' battle for abortion rights makes sense. However, Western feminists' demands concerning their right to enjoy sex without bearing the burdens of reproduction are sometimes puzzling to women in cultures where motherhood is an almost universal, taken-for-granted and valued destiny for women. In many countries beyond the West, women are most vulnerable as adolescents, increasing their status when they marry, and when they bear children, especially sons. As post-menopausal mothers-in-law and widows, they may control a large extended household and a family business. Women's birth-giving role is perhaps more respected, even if sometimes expressed in awe for the polluting power of menstruating or birth-giving women, while children are cared for and loved by an array of relatives, including men.

Furthermore, white Western women's abortion campaigns occurred at the same time as women of colour were exposed to forced sterilizations or given harmful contraceptives like Depo-Provera. Nationalist government-inspired *population policies* in some Western countries like the USA and Australia encouraged white women to have more children and indigenous women to have less. Thus where white women struggled for the right to choose not to have children through abortion or contraceptive availability, indigenous, African-American and migrant women have struggled for the right to have and raise healthy children. Such national population policies, tinged with eugenics, are not the preserve of white nations, however. In 1983 the Prime Minister of Singapore, Lee Kuan Yew, urged 'graduate mothers' to raise their reproduction rate from 1.65 children by offering tax breaks and entry into the best schools. Less educated mothers were encouraged to reduce their fertility rates from 3.5 children with cash incentives. In fact the two groups thus identified were respectively largely Chinese professional women and working-class women of Malay and Indian background (Heng and Devan in Ong and Peletz, 1995).

Here it is useful to make a distinction between reproductive rights and population policies. National population policies exhort women to either have or not have children because women's fertility is interpreted in terms of development or other national goals. In population policies, emphasis is placed on strategies which allow control of women's fertility by government agencies, for example female sterilization or the implantation of the contraceptive Norplant, often in the forearm and so visible beneath the skin. The notion of reproductive rights, in contrast, refers to women's rights to *choose* whether, when, how many children they will have and by what means they will control their fertility. Feminists of many nations, whether they campaign for abortion rights or health care and social welfare, are united in believing that women should be the agents of their own reproduction. Reproductive rights focus on access to contraception which does not threaten women's health; indeed, condoms and vasectomies are less expensive and involve lower health risks than most contraceptive techniques targeted to women. It is from this feminist perspective that China's one-child policy is condemned (see Box 8.4). Indeed, in the long term, contraceptive services are far more effective when offered as part of a wider health-care delivery system than when they are part of a state population-reduction policy.

Female literacy has shown the strongest, most widespread and enduring correlation with women's fertility. Education gives women wider access to paid employment, wealth, family planning strategies and health programmes, knowledge of their legal rights (for example inheritance rights and rights to dissolve marriages). Women tend to delay marriage beyond their teenage years, because they complete their schooling and thus have greater job opportunities. This correlation between increased education and reduced fertility for women has produced a happy coincidence between Western fears of over-population in the Third World and non-Western women's desire for women's improved status. While targeting

> **Box 8.4 China's one-child policy: the effects of 'gender neutrality'**
>
> Where population policies are often discriminatory against minority ethnic groups and may favour boy-children, China's one-child policy, at least officially, is discriminatory against the Han majority and is gender-neutral. The policy is not meant to cover minority populations, for example in Tibet (although there is debate concerning the effects of the policy in practice, for example requiring Tibetan families to buy the right to have additional children). Nevertheless, given the enormous desire for the birth of a boy in rural areas, by 1988 two-thirds of China's provinces had incorporated gender considerations into their policies, for example allowing a second child only if the first born was a girl. Thus the one-child policy would have been more acceptable if the central government had not framed it in gender-neutral terms (Greenhalgh and Li, 1995).

increased literacy and further education for women meets both these goals, whether aid agencies and governments are more interested in women's autonomy or national population goals is reflected in the kinds of family planning pursued.

However, equally important is a focus on women's economic independence, both income-earning capacity and access to land or other 'social security' for their old age. The famous 'marriage resisters' of southern China in the nineteenth and early twentieth centuries were able to avoid marriage because of employment in the silk industry. Paying much of their wages to their families, they joined sisterhoods and sometimes chose lesbian relationships. Little wonder then that in the 1930s, Agnes Smedley's male escort told her that women spinners were 'too rich' and thus became 'proud and contemptuous' (Smedley, 1995, p.48). Today in parts of China and Taiwan, more women have access to paid employment. Interestingly, this is reflected in a reduction in son preference by parents. A son was one's old-age pension, inheriting the farmland and being obliged to support his parents until they died. Now that some daughters can also support their parents, they are often found to be more reliable in meeting their obligations. Alternatively, one Chinese province has established one-child co-operatives to provide for parents in their old age.

When Hillary Clinton, wife of the US President, condemned China's one-child policy at the Beijing forum because it infringed women's reproductive rights, she omitted to mention that in the USA abortion continues to be a very contentious issue. Despite the US Supreme Court's creation of a constitutional guarantee of a right to an abortion in the first trimester of pregnancy, a large section of opinion has continually challenged the court's judgement. Those arguing for the 'rights' of the foetus were successful in removing federal funding for abortions and even for providing advice on their availability; in taking pregnant women to court for drug use, refusing doctors' orders, eating only 'the foods that tasted good to her', and for having sex; and in winning court orders that pregnant women submit to caesarean sections or hospital rather than midwife delivery (Faludi, 1991, pp.412, 425, 430–1). In 1986 there were at least 21 cases of attempts at court orders to override the mother's wishes, including fifteen of court-ordered caesarean section and three of hospital detention. In 86 per cent of cases the mothers lost and in 81 per cent of cases the women were black, Asian or Hispanic (Graycar and Morgan, 1990, pp.225–6). Despite constant reference in court decisions to the interests of the 'state' in protecting the life and viability of children born and unborn, the government provides neither free medical care nor government-funded day care to help women raise their children.

Women's reproductive rights are expressed in Paragraph 96 of the Beijing Platform of Action as the right of 'couples and individuals' to choose the number, spacing and timing of children, although these choices should be balanced against the needs of other children and responsibilities to the community. Does either China or the USA guarantee women's reproductive rights in these terms?

Violence and women's rights

Despite the UN *Universal* Declaration of Human Rights in 1949, it required long campaigning by women before 'gender based violence' was recognized as an infringement of human rights. In 1993, the UN General Assembly recognized that rape, domestic violence and so on were limitations on women's human rights. During the NGO Forum in Beijing a petition demanding that the UN report on the steps it has taken to promote the human rights of women since this UN declaration was sponsored by over 1,500 groups internationally.

Even so, Western feminists have sometimes tended to associate domestic violence with foreign customs, for example the payment of a dowry or a bride-price. The dowry deaths in India are thus attributed to the revival of *sati* or widows throwing themselves on their husbands' funeral pyres. In its modern variant, husbands and their families conspire to burn the wife in a kitchen fire so the husband can remarry and extract a second dowry. In some African and Melanesian nations, violence has been attributed to the payment of a bride-price to the wife's family. The husband then feels he owns his wife and has the right to beat her. In retort to these explanations, women activists in non-Western nations point out that statistics on violence against women suggest a much higher incidence in the USA and Australia, where neither dowry nor bride-price are paid, than other Asia-Pacific nations.

They further claim that the rising incidence of violence against women is due to the corruption of traditional practices by Western influences. Thus some women in India and Melanesia argue that the dowry or bride-price were a sign of respect for the women's capacities, both to bear children and contribute to the household economy of her husband. When paid in traditional forms like jewellery or pigs, the meaning of respect was retained. However, now that money or modern consumer goods are increasingly demanded, dowry means daughters are too expensive to raise and bride-price means that women are paid for and owned like other commodities. The breakdown in traditional mechanisms by which the wife's family or husband's kin controlled domestic violence, for example when couples move to towns and cities, allows men to beat their wives without reprisal.

Box 8.5 shows the response of some women activists in the Pacific Islands to these issues. These examples show that South Pacific women activists combine Western notions of rights, drawn from both law and religion, with responses to their own particular situations. However, the Vanuatu Women's Centre is primarily supported by overseas aid monies, particularly from Australia and New Zealand. Might this influence the local campaign against violence? The final section explores the economic relations between women across national borders, of which aid is a tiny fraction in comparison with trade and investment.

Box 8.5   Papua New Guinea: wife-beating is a crime

With 111.7 men to every 100 women in PNG, the country has been described as 'the most masculine country on the face of the earth' (Denoon *et al.*, 1989, p.91). This has been attributed to a combination of the indigenous culture's preferential treatment for men and boys and the Australian colonial administration's neglect of women. Melanesian society describes women as 'bouncing coconuts' who marry into another village and so confer no benefit on their own village. In 1990 and 1991, the Women and Law Committee in Papua New Guinea distributed 150,000 leaflets entitled 'Wife-Beating is a Crime'. During the parliamentary debate to make wife-beating illegal, the following comments were made: most ministers 'were violently against interfering in traditional family life' and 'I paid for my wife, so she should not overrule my decisions, because I am the head of the family'. (What is the representation of women in the PNG parliament?)

Vanuatu: women's rights are human rights

The Vanuatu National Council of Women have prepared the booklet *Women Ikat Raet Long Human Raet O No?* (Are human rights also women's rights?) When answering this question in relation to domestic violence, Ni-Vanuatu activists call on Western notions of women's equality and rights, the idea that romantic love is liberating in contrast with traditional 'forced' marriages, and Christianity's rhetorical commitment to familial love and respect. But they also suggest that men are misinterpreting *Kastom* (custom) when they claim their rights to beat their wives. Similarly, the Women's Crisis Centre in Fiji points out that wife-beating is hardly a Fijian custom as it occurs world-wide and that not all traditional things need to be accepted anyway. Ni-Vanuatu campaigner Merilyn Tahi claims that the roots of violence are cultural; then so must be the means of digging up those roots. She suggests that collective values must be changed by men and women acting in concert (see Jolly, 1996).

8.4 The international traffic in women

In this section, three examples of the impact and response to the international traffic in women will be outlined: responses to the exploitation of non-unionized labour in the free-trade zones and elsewhere in the Asia-Pacific; the relationship between domestic workers and their female employers; and the relationship between women in the developed nations and Thailand and the Philippines constructed via sex tourism.

Responses to exploiting women's labour in free-trade zones

Despite the criticisms of non-sustainable development programmes made by commentators like Marilyn Waring, the World Bank and the IMF, at least until the 1996 economic 'melt down', recommended that all developing nations emulate the 'Asian tigers'. The World Bank recommended such so-called structural adjustment programmes for 22 Pacific Island countries. In these countries, as in East Asia, women are the most exploited of the free-trade zone workers, notably in fish processing plants, garments making in Fiji, and automotive wire assembly in Western Samoa. The majority of workers in Asia-Pacific free-trade zones are women, who receive wages as low as half those of men; have few career prospects, which fuels their desire to marry a 'man with a necktie' (a white-collar worker); and suffer occupational injury and disease which may force them to stop working in their thirties. Workers have been burned to death in fires because they were locked in dormitories attached to factories. In the Pacific Island nations, where women are the sole breadwinners, men have not necessarily taken on child-care and other support roles, while levels of domestic violence, child malnutrition and behavioural problems in children have increased.

The ever-lower prices for clothing, electronics and household goods in Western department stores allows Western consumers to benefit from the cheap labour of women in free-trade zones in developing countries. Women activists are developing strategies to redress this exploitation. In South Korea, women were the leaders of the labour clashes of the early 1980s and the Korean Women Workers Association is an active campaigner for working conditions, including maternity leave, menstrual leave and day-care facilities (Louie, 1995). The Committee for Asian Women organizes exchanges between women workers in various Asian countries to explore the international effects of globalization on women's working conditions. From Western nations, both aid and ethical trading attempt to counter the impact of exploitation of workers in East Asia and the Pacific Islands. Unifem has a successful revolving loan scheme to help women establish small businesses, while Oxfam and Community Aid Abroad focus on the needs of women in economic development. Apart from programmes to increase women's self-sufficiency in the developing world, some of these groups have established Alternative Trading Organizations (ATOs). Not only do they investigate and expose exploitation of labour by other suppliers, they also help producers with marketing, stock control and design advice. Although this 'ethical market' now reaches 10 million people in North America, ATOs are small international players. Another strategy has been to lobby governments to require that imported goods produced in unacceptable labour conditions, for example using child labour or where free trade unions are not allowed to exist, are thus marked. The International Coalition of Trade Unions is calling on national governments to attach a social clause to trade agreements so that governments which do not respect workers' rights lose trade privileges.

Domestic workers: Hong Kong women and Filipinas

In the Philippines, beside the textiles and garments industries, the biggest foreign exchange earner is remittances by overseas contract workers, half of whom are women and most of whom work in Singapore and Hong Kong. Domestic workers may work in more hazardous, isolated, lower-paid conditions and for longer hours (for example 5 a.m. to 11 p.m.) than even the free-trade zone workers. Sri Lankan, Indonesian and Filipino women work in the Gulf states; Filipino and Thai women work in Hong Kong and Singapore. Because employers often retain their passports, domestic workers can become virtual slaves with few avenues of redress for non-payment of wages, exploitation or sexual assault. The jobs of middle-class Chinese and expatriate women in Singapore and Hong Kong are supported by the work of low-paid domestic workers. As an attempt to forge counter-connections to the links of exploitation, the Women's Centre in Hong Kong offers legal advice to Filipino domestic workers complaining of ill-treatment.

Sex tourism: Australian and Filipino women

Where the issue of comfort women is an expression of military dominance by one nation over another, sex tourism is an expression of economic superiority, as well as the commodification of women's sexual services, not unique to capitalism but practised in different forms in most countries prior to the arrival of Western men. Male tourists visiting the Philippines increased from 166,000 in 1972 to over 1 million in 1980, coming predominantly from the USA, Australia, Japan, Germany and other European countries. Given comparative wages and the exchange rate, sex tourists can 'live like lords' for several weeks, in a well-appointed hotel with the companionship of a woman who provides cleaning, massaging, tour guiding and sexual favours. Sex workers in the developed countries conclude specific contracts by the hour, but Thai women act 'more like girlfriends' receiving an uncertain reward at the conclusion of the encounter. Sex tourism is commonly associated with Thailand (where 80 per cent of clients are Thai men) and the Philippines, where government officials have stated that female sexuality is to be regarded as an economic asset for national development. However, Filipino sex workers have moved to Tahiti and Guam following the closure of the US military bases. Sex tourists from Britain are increasingly choosing Ho Chi Minh City, Hanoi and Phnom Penh as destinations where the girls are 'less commercial' than the now 'spoiled' women of Thailand (see Davidson, 1995).

While sex tourism highlights income differences between nations, like sexual exploitation of women in war, it is also a relationship between men and women. In the mid 1980s, 85 per cent of the tourists visiting the Philippines were men, and Japanese-Korean women's groups attribute sex tourism to both the imbalance in the international economy and the systematic commodification of women's bodies. Many white Western feminists have shifted attention from this issue of male exploitation of women's bodies to accept prostitutes' claims that they are doing *work* as much as sex. Thus workers should be legally protected to preserve their health and working conditions. The conditions of sex workers in the West have improved – hence the complaints of Western men that Western prostitutes demand payment for specified services. In relation to international prostitution, a united response from Western nations has been formulated only in the case of child prostitution, particularly where girls are sold into the trade. (Thus the fire in Phuket in 1984 revealed the burnt bodies of young girls chained to their beds.) Following Germany, the Australian government passed a law in November 1993 providing a gaol sentence for Australians overseas who have sex with a child under 16 years old (14-year sentence) or under 12 years of age (17-year sentence).

Japanese, American, British and Australian sex tourists often contrast the smiling subservience of prostitutes with their own womenfolk who are described as whining, assertive or unfeminine. In this climate, some Australian and American women initially condemned emigrating Filipino brides for 'taking their men'. However, violence (including murder) against Filipinas was exposed by activist women in Australia such as Melba Marginson's Collective of Filipinos for Empowerment and Development. Special services now support this vulnerable group of women, including refuges. The Australian Government has established a counselling service in the Philippines for intending migrants. They pass on the names of Australian men who have previously sponsored a Filipina. Such evidence of serial sponsorship may indicate sponsorship for the purposes of 'selling' women into Australian brothels or of previous domestic violence. The government allows women to retain eligibility for permanent residence if their marriage breaks down because of proven domestic violence.

8.5   Conclusion

Neferti Tadiar (1993, p.185) claims that the idea of a Pacific community is 'a baby whose putative parents are Japanese and American and whose midwife is Australian'. The Philippines is a child of this marriage, and a female child at that. Thus the Philippines is a feminized nation, made subservient by colonial subjugation to the USA, which was expressed until recently in military bases on its shores. The Philippines is further feminized in a relationship of debt and dependence on the USA, the World Bank and the IMF. As hosts to multinational capital and the military, Philippines sex tourism produces surplus pleasure which is extracted from the bodies of women. The vectors of exploitation marked out by the traffic in women's bodies through sex tourism and domestic service both connect and separate poor nations of the Asia-Pacific with wealthier members like Japan, the USA and Australia. The international action of women which gained momentum as a result of the UN Decade for Women struggles against the grain of economic inequality in the region.

As noted above, the slogan for the UN Decade for Women was peace, equality and development. At the Beijing conference, the notion of empowerment gained almost co-equal status. The Platform of Action noted that women have been denied access to 'the traditional avenues to power, such as ... political parties, employer organizations and trade unions'. Instead women have made their presence felt through non-governmental and grass-roots organizations. The Platform recommended the equal representation of women in all their diversity in all decision-making structures. One can imagine the challenge to the IMF if it were to be guided by the female voices of Vancouver economists, Vietnamese rice farmers, and Fijian textile workers. Perhaps then the larger visions of debt forgiveness, environmental preservation, valuing and cherishing women's unpaid community and family maintenance work, supporting women's reproductive autonomy, denying the rights of men to women's bodies will compete more effectively with notions of development and progress written in national rhetorics which are not always sensitive to the particular needs of women.

References

Boserup, E. (1970) *Women's Role in Economic Development*, London, Allen & Unwin.

Davidson, J.O'C. (1995) 'British sex tourists in Thailand' in Maynard, M. and Parvis, J. (eds) (1995) *(Hetero)sexual Politics*, London, Taylor & Francis.

Denoon, D. with Dugin, K. and Marshall, L. (1989) *Public Health in Papua New Guinea: Medical Possibility and Social Constraint, 1884–1984*, Cambridge, Cambridge University Press.

Faludi, S. (1991) *Backlash: the Undeclared War Against American Women*, New York, Crown.

Graycar, R. and Morgan, J. (1990) *The Hidden Gender of Law*, Leichhardt, Federation Press.

Greenhalgh, S. and Li, J. (1995) 'Engendering reproductive policy and practice in peasant China: for a feminist demography of reproduction', *Signs: Journal of Women in Culture and Society*, vol.20, no.3, pp.601–41.

Hicks, G. (1995) *The Comfort Women: Japan's Brutal Regime of Enforced Prostitution in the Second World War*, New York, W.W. Norton.

Jayawardena, K. (1986) *Feminism and Nationalism in the Third World*, London, Zed Books.

Jolly, M. (1996) 'Women ikat raet long human raet o no? (Are human rights also women's rights?)', *Feminist Review*, vol.52, pp.169–90.

Kameda, A. (1995) 'Sexism and gender stereotyping in schools' in Fujimura-Fanselow, K. and Kameda, A. (eds) *Japanese Women: New Feminist Perspectives on the Past, Present and the Future*, New York, Feminist Press.

Louie, M.C.Y. (1995) 'Minjung feminism: Korean Women's Movement for Gender and Class Liberation', *Women's Studies International Forum*, vol.18, no.4, pp.417–30.

Mies, M. (1986) *Patriarchy and Accumulation on a World Scale: Women and the International Division of Labour*, London, Zed Books.

Miller, F. (1991) *Latin American Women and the Search for Social Justice*, Hanover, University Press of New England.

Ong, A. and Peletz, M.G. (eds) (1995) *Bewitching Women, Pious Men: Gender and Body Politics in Southeast Asia*, Berkeley, University of California Press.

Pakpahan, D. (1996) 'Women and culture in Indonesia: images in religion, customary law and the state', *Lila: Asia-Pacific Women's Studies Journal*, vol.6, pp.1–11.

Smedley, A. (1995) 'Silk workers' in *China for Women: Travel and Culture*, North Melbourne, Spinifex Press.

Tadiar, N.X.M. (1993) 'Sexual economies in the Asia-Pacific community' in Kirlik, A. (ed.) *What is in a Rim? Critical Perspectives on the Pacific Region Idea*, Boulder, Westview Press.

Tomasevski, K. (1995) *Women and Human Rights*, London, Zed Books.

United Nations (1991) *The World's Women 1970–1990: Trends and Statistics*, New York, UN.

Waring, M. (1988) *Counting for Nothing*, Wellington, Allen & Unwin and Port Nicholson Press.

Watanabe, K. (1994) 'Militarism, colonialism, and the trafficking of women: "Comfort Women" forced into sexual labor for Japanese soldiers', *Bulletin of Concerned Asian Scholars*, vol.26, no.4, pp.3–17.

Further reading

Dixon-Mueller, R. (1993) *Population Policy and Women's Rights: Transforming Reproductive Choice*, Westport, Praeger.

Greenhalgh, S. and Li, J. (1995) 'Engendering reproductive policy and practice in peasant China: for a feminist demography of reproduction', *Signs: Journal of Women in Culture and Society*, vol.20, no.3, pp.601–41.

Jayawardena, K. (1986) *Feminism and Nationalism in the Third World*, London, Zed Books.

Kabeer, N. (1994) *Reversed Realities: Gender Hierarchies in Development Thought*, London, Verso.

Mies, M. (1986) *Patriarchy and Accumulation on a World Scale: Women and the International Division of Labour*, London, Zed Books.

Ong, A. and Peletz, M.G. (eds) (1995) *Bewitching Women, Pious Men: Gender and Body Politics in Southeast Asia*, Berkeley, University of California Press.

Pacific images

Stephanie Taylor

9.1 Introduction

The aim of this chapter is not simply to present an array of Pacific images, with all that title may imply and evoke for different readers. The previous chapters of the book have considered different aspects of 'culture', from apparently concrete and measurable features like population to more abstract and slippery ideas like religion and ethnicity. The aim here is to use 'images' to draw further attention to certain problems associated with the study of culture. The broad argument is that statements about a culture cannot be objectively checked against the reality of what is being described: it is always necessary to ask whose knowledge is being proffered, and what consequences may follow from it. The examples chosen are mainly from the Southern Pacific, that is, the 'Pacific' part of the 'Asia-Pacific'. This is for several reasons. The smaller and less populous parts of the region have, inevitably, featured less in this book, so, in focusing on them, this chapter fills a possible gap. However, these places have also been important in encounters which shaped Anglo-European and later Anglo-American understandings of the region. They are therefore very relevant to any study written for and by English-language speakers, including, of course, this one.

The chapter begins with a discussion of what is meant by 'images'. The Asia-Pacific can be understood as a new entity which is still in the process of being defined and constructed. Section 9.3 explores the relevance of images to the study of the 'Asia-Pacific' and then outlines the main questions to be considered. The next two sections discuss how European explorers established ways of seeing the lands around the Pacific Ocean which had far-reaching and still pertinent consequences. The two images considered here are, in Section 9.4, the image of emptiness and, in Section 9.5, the image of the Pacific as primitive and natural.

Another aim is to consider how images can change, for example in response to economic factors. Section 9.6 takes the example of place in New Zealand. Finally, the chapter aims to show how images can establish relationships and define peoples as culturally different. Section 9.7 looks at how contemporary relationships can be influenced by images which establish 'cultural difference', taking the example of new 'Asian' migration into one of the European-settled countries of the Asia-Pacific, again focusing on New Zealand.

9.2   The nature of images

The word 'image' has varied meanings and associations. To 'imagine' or use the 'imagination' is to depart from reality and fantasize. In photography an image is visual. A public image refers to the way that something, or someone, is regarded by others, so that in commerce and public relations the task of creating an image for a product, organization or person involves manipulating appearances and also the ideas which people hold and the chains of association by which one idea is linked to another. Underlying each of these uses of 'image' is a contrast with truth or reality. For example, there is the assumption that it is possible to go behind a public image in order to discover the real person or true situation. Images are therefore often considered superficial and even false, a temporary and 'second class' form of knowledge compared with 'real' knowledge, like facts, figures and true information. Dreams or the pictures and ideas taken up idly from advertising or cinema are not conventionally associated with academic study, except perhaps as evidence of illusion or ignorance, to be contrasted and corrected, again, with reality.

This chapter will argue against drawing such a clearcut distinction between 'images' and other kinds of knowledge. It is, of course, widely accepted that preconceptions can affect perceptions: the expression 'beauty is in the eye of the beholder' is one way of saying that people see what they are looking for. On the other hand, objectivity is assumed to be possible. When someone is described as a 'prejudiced' or 'biased' observer, implicit in the criticism that she or he selects evidence to support already-held beliefs is the idea that there can be neutral and impartial observation. In contrast, this chapter will argue that preconceptions and beliefs are more pervasive and less avoidable than is commonly assumed. The images which people hold will shape, and often limit, their understanding of places, situations and relationships with others. Images have important consequences because they can serve certain interests and warrant certain practices. They can be modified and superseded but never completely set aside. To 'see' or 'understand' something inevitably involves drawing on ideas, and these are always limiting. People do not enter new situations as neutral observers but as interpreting machines equipped with the ideas and biases, the images, received from their particular social and cultural environments.

This chapter also challenges the neat assumption that there is a reality 'out there' against which an image can be checked. It suggests that pictures and words, ideas, practices cannot easily be separated from the world that is their object. There is an intricate connection between the way a place or thing is described, the ideas people hold of it, their behaviour towards it (whether, for instance, they are respectful or exploitative) and the consequences of that behaviour.

These notions raise a number of problems. Where do images come from? Does an individual observer or thinker see or understand the world in a particular way because of the images she or he has chosen to hold? Can that individual imagine a world which is quite different to anyone else's, so that every person inhabits a unique and solitary 'bubble' of experiences and ideas? The answer proposed here is that each individual has some freedom to innovate and 'think' a unique personal world but is limited, like a sculptor or builder, by the materials available. These materials are the ideas and assumptions received from society and culture, mainly in the form of language. It is possible for any one person to build new images, to introduce new ideas and develop new theories, but without drawing on the existing shared ideas and language she or he will be unable to communicate and interact with others. As social beings people depend on understanding and being understood rather than being isolated in their private worlds of meaning. In addition, to use the analogy of the builder again, in most situations people are likely to follow traditional practices and designs. Innovation is difficult, total 100 per cent innovation is probably impossible, so in making individual images people use the resources, the ideas and explanations, and arguments and words which are already around them.

9.3   The relevance of images to the study of the Asia-Pacific

Some of the issues which these ideas raise for a study of the Asia-Pacific have already been encountered. For example, there is the problem of terminology. To write or speak of the 'Asia-Pacific' raises debates about the validity of using this one term to group together all the varied economic and political entities, the different nations, economic partners, parties and treaty signatories included under its umbrella. The use of the term could also be seen as part of the process by which the entity is constructed. On the one hand, new relationships make it necessary to postulate a new entity (rather than, for example, continuing to talk of 'Asia and the Pacific', or 'Asia, South-East Asia and Oceania', etc.); on the other, the use of the term more firmly establishes the collective entity which it refers to.

If terminology is significant, then it should be noted whose terms are used. The name 'Pacific' means 'peaceful', from the Latin word for peace 'pax'. 'Polynesia' comes from the Greek words for 'many' and 'islands' (see **Eccleston *et al.*, 1998, p.249**). These names are not, therefore, derived from the languages of the people who are native to this part of the world. In other cases, there are two alternative place names, such as 'New Zealand' or 'Aotearoa', and 'Nouvelle-Caledonie' and 'Kanaky', and a political contest over which is appropriate. Similarly, the persistence of the European images described in the following two sections of this chapter can be seen as an indication of continuing Euro-American cultural influence which in some cases may obscure local resistance. The next two sections also suggest that certain images of the Pacific derived more from the early European explorers who first propagated them than the places they supposedly referred to. However, for a contemporary observer or resident this may not be just a problem of sweeping away myths and misconceptions: earlier understandings of different parts of the Pacific shaped and influenced later interactions and activities, and continue to do so.

Like the major entity 'Asia-Pacific', many of the terms for its constituent entities can also be challenged. For example, the term 'nation' or 'nation-state', like the name of a particular nation, generally groups together disparate individuals and communities, as if implying that all differences between them, whether of religion, language, wealth, physical appearance, political sympathy or whatever, are mysteriously smoothed out by their sharing a single official government. Again, the use of such a term for a nation or region is part of the process of creating important links. When certain places and peoples are talked of and thought of as connected, marked off as a separate group or category and then treated as such, it is clear that shared interests may be established. This is the reason that images are important for nations or nation-states. Their foundation and then their maintenance always includes the production of visual, literary, poetic and historic images, not only for 'outsiders' but also for the home population. (For example, Chapter 10 discusses the role of cinema in producing such images.)

However, out of all the possible images for a place, only a few persist and any single image is inevitably selective. This raises the key question of why certain images, including some features but not others, arise and persist, and why other images change. The discussion of images of place, in Section 9.6, will consider the influence of economic factors in this. Furthermore, images are often based on distinctions and contrasts, for example, between insiders and outsiders, European and non-European, modern and traditional. Section 9.7 will consider how real these cultural differences are and why they are perceived.

Sections 9.2 and 9.3 have introduced the idea of images and suggested that people's knowledge about the world is not simply neutral information. They have suggested that their images of the world, the ways in which they describe and understand it, can precede and then influence what they perceive. The next two sections look in more detail at particular images which have operated in this way.

9.4   The image of emptiness

Contemporary images of the Pacific Ocean and its environs, among European and English-speaking populations, still owe a great deal to the ideas and representations disseminated by the first Europeans to go there. The early European exploration of the Pacific Ocean, in the sixteenth, seventeenth and eighteenth centuries, was in search of an unknown southern continent, *Terra Australis Incognita*. The assumption was that if the world was spherical this 'last great continent' must exist in the south in order to balance it. There was competition between European powers, such as France and Britain, to be the first to claim new territories and control the wealth they might contain, including new goods, markets and places for settlement, as Asia, Africa and the Atlantic side of America had already provided.

Box 9.1 *Terra Australis Incognita*

The expectations attached to the undiscovered but already named southern continent of *Terra Australis Incognita* have been described by two historians:

> 'The great southern continent was to most thinkers of the time more than mere knowledge founded on discovery and experience – it was a feeling, a tradition, a logical and now even a theological necessity, a compelling and inescapable mathematical certitude' (Beaglehole, 1934, p.9).

> 'It was a dream of gold, of strange races, of entire populations to be saved for Christ, of wealth and of conquest. There both El Dorado and Utopia had their last refuge' (Dunmore, 1965, p.3).

These short extracts indicate some of the images which preceded and might have influenced European encounters with Pacific lands and peoples. As well as fantasies of money and happiness ('El Dorado and Utopia'), there was a strong expectation of difference and novelty ('strange races'), rather like later ideas about the possible life-forms on other planets. What is different from science fiction, however, is the strength of the belief that this new place and its inhabitants did exist and could be found. This confident 'certitude' (certainty) suggests that the explorers would feel they were claiming something over which they already had rights, like an inheritance. And there was another right conferred by their religion: peoples who were not already Christian had to be 'saved for Christ'. It is easy to see how these assumptions would lead to conflict, immediately and subsequently, and of course all the peoples the Europeans encountered would have had their own, equally strong ideas about the world and their own place in it.

The invisible peoples

Despite being 'incognita', or unknown, to Europeans, most of the places 'discovered' by the explorers were, of course, already populated. Yet one of the images which has persisted is of the Pacific and its environs as empty space. Partly this is because the areas of ocean are so large. (In some Pacific legends the ocean is compared with the expanse of the night sky.) However, the image of emptiness also expresses the European tendency to disregard the peoples of the Pacific, to consider them as relatively unimportant and no obstacle to the (re)settlement of the lands they inhabited.

This assumption was not always overt or unqualified. For example, on Captain James Cook's 1768 voyage, he carried instructions from the Royal Society in Britain which were intended to guide him in his treatment of any peoples encountered during the exploration of the Pacific region. Cook was advised that, 'They are human creatures, the work of the same omnipotent Author' and 'They are the natural, and in the strictest sense of the word, the legal possessors of the several Regions which they inhabit'. Individual records from those on the voyage, including Cook's journals, describe some aspects of the lives of the 'creatures' with admiration and respect, including the excellence of their sea vessels (referring to the Maori), the quality of their cultivation and wood-working methods, and their good general health. However, another instruction from the Royal Society was that, 'There are many ways to convince them of the Superiority of Europeans, without slaying any of those poor people', and, despite the reservation about legal possession, at each landing a British flag was hoisted to mark the claiming of the 'new' territory for the Crown. In these and subsequent encounters the predominant European understanding was that the peoples of the Pacific were inferior and therefore relatively unimportant.

This perception possibly had the most extreme consequences in the case of the Aboriginal people of Australia. The Europeans had been aware of their presence from the occasion of Cook's first landing, in 1770. However, unlike some other Pacific peoples, such as the Tahitians, the Aborigines had shown little interest in the material possessions of Cook's company, nor had they presented as overt a military challenge as, for example, the Maoris had done in New Zealand/Aotearoa. Nine years after the landing, Joseph Banks, the botanist who had accompanied Cook, gave evidence to a British parliamentary committee which was investigating suitable sites for the establishment of a penal colony. Banks recommended that a colony be started in Botany Bay, on the east coast of Australia, and his advice was followed.

In deciding to establish this and subsequent settlements, the British therefore disregarded the Aborigines and moved onto their territories as if Australia was empty and uninhabited land. This concept was formalized in the legal doctrine of *Terra Nullius* which persisted for 205 years until the 1992 Mabo ruling in the High Court recognized that indigenous land ownership had existed in Australia before Europeans arrived. Banks also advised the committee that Botany Bay had a sufficiently good climate and soil to enable a new colony established there to become self-sufficient in food production within a single year. It can be argued that his assessment of the fertility of the land was not inaccurate because Australia did, eventually, become an agricultural and horticultural producer. However, the initial attempts to cultivate it were so unsuccessful that in the first few years of the colony the convicts and those sent out to take charge of them almost starved to death together.

In Banks's advice to the committee it is therefore possible to see how his images of Australia, as both uninhabited and fertile, had enormous consequences, immediately and continuing into the present day. It is also clear how much suffering and conflict developed out of the different

Contesting the image of Australia as European: During the official celebrations of the Australian Bicentenary in January, 1988, tall ships arrived from England to commemorate the arrival of European settlers but Aborigines and their supporters demonstrated in protest, their placards reading '200 years of white lies'

images and ideas held by the two peoples. The British forms of farming and cultivation which initially failed in the Australian context were based on certain understandings of what it meant to own and occupy land. In Britain and Europe land was a commodity which was occupied permanently and used to produce food and other goods for sale and exchange. It was essential to the whole economic system that the land produced a surplus, so that agricultural workers could feed themselves and in addition produce an extra amount which, whether traded or passed on as rents or taxes, would feed non-agricultural workers and other classes. This is so obvious as to be unnoticeable to people living within such a system, but the existence of city dwellers, full-time politicians and religious leaders and, indeed, explorers is based on such a surplus.

In contrast, the Aborigines, in a very different natural environment, survived with a form of economic organization which was not based on a surplus. Living in small groups in which all the members, except perhaps small children, participated in the work to find food, they did not cultivate food but obtained it by hunting and gathering. They lived nomadically, moving around within large tribal territories. An indication of the success of this form of economic organization is that, it has been suggested, in the most arid parts of Australia Aborigines living traditionally could sustain a greater population density than has been achieved since with any alternative technology, including present-day equipment and communications.

However, the nature of their economy meant that the Aborigines encountered by the early European explorers and settlers did not have the permanent settlements or material wealth which the Europeans associated with religion, culture or civilization. They had no monarchs or ruling class whom the Europeans would recognize as leaders appropriate to negotiate with. As nomads, they carried few material possessions. Although some sacred sites have rock paintings and engravings, religious meaning for Aborigines is traditionally attached to natural features of the land and environment rather than to artificial objects.

The consequence of these differences was that most aspects of the Aborigines' lives were misinterpreted or scarcely seen by the Europeans who encountered them. The 'empty' land was settled. When the Aborigines responded to the damage and threat to their territory by attacking farm buildings, herds and the settlers themselves, these actions were not recognized as resistance but seen only as irrational and unwarranted destruction. The image of the Aborigines as primitives, or, in one writer's words, as 'an economic pest', then obscured brutality and murder; they were not acknowledged to have rights because they were not seen as fully human.

The image of emptiness can therefore be seen to have continuing relevance for any understanding of contemporary Australia and the peoples who live there. The same image can also be seen to have prompted decisions by different twentieth-century governments about their activities in this part of the world.

The illusion of safe distance

Linked with the search for *Terra Australis Incognita* and the claiming of empty 'new' lands was an image of the world as a chart marked with all 'known' and 'unknown' areas. This way of thinking about places, based heavily on the documents produced for European sailing vessels, continues to be influential. Contemporary world maps still tend to be laid out with Europe in the middle, reflecting the experience of the European explorers that the Pacific is a long way from the centre. As a result, it has appeared a logical place to carry out certain potentially dangerous activities, well away from home. From the Second World War onwards, European powers and the USA have used the Pacific Ocean and also the Australian outback – the emptiness in the middle of the unknown southern continent – for nuclear testing and, more recently, chemical dumping. Both France and the USA moved their nuclear test sites to the Pacific from other 'empty' and remote sites, in the Algerian Sahara and the Nevada desert; the Pacific seemed even further away.

The history of nuclear activity in the Pacific contains more incidents and accidents than is generally remembered. The most serious were undoubtedly the two bombs dropped on Japan in 1945, in Hiroshima and Nagasaki. In addition, between 1944 and 1963 Britain exploded nuclear devices on Christmas Island (in Kiribati) and, with the co-operation of the Australian government, in the Australian desert and also on the Monte Bello islands off the west coast of Australia. The USA tested nuclear weapons in the Marshall Islands until 1962 and also over Johnston Island and Christmas Island. France began testing devices in Mururoa in 1966. A series of tests there in 1996 were announced to be the last.

All of these nuclear explosions have left dangerous radioactive material. Both Japan and the USA have also established nuclear waste dumps in the Pacific and the USA has disposed of dangerous chemicals there. As well as the future threat from residues, a number of the explosions had more immediate consequences. Populations have had to be evacuated from the Marshall Islands and Mururoa. Some of the Rongelap Islands, Enjebit and Runit Island remain too contaminated for their former inhabitants to return to. The people of Kwajalein Island were relocated when it was made an American missile range and parts of the Australian outback are still closed to Aborigines for whom it is part of their territory.

In a particularly serious incident of accidental contamination, in 1954, Rongelap Islanders were exposed to nuclear fallout from an enormous explosion near Bikini Atoll in the Marshall Islands. They suffered from radiation sickness, burns, hair loss and conjunctivitis. In the longer term, children have developed cancers and growth-retarding thyroid malfunctions, and there have been foetal abnormalities. The crew of a Japanese vessel which was fishing near the explosion also suffered radiation sickness. The Australian tests are reported to have exposed Aborigines and other outback residents and also British soldiers to radiation, although there is not enough data to confirm this; service veterans from both Australia and Christmas Island have since demanded compensation for radiation-induced illnesses.

The decisions to carry out these activities in the Pacific led to opposition and protest, much of which continues. In the late twentieth century there is strong pressure to have the Pacific declared a nuclear-free zone. Both the protests and resistance and the activities against which these are directed can be understood to draw on conflicting images. On the one hand, there are the linked images of emptiness and distance from the centre which were inherited from the earliest European visitors. Against these are more recent images, for example, of the ocean as a single and elaborate ecosystem; radioactivity as a corrosive and long-acting invisible force which threatens it; and the Pacific Ocean as a unified political and social region. These were brought together, as one example, in a 1990 statement from the President of the Pacific Council of Churches who said: 'The Pacific is not just an ocean. It's a people – people who see themselves as trustees of the environment'.

This section has suggested that a broad image of the Pacific as empty has operated in different contexts, both of place and time. It has influenced and warranted certain activities with negative consequences for people of the Pacific region. The images have therefore led to certain outsiders' interests being prioritized over the interests of people within the region; local interests, like many of the local people, were either not recognized or seen as irrelevant. The next section considers a different and apparently more positive image which can also be traced back to early European exploration.

9.5   The primitive islands of love and happiness

The previous section showed how images of a place and a people can be closely linked. In certain Pacific Islands, European attitudes to indigenous peoples were heavily influenced by a different image, derived from the eighteenth-century French philosopher, Jean Jacques Rousseau. He had contrasted the misery of people corrupted by the false existence within a civilized society with an ideal of a happy and natural life away from civilization. In the context of French society his writings could be understood as a criticism of Versailles, an attack on the privilege and artifice of the royal court there. However, when the French navigator Louis Antoine de Bougainville visited Tahiti in 1768, he and many of his companions saw its society as an example of the natural state that Rousseau praised. For example, one of those on board Bougainville's ship, C.F.P. Fesche wrote

> If happiness consists in an abundance of all things necessary to life, in living in a superb land with the finest climate, in enjoying the best of health, in breathing the purest and most salubrious air, in leading a simple, soft, quiet life, free from all passions, even from jealousy, although surrounded by women, if these women can themselves even disperse happiness, then I say that there is not in the world a happier nation than the Tahitian one.
>
> (quoted in Dunmore, 1965, p.111)

On their return to France, Bougainville and others on the voyage published accounts of life in Tahiti which emphasized the beauty and apparent sexual freedom of women. Bougainville also took back a Tahitian man, Aoutourou, and the spectacle of this visitor contributed to interest in the published accounts. Aoutourou's own accounts of Tahitian society eventually led Bougainville to realize that it did not conform to Rousseau's ideal, but the legend was established in France of the Pacific as a romantic place of sunshine, freedom, and sexual happiness where the natural diet of fruit and fish was so easily available that no one had to work to obtain food.

These images of the South Pacific as primitive, natural, idle and idyllic persisted and influenced the interpretations and expectations of subsequent European visitors. For example, a 1889 book published by the French Colonial Department commented on the Tahitians: 'For them, to live is to sing and to love'. The painter Paul Gauguin went to Tahiti because his friend had chosen the destination after reading a popular novel which described it as a place of 'utter idleness and perpetual dreams'.

Gauguin arrived approximately 130 years after Bougainville's visit, expecting to find a 'natural' society. He was disappointed. However simple or complex Tahitian society had been before European contact, at this point it was organized economically and socially as a French colony. For example, the capital, Papeete, was a busy, relatively large port and the Christian church and its teachings were extremely influential. However, neither Gauguin's paintings of Tahiti nor the book, *Noa Noa*, which he wrote (begun in 1893) to promote their sale back in Europe, reflect these aspects of Tahitian life. Rather, they perpetuate the illusions which had brought him there. For example, in the following extract he describes his life at a point shortly before lack of money forced him to leave Tahiti. At the time he was renting accommodation in a place where he had to live on expensive tinned food from the local store and was unable to communicate with his neighbours because he did not speak Tahitian; however his account conforms to the images of life in a natural paradise:

> Every day gets better for me, in the end I understand the language quite well, my neighbours ... regard me almost as one of themselves; my naked feet, from daily contact with the rock, have got used to the ground; my body, almost quite naked, no longer feels the sun; civilisation leaves me bit by bit and I begin to think simply, to have only a little hatred for my neighbour, and I function in an animal way, freely – with the certainty of the morrow [being] like today; every morning the sun rises serene for me as for everyone, I become carefree and calm and loving.

> (Gauguin, 1961, p.23)

In his paintings, as in his writing, Gauguin did not, of course, simply 'reflect' what he saw; he shaped, interpreted and presented it, as his accounts of the process of painting acknowledge. For instance, he wrote that it was important not to paint too much from nature, and many of his strongly coloured paintings were developed from (black and white) sketches when he was working in his studio away from the scenes 'depicted', and in some cases, after his first visit, away from Tahiti, back in Europe. However, the paintings, of passive women, sunlit landscapes, fruit and flowers, resemble Rousseau's natural paradise and the island of love described by the early explorers.

Nave, Nave, Fenua *(The Delectable Earth) woodcut by Paul Gauguin (Courtauld Institute of Art). Gauguin's depictions of Tahiti, such as this scene of a naked woman waiting in a landscape of exotic plants and animals, perpetuate earlier images and still influence tourist advertising for the Pacific Islands*

Recognizably similar images of a different Pacific Island society recur 30 years later in an academic book which became a popular bestseller. In 1928 an American anthropologist, Margaret Mead, published *Coming of Age in Samoa: a Study of Adolescence and Sex in Primitive Societies.* The book claimed that in Samoa sexual freedom and promiscuity among young unmarried people were widely accepted and that, as a result, adolescents there did not experience the crisis or stress associated with this transitional age in the West. This account supports the theory of 'cultural determinism', that 'nature' is less important than 'nurture', which implies that many social problems can be eradicated by changing society itself, an assumption which was popular at the time Mead was writing.

Mead's account of Samoa as a sexually free society was challenged by the Samoans themselves and also by a number of contemporary studies by other non-Samoans. There are also contradictions within Mead's own work (for example, she writes that young Samoan women are expected to be virgins when they marry). However, the book was highly influential. This raises two questions. The first is whether Mead could have drastically misunderstood the society she studied. The second is why, if she had done so, her account was accepted over those of her critics, both at that time and for many years subsequently.

The first question can be approached as an issue of individual competence. Mead was a young and relatively inexperienced academic who had spent only six months in Samoa and did not speak the language well. Most of her information came from her interviews with young girls who a more recent writer, Derek Freeman (1983), has suggested, deliberately misled her, partly as a kind of joke and partly because they were shocked at being asked about sexual behaviour. The inaccuracies of the book can therefore be seen as the responsibility of a single person, the author. If this is the case, however, it does not resolve the second problem, of why Mead's account was so widely accepted.

An alternative approach is to see this as another situation in which existing images were taken up and perpetuated. In other words, it can be argued that both the research and its reception, by both academic and general readers, were influenced by the old images of Pacific societies as simple and sexually free. The terms in which Mead describes Samoa do suggest that she had been influenced, perhaps unknowingly, by earlier images. Even the sub-title of her book, juxtaposing 'sex' and 'primitive', recalls the nineteenth-century European myths. In the introduction she also suggests that a scholar studying such a 'primitive society' needs less time to understand its structure than would be necessary for 'complicated civilizations like those of Europe, or the higher civilizations of the East'. Her account emphasizes the pleasantness of the climate and physical surroundings, and the ease, leisure and shallowness of the people's lives. Despite the apparently positive thesis that Samoan adolescents escape the crises experienced by the same age group in the West, there is a strong suggestion of Western superiority in the assumptions that these adolescents are less complicated and sensitive than those in, for example, the USA.

This section has looked at three situations in which similar images of Pacific societies, as idle and sexually free, were held and perpetuated by outsiders. It has suggested that in each case there was a tendency for existing images to persist and be perpetuated; alternative accounts were ignored. Despite their superficially positive nature, the images described in this section set up unequal and potentially exploitative relationships. This point will be explored in more detail in Section 9.7. Now, after these two examples of the way that images can persist, the next section will investigate why they might change. It takes as an illustration the changing images of the land in New Zealand/Aotearoa.

9.6 Changing images of place

Land, place, territory are all terms which refer to perhaps the most enduring feature of people's physical environment. It would seem easier to disagree about people's society and beliefs than the place they live in, the landscape around them and the ground they stand on. Yet Section 9.4 suggested that conflicting images of land in Australia were held by the Aborigines and the settlers. This section will look at another example in which economic factors are also highly relevant, the changing images of the natural environment in New Zealand/Aotearoa.

The first economic value which Europeans placed on New Zealand/ Aotearoa was as a source of certain natural commodities: wood, for ships' masts; sealskin; and the various products derived from whales. When more permanent British settlement began, in the early nineteenth century, it was focused on agriculture. The land was 'broken in' as large areas of native forest were cleared for the establishment of farms. Inevitably, agricultural production was not achieved without environmental damage. Both the land clearing and the intensive grazing which followed led to soil erosion, which still continues. Other contemporary problems also originated in the settlers' attempts to recreate aspects of the British landscape. The introduction of foreign species of plants, birds and animals led to further environmental damage. For example, gorse plants which provide effective hedging in Britain spread over large areas of land in New Zealand, making it unusable. Common British birds, such as sparrows, blackbirds, thrushes and starlings, competed effectively with native species, taking over their habitats and reducing their numbers.

These activities were prompted by a certain image of the land and were also at least partly successful in making the new place conform to it. It is an image of lush green farmlands scattered with sheep, reminiscent of the countryside in the British Isles which many of the settlers had known. This image is still widespread and is used commercially to advertise New Zealand agricultural products, such as meat and butter. It is also, inevitably, selective, omitting, for example, the environmental damage and also other aspects such as native species of birds and plants and non-agricultural uses.

In the 1970s and 1980s the New Zealand economy changed and, although agriculture remained significant, tourism was promoted as a major new industry. New Zealand was marketed as a place of outdoor leisure activities, such as skiing, sailing and hiking. Linked to this was 'eco-tourism', drawing on a new image of New Zealand as an unspoilt natural environment. This commodification of nature operated in the domestic market as well. New Zealanders began to describe their country in similar terms, for example, as 'clean and green' and also to consume more of the newly perceived attractions, for example, by going hiking in national parks.

The man-made landscape in New Zealand/Aotearoa: Henry James Warre, Bush Clearing, Ratahihi, *Hocken Library, University of Otago, Dunedin. The drawing shows land cleared by settlers in 1863. However, more recent images of New Zealand tend to present it as an unspoilt natural landscape, as if this settlement and breaking-in had never occurred*

Instead of the landscape which had been broken in and cleared by settlers for farming, a new image prevails, of New Zealand as an undeveloped and unspoiled natural landscape, as if it had never been colonized.

The above account of this change in the way that New Zealand is both depicted and perceived emphasizes the influence of economic factors. The diverse images of the land are linked to different forms of economic exploitation. However, this explanation can itself be criticized as selective. For example, it does not refer to the indigenous people of New Zealand, the Maori. They are, of course, participants in the New Zealand economy like the other members of the population, including the majority who are of white British descent. In addition, the Maori can be presented as the inheritors of a separate culture and traditions in which the land has spiritual and religious meanings. Over approximately the same period that the economy was being reorganized, there was an increase in awareness of this cultural heritage, among Maori and non-Maori. Long-standing claims for the return of tribal lands, in some cases taken at the time of the first European settlement, were finally officially acknowledged. The ensuing legal hearings have offered new ways of thinking of land, for example, as cultural heritage, sacred sites (wahi tapu), an object of veneration, stolen goods or the spoils of conquest. A different set of concepts, such as fragile ecosystems and scarce natural resources, have come from environmental movements. All may have contributed to the new image of New Zealand as a precolonial landscape which must be respected and preserved.

Changing images of Maori soldiers: The engraving of a tattooed warrior (Sydney Parkinson, Warrior of New Zealand in the South Pacific Ocean, *Hocken Library, University of Otago, Dunedin) is based on a drawing by an artist who accompanied Cook in 1773 on one of the first European voyages to New Zealand. The photograph shows a traditional greeting between two Maori peacekeepers on duty with the UN in Croatia in 1995*

A 'realist' explanation for these varied images would be that they are all true, in that they describe the world as it is: New Zealand developed an economy based on agricultural production and is now, in addition, obtaining income as a tourist destination in which the main attractions are mountains, beaches and open spaces. For Maori people, the land also has religious and cultural meaning. In some situations Maori culture can itself enhance New Zealand's attractiveness to tourists. The diversity of images of New Zealand therefore reflects its multiple real features.

However, this ignores contradictions and conflicts. New images are not necessarily compatible but work to contest those that preceded them. For example, Maori claims of traditional ownership and rights over a piece of land or stretch of coast or river contest the accounts of New Zealand as discovered, settled and broken in by Europeans, and have sometimes been themselves contested by arguments for conservation and protection of nature.

The example discussed in this section has indicated how economic factors may influence and change the prevailing images of a place. Alternatively, it can be argued that the changes described here were brought about by political and ecological movements.

9.7 The power of images to construct relationships

Section 9.5 described how certain images of Pacific Island societies have persisted across different periods and contexts, indicating the continuing dominance or influence of certain groups and viewpoints. The examples also showed how each time the images recur they contain an implicit contrast with the society of the observer. This section will look in more detail at the significance of these contrasts. To understand their implications it will first summarize ideas from two theorists and apply these to another contemporary example.

In a discussion of a similar contrast between two other parts of the world, 'the West' and 'the Orient', the writer Edward Said coined the term 'Orientalism', which has three connected meanings. It refers, firstly, to an area of academic study in which the objects, in several senses, are the peoples who live in the areas variously described as the East, the Middle East and the Orient. When studied by Western experts, the Orientals are reduced to the status of objects, rather like museum exhibits, and in a certain sense become the possessions of experts who claim to know them better than they can know themselves. There are clear parallels here in Margaret Mead's study of the Samoans, described in Section 9.5. In that case, the account of Samoan customs contained in Mead's book carried more authority than the Samoans who challenged it: she was thought to 'know' them better than they knew themselves.

Said's term, Orientalism, can also mean a way of thinking in which the two entities, the Orient and the West, however defined, are contrasting opposites: the Orient and the Oriental are 'Other' to the West and the

Westerner. Again, there are parallels in the examples described in Section 9.5. The Pacific image can be understood as half of a pair, with an opposing image of European or American society: if Pacific Islanders were sexually free, idle, primitive and natural, the Europeans/Americans who described them could be understood to be sexually inhibited but also industrious, sophisticated and civilized. This, however, is not explicitly stated. Another point to be noted about 'Others' is that they are normally the 'marked' identity, named and described as in some way different. The 'unmarked' identity of the observer or speaker is not usually discussed; it stands as the taken-for-granted standard of normality against which any difference is measured.

The third meaning of Orientalism suggested by Said is 'a Western style for dominating, restructuring and having authority over the Orient' (Said, 1978, p.2). Part of this dominance derives directly from the contrast, from the Western understanding of the Orient as a negative opposite. The culture and values of the Orient are thought to be the opposite of those the West perceives itself to have, and these opposing values are both inferior and desirable. Exactly as with the French images of the Tahitians, nineteenth-century Western travellers and colonial servants depicted Oriental peoples as sexually licentious and wanton. This image simultaneously distinguished East from West and allowed the Western visitors certain 'forbidden' practices. More importantly, because the inferior peoples are understood to need leadership and education to improve them, the images then warrant and facilitate further dominance, such as that of imperial and neo-colonial rulers.

Said suggests that these images therefore function to 'make' both the entities they depict, the West and the Orient. This does not happen quickly or simply but in a complex process which involves naming, defining and justifying. His account does not deny that differences of language and religion, etc. are significant. The point being made is that relationships are established across 'cultural differences' which have been defined and then constructed from the point of view and interests of one party only. In this theory, Said is drawing on the ideas of the French philosopher, Michel Foucault. In particular, he draws on Foucault's notion of language/ knowledge constructing what it describes (rather than neutrally describing what already exists). This active, constitutive quality is what is being emphasized in this chapter in the concept of images. Foucault analyses the way that definitions, classifications and categories establish relationships between people and things, conferring value and status and meaning upon them. This is not a once-for-all event but an ongoing process in which power is created and denied, exercised and resisted in the changing relationships which are set up.

Once again it is necessary to ask how this relates to the 'Asia-Pacific'. The importance, and difficulty, of defining this new entity has already been discussed. In Chapter 3 Hull proposes the image of the Asia-Pacific as a 'negative' continent, of water surrounded by land. This is complemented by Kathirithamby-Wells's account, in Chapter 2, of some of the crossings which have brought different goods, people, languages and ideas to the land edges of the negative continent. This new image emphasizes the successive contacts and communications which have occurred between the composite cultures of the Asia-Pacific. If people are understood to approach each other as neutral, information-gathering observers, the sheer volume of these encounters might be expected to have resulted in groups being well-informed about each other's similarities and differences. However, the concept which has been developed in this chapter would predict, and account for, less harmonious relationships. It has been argued that images precede encounters, have far-reaching consequences, and persist or change in ways which are not easily predicted. The images themselves may produce and justify so-called cultural divisions. The remainder of this section will outline one particular example of such a division.

Creating 'Asians'

The example which will be discussed is the division between the majority populations, on the one hand, and Chinese and other Asian minorities, on the other, in the countries settled mainly by Europeans, that is, the USA, Canada, Australia and New Zealand. These last three are often referred to as the 'settlement colonies', since the colonists who went there established permanent and white majority populations. In all four countries there was a long history of opposition to Chinese and other Asian migration. This has been attributed to a collective and undifferentiated image of China, South-East Asia and the Indian subcontinent as overpopulated and poor. It was believed that migrant workers from these places would flood labour markets, competing for jobs and undercutting wages. In response to this fear and stereotyping, migration was restricted, and when Chinese and other Asians were permitted to enter they were usually kept separate, paid lower wages and generally discriminated against.

The first migrants from China to come to New Zealand, for example, in the 1860s, had been invited there by British settlers in the hope that they would start businesses in an economy which was at that time unbalanced by the goldrushes. However, in spite of the invitation the newcomers encountered immediate hostility. An 1871 government report, seeking to subdue this, concluded that they should not be excluded. The points it stated in their favour were that they were hardworking, careful with money, moral and adaptable, and would eventually return to China! Yet the hostility continued and ironically they were criticized for the same qualities that they had been praised for, that is, as one writer says, 'because they were industrious, unfairly competitive, because they were adaptable or of questionable morality with too much ability, and now apparently were not going back to China as formerly anticipated' (Sedgwick, 1984, p.49).

Laws were passed to impose special taxes on Chinese, limit their right to naturalization and restrict further migration. In 1907 a special reading test in English was introduced for prospective migrants. A few years later there was opposition to intermarriage between Chinese men and Maori women, apparently because this might lead to an increase in the (very small) Asian population. Similar hostility arose elsewhere and similar restrictions were established in response to it.

More than a century after the first Chinese had been invited, the New Zealand government introduced a 'business immigration scheme' to attract 'Asian' entrepreneurs who would start businesses and improve the national economy. Just as the scheme was apparently based in the same image of Chinese as natural businesspeople which had prompted the earlier invitation, it also led to the new migrants being criticized in the same terms as before. They were said to work too hard and be too competitive in business and in schools. Their morals were challenged, in contemporary terms: for example, they were reported to be greedy and materialistic and said to damage the natural environment, by building overlarge houses which 'used up' the land, and by 'stripping' beaches of seafood. Another accusation was that they had introduced organized crime to New Zealand (the triads). Also, as had happened in the nineteenth century, there were disputes around whether or not they would stay: on the one hand, there were complaints that too many migrants were being allowed in, and on the other, that those who had been admitted were not really settling but just buying up property and then leaving again. The measures proposed were also similar to those introduced previously. Language tests were suggested for prospective migrants and also for children coming into schools. There were calls for Asian immigration to be stopped.

This situation can be taken to illustrate several ways in which images construct and perpetuate cultural divisions. First, it shows how images persist even when it would seem obvious that they are inaccurate and inadequate. Over a long period of time the same few labels are used to refer to an enormous number of people. As with Said's 'Orient' and 'Orientals', the categories invoked in these disputes are extremely broad and vague. In the New Zealand case, 'Asian' and 'Chinese' both continue to be widely used umbrella terms for people of different original nationalities, including from China, Hong Kong, Taiwan, Japan, Korea and Vietnam; different language and religious groups; and different economic positions, from short-term business visitors to refugees. Attached to the labels are a similarly simplistic but enduring set of characteristics. One way to understand how this categorization is perpetuated is with (the image of) a circular diagram: people are labelled a certain way, then presumed to have the character which goes with the label, which then seems to justify the use of the label, and so on.

Secondly, the example shows how images can create contrasted and opposed groupings, in several senses. 'New Zealanders' and 'Asians' are made when they are understood to fall into two neat groups in which any individual resembles the members of her or his group, but is completely unlike the members of the Other group. Then, the images make the groups in another sense, for example, by warranting 'anti-Asian' feeling which has led in some cases to physical attacks. Such treatment, and the fear of it, inevitably leads people to take sides and in that way to define themselves as they are being defined. The different meanings of image converge: the world is 'seen' through the images of cultural difference and social division, then laws and special tests are introduced, conflict occurs, the division becomes part of people's experience and opportunities, and so the groups must divide off and the image becomes material.

9.8   Conclusion

This chapter has challenged conventional notions of knowledge and information. It has suggested that people's images of the world are not transparently neutral and accurate. Instead of assuming that reality precedes images, it has aimed to show that images are made, by different individuals and groups drawing on shared materials, and in turn the images make or affect what they describe. In other words, images are constructed and constitutive, as well as collective and also contradictory. The chapter has drawn attention to the way that certain images have persisted or changed over time and the factors which contributed to this.

The examples which have been discussed are taken from some of the areas of the Asia-Pacific covered in less detail previously. The chapter has shown how early contacts between Europeans and peoples of the Pacific established ways of understanding places which served European interests and obscured those of indigenous people. It has also considered the way that the same place can be differently depicted, in response to different interests. It has therefore shown how diversity can in some situations be denied and in others increased. The final section looked at how images can establish relationships between people, preceding and creating 'cultural' differences.

The various situations, of early exploration, settlement, nuclear testing and tourism, in the places mentioned, Australia, Tahiti, Samoa, the Marshall Islands, Nouvelle-Caledonie and New Zealand, can be understood in terms of relations of power, between latercomers and indigenous peoples, and between different groups of migrants and colonizers. In each case the images which are available are a clue to the point which has been reached in an ongoing contest and are also one means by which that contest is being conducted.

References

Beaglehole, J.C. (1934) *The Exploration of the Pacific*, London, Adam and Charles Black.

Dunmore, J. (1965) *French Explorers in the Pacific*, Oxford, Clarendon Press.

Eccleston, B., Dawson, M. and McNamara, D. (eds) (1998) *The Asia-Pacific Profile*, London, Routledge in association with The Open University.

Freeman, D. (1983) *Margaret Mead and Samoa: the Making and Unmaking of an Anthropological Myth*, Cambridge, Mass., Harvard University Press.

Gauguin, P. (1961) *Noa Noa: Voyage to Tahiti*, Oxford, Bruno Cassirer.

Said, E.W. (1978) *Orientalism*, London, Penguin.

Sedgwick, C. (1984) 'The organizational dynamics of the New Zealand Chinese' in Spoonley, P., Macpherson, C., Pearson, D. and Sedgwick, C. (eds) *Tau Iwi: Racism and Ethnicity in New Zealand*, Palmerston North, Dunmore Press.

Further reading

Hughes, R. (1987) *The Fatal Shore: a History of the Transportation of Convicts to Australia 1787–1868*, London, Collins Harvill.

Salmond, A. (1991) *Two Worlds: First Meetings between Maori and Europeans 1642–1772*, Auckland, Viking, Penguin.

Stasiulis, D. and Yuval-Davis, N. (eds) (1995) *Unsettling Settler Societies: Articulations of Gender, Race, Ethnicity and Class*, London, Sage.

CHAPTER 10

Asia-Pacific cinemas

Mary Farquhar and Linda Erlich

10.1 Introduction

In 1996, people across the Asia-Pacific watched the Olympics in Atlanta. In 2000, they will tune into Sydney. On the outskirts of Beijing, during mid-autumn festival, guests left a concert of stars after a lavish banquet to sing karaoke in a series of upstairs rooms, styled after famous cities: New York, Tokyo, London and Paris. In Auckland and San Francisco, Shanghai and Osaka, movie-goers see films from Hong Kong as well as Hollywood. Indeed, it was Hong Kong, not mainland, audiences who pronounced the birth of New Wave Chinese cinema with the screening of *Yellow Earth* in 1985. It was Americans, like Jack Nicholson and Andy Warhol, who defended Oshima's *In the Realm of the Senses* from New York police in 1976.

These snapshots show not only the diversity and dynamism of the region's visual media, now capable of mass delivery by new technologies. They also point to the blurring of national cultures through global mass media and audience cross-participation. Nowhere is this blurring more evident or, in some cases, more hotly debated than in the various national film industries. This chapter therefore focuses on film as a window on arts across the Asia-Pacific this century.

10.2 The significance of film

What can cinema tell us about arts in the Asia-Pacific? Why should we look at cinema, for example, rather than painting or music? There are several reasons. One is that film is a composite art form. A second is that, through film, we can read different stories told by the people themselves in a highly accessible form. A third reason is that film is increasingly a global medium and demonstrates the growing internationalization of the arts.

As a composite art form, film combines images and sound. It deploys a wide range of arts and music – classical, popular and modern – and so absorbs and transforms discrete art forms from various countries. Thus, theatre is a major influence on Japanese film and contributes to a certain style or 'look'. Music may range from traditional percussion music in

Behind the fusuma *(door): at sex and play (*In the Realm of the Senses*)*

martial arts movies to the latest pop group in exploratory Sixth Generation Chinese films. We even see what people wear and how people live (such as cars and kitchens in American movies). This matters, as we will discover from Japanese responses to American movies. Film assimilates the old and the new, the elite and the everyday, the arrangements of time and space, into an art form based on the moving image.

This leads to the second reason. Narrative films tell stories in a highly accessible visual language, unlike prose and poetry which lose immediacy in translation. Taking China as an example, Rey Chow (1995, p.x) states that the advent of film signalled the end of an ancient, word-centred culture and the beginning of a modern and post-modern technological culture captured as visual images. Film and national transformation in China share certain concerns: technology, visuality and spectatorship. Thus, cinema is both writing about the self as well as national conscious-ness, exhibition and spectatorship. This individual/national story-telling may be mythical or historical, dreams or documentary. It both transcribes and transforms culture. Thus, a major theme in this chapter is that, across the Asia-Pacific as elsewhere, cinema mirrors turbulent twentieth-century histories.

The third reason for focusing on film is that it is part of the telecommunications revolution at the end of the twentieth century. Film is a medium in an increasingly global industry. Thus, the second main theme in this chapter is that film is an international industry, whether as entertainment, propaganda, big business or art. As the world moves on-line, audiences have more choice and so more power. Increasingly, global audiences can make or break a film at the box or censor's office, in art houses, through television, or at international festivals around the world.

10.3 National cinemas in three locations: Hollywood, Japan and China

Cinema in the Asia-Pacific is not just about making movies in different places for audiences around the world. Indeed, it is impossible to cover cinema in the region in one long shot. Instead, this chapter looks at three regions in the Asia-Pacific: Hollywood, Japan and China. These are major locations. Hollywood dominates the field while Japanese and, more recently, Chinese film belong to internationally recognized national cinemas with their own film traditions. National cinemas refer to, first, films made within a particular nation that share stylistic and formal features, and, second, film makers who share assumptions about film making and work within a common production structure (Bordwell and Thompson, 1990, p.371). These national cinemas are usually distinguished from Hollywood, the dominant cinema.

Each national cinema has its own complex history. So the focus of this chapter is further narrowed to three areas: background, narrative and aesthetics. While the backgrounds of both Japanese and Chinese film show the important influence of Hollywood which, with subsequent modifications, produced vibrant industries, national cinemas used film as a medium to tell their own stories in their own ways. Modifications of the medium include assimilating alternative – often traditional – narrative and aesthetic conventions to produce recognizable film-making styles. Thus, this chapter cuts between the three locations to discuss their respective film industries in terms of:

- historical background, especially different modes of production,
- film narrative, and ways of viewing within and across cultures, and
- film aesthetics, concentrating on famous films.

10.4 Backgrounds

Hollywood represents both national and international cinema. It is called dominant cinema because, from its earliest years, it shaped not only film institutions but also film form around the world, including in Japan and China. Throughout its history, its influence has sometimes been welcomed, such as in Japan early this century, and sometimes rejected, such as in China during the Mao years. Welcome or not, Hollywood has frequently set the standards by which films are produced, received and analysed.

Given this influence, how do we understand Japanese and Chinese films as works belonging to distinctive national cinemas? One answer lies in the extent to which their traditions, modes and principles of film making run counter to the dominant Hollywood model. So the first question is: what is 'Hollywood'?

Hollywood is an ideal-type of mainstream American film making. While there are many variations, its classic form between 1917 and 1960 had certain fundamental characteristics. One of these was the sheer vitality of the industry, producing at least 15,000 feature films in this period. Hollywood is often conflated with cinema itself. Overall, it represents a commodity for entertainment, a cultural industry and a 'dream factory' which is pervasive as a model for other national film industries. In this section, the concern is less with Hollywood itself than with its trans-Pacific influences, specifically Japanese and Chinese cinemas in terms of audience expectations and modes of production in changing political circumstances.

Expectations

Certain basic Western and Asian expectations about cinema arise from Hollywood practices, such as paying for a ticket to watch a film as a collective activity in a specially designed theatre. However, while this is the norm, there are variations according to time and place. Thus, in socialist China during the period from 1949 to 1976, when Mao Zedong was in control, film tickets in the cities were usually allocated to members by work units. In rural villages with no theatres, a truck would drive in with a projector set up in the back, a screen was erected in the fields, and villagers brought along folding chairs to watch in the sometimes very cold open air. Despite the weather, the fields were packed.

Other expectations relate to film itself. Kuhn states:

> Most of the millions of people throughout the world who have had contact with cinema would share certain assumptions about it: for example, that 'cinema' is constituted of films of a certain length (between one and two hours, say), which tell stories with beginnings, middles and ends, stories which usually involve fictional characters as pivots of narrative action.
>
> (Kuhn, 1994, p.21)

Even here the transplant involved cultural variations. The earliest Japanese and Chinese films, in 1899 and 1908 respectively, were of traditional operas. Operatic conventions influenced not only the acting styles of both cinemas, but also their distinctive 'looks' even today. Indeed, in the early years of Japanese cinema, film sequences were sometimes alternated with live stage performances. More significantly, until the early 1930s, a silent film narrator (*benshi*) imitated characters' voices, commented on the action, made sound effects, and provided narrative coherence. This represents the early adaptation of a foreign film form to traditional Japanese 'co-mingled media', despite the strong influence of American movies before the Pacific War. Sato (1982, p.31) writes that a distinguishing feature of modern Japan, including cinema, is the complicated mix between traditional culture and Western imports so that 'it is difficult even for the Japanese to distinguish between them'.

Modes of production in different political contexts

Classic Hollywood also refers to a particular capitalist mode of film production which sets strict limits on individual innovation. Its apogee, in the 1930s and 1940s, took the form of monopolistic, monolithic and hierarchical studio systems, which have been likened to factory production or, given that each film is unique, serial manufacture. This system was adopted in Japan and, to a much lesser extent, in China before 1949 where it was afterwards reorganized according to state-controlled, but still highly centralized, soviet models. Even with the vehement Chinese rejection of Hollywood after 1949, certain Hollywood practices, such as production stages, remain common in China as well as in Taiwan, Hong Kong, Japan and the West.

In different ways, on the home fronts, the Japanese and Chinese film industries contested Hollywood's dominance. This arose in part because of the political conditions in which the various cinemas developed. The Second World War, in particular, affected film making.

In the pre-war period, many Japanese film makers studied abroad, actor/director Kinugasa with Eisenstein, for example; Hollywood films were remade, such as *The Adventures of Robin Hood* and Griffith's *Broken Blossoms* (twice); and both the star system and the Hollywood studio model were copied. By the late 1920s, this mastery of the medium combined with Japanese aesthetics and social concerns to produce an original Japanese cinema which ran counter to Hollywood in many ways. For example, the short-lived genre of 'tendency films' adopted a Marxist position. It rejected Hollywood, centring on contemporary social problems in a style influenced by Italian neo-realism and Soviet cinema's experiments with montage.

In the Second World War period, all foreign films were banned and all Japanese film scripts had to be approved by the censors. Wartime films, which treated war as a kind of spiritual training ground, tended to stress group solidarity and self-sacrifice rather than the portrayal of an evil enemy. With the post-war occupation period American films returned, and the Supreme Command of the Allied Powers (SCAP), under General MacArthur, condemned and confiscated 225 of the 554 Japanese wartime films. SCAP also censored all films showing feudal values such as swordplay (but not gunfights), loyalty to a lord, and the degradation of women and children. This effectively meant banning one of the two main types of Japanese movies, 'period dramas', as distinct from 'contemporary dramas'. At the same time SCAP promoted kissing in movies, for example, as a democratizing influence.

During the 1950s, Japanese studios maintained control of all phases of the industry. Under the studio system, directors began to examine Japanese behaviour during the war, such as Shindo Kaneto in *Children of the Atom Bomb* (1952) and Ichikawa Kon in *Harp of Burma* (1956). A famous series examined the trauma of the atomic bomb. The *Godzilla* film (1954) originally had an anti-nuclear message as Godzilla is awakened by undersea nuclear testing. It inspired sixteen sequels and many more monsters like Rodan and Mothra. While the series was influenced by American films, such as *King Kong* (1933) and *Beast from Twenty Thousand Fathoms* (1953), it also symbolically re-enacted a problematic US–Japan relationship and a Cold War mentality. Numerous critics have also noted that the moral decay and physical violence in Kurosawa's famous film *Rashomon* (1950) – about a rape but including the 'democratizing' kiss, prolonged and passionate between rapist and victim – also come from the Japanese experience of variously the bomb, the war and US occupation.

Like Japan, American influence dominated the Chinese movie scene until the War of Resistance against Japan (1931–45), the Chinese term for the Japanese invasion and the Second World War. In 1929, for example, 90 per cent of the films shown in China were American. China's film industry was centred on Shanghai but, like the country itself, much more chaotic than the studio systems of Hollywood or Japan. Film grew along with Chinese nationalism and revolution until, combined with left-wing cultural policy, it offered a strong critique of Western film. In 1930, Lu Xun (1881–1936), China's greatest twentieth-century writer, added a postscript to his translation of a Japanese text on film and propaganda: 'European and US imperialists dispose of their old guns to give us war and unrest, then they use old films to astound and stupefy us' (Leyda, 1972, p.61). When the Japanese invaded China in 1931 they, not the Western imperialist powers, became the main enemy – on the battlefield and on the screen – until the Civil War period (1946–49) when America, again, became an arch-villain because of military support given to the Nationalists under Chiang Kai-shek. These enmities remained for half a century. Even in the post-Mao period, scenes of the Japanese invasion remain some of the most compelling in the new cinema; examples from international prize-winning films include the chilling sequence of Japanese soldiers skinning a Chinese alive before his village in *Red Sorghum* (1987) and vast vistas of death and destruction in *To Live* (1993).

The war background is therefore crucial to understanding both Japan's and China's film industry this century. The crisis of Japanese invasion gave Chinese leftist war films a revolutionary excitement and patriotic fervour. Nationalist and Japanese repression meant the left-wing film industry was dispersed, chaotic, and underground.

> the most dramatic, and the most astonishing, period of Chinese film history is the maintenance of an active underground movement in the film industry for almost twenty years [1931–49]. More than any other factor this record distinguishes Chinese films from the films of other countries
>
> (Leyda, 1972, p.71)

Leyda adds that what is more extraordinary is the fact that these films, made in 'exceptional, bitter, difficult, and often bloody circumstances', are better than films of any other period, except in recent times. Nevertheless, American influence lingered. For example, *Street Angel* (1937), a left-wing Chinese classic from this period, was based on an American film of the same name.

When the Chinese Communist Party won power in 1949, the Chinese film industry divided into what are usually seen as separate national

*Wartime: death and destruction (*To Live*)*

cinemas, in Taiwan, Hong Kong and China itself. By the end of the century, all three cinemas are vital and increasingly intertwined. Taiwan boasts world-class directors, such as Hou Xiaoxian. Hong Kong's industry, revitalized in the 1980s by directors returning from study in America and Europe, now produces more films each year than Hollywood – Jackie Chan movies and *A Chinese Ghost Story* series are well-known examples. All three cinemas have retained characteristics of the Hollywood studio system – albeit along Soviet lines in the PRC, where studios were state-owned under the Ministry of Culture, hierarchical, and subject to strict censorship and production targets. Cultural authorities insisted on art with 'Chinese characteristics' and carefully controlled films for mass education according to set formulae. Western films were banned. In China, the century of cinema was also a century of struggle for revolution, independence and national status.

In Hollywood, Japan and China, the studio system excluded much experimentation outside the commercial or state-controlled guidelines dominating the respective film industries. It was only with the onslaught of television and the decline of audiences for centralized studio productions that space was made for alternative and independent film making. In America, film lost its status as the most popular art in the 1950s. By 1970, in Japan, moviegoers dropped to less than a quarter of the peak of over a billion viewers in 1958; Daiei studio went bankrupt in 1971 while Nikkatsu studio saved itself only by capitalizing on so-called 'roman-porno' (romantic pornography) films which were quickly produced on a low budget with indirect sex scenes. This loss of audience led to New Wave cinema in Japan in the late 1960s with commercial studios promoted young directors to stem the tide. In China, where television arrived much later as mass entertainment, the record of 29 billion viewers in 1978 fell to about 18 billion a decade later. However, China's New Wave in the 1980s is more directly attributable to the decline in state control of film studios, with studio heads in the provinces allowing young film makers, now called the Fifth Generation, to direct for the first time. This young directorial talent led to national *and* international cinema industries in both countries.

The New Wave cinemas of both countries were strongly political and involved rethinking their own societies. Japan's New Wave arose in part out of a sense of betrayal when the Japanese-American Security Pact was renewed in 1959, despite one of the largest mass movements against it in Japan's history. A frequent symbol is disaffected and alienated youth. Oshima's *Night and Fog in Japan* (1960), for example, was explicitly set around the politics of the post-war period, juxtaposed against the student protests surrounding the renewal of the Security Pact. It passed through the commercial studio process because the film superficially focused on a wedding but was quickly withdrawn on its fourth day of release because of its overt politics. Thus, the New Wave from 1960 to 1970, when the leftist student movement declined, represents a political as well as cinematic *avant-garde*.

New Wave cinema in China also happened because of political change: the opening up of China under Deng Xiaoping in the late 1970s. The ramifications touched all aspects of life, including the commercialization of studio production so that commercial successes could pay for less popular, exploratory Fifth Generation cinema. Unlike their Japanese counterparts two decades previously, the new film makers' politics were covert to bypass the censorship system – at the studio, central government, distribution and exhibition levels. Also unlike their Japanese counterparts, Chinese films looked inwards at re-telling China's own recent history rather than outwards. Despite the deliberate ambiguity in many of China's New Wave films, the censors caught on and many were either distributed in pitifully small numbers or banned outright, although some were shown internationally.

By the end of the century, it is clear that national cinemas face two problems. The first is that the revitalization in New Wave cinemas did not stop television's assault on film audiences. Independent productions, such as those by China's young Sixth Generation directors, have partly replaced the monolithic studio systems in all three countries, with many films becoming part of television's menu after initial screenings. A second problem is that Japan's New Wave was short-lived and China's Fifth or Sixth Generation films are not popular with ordinary Chinese. Yet even Chinese schoolchildren know of Rambo and Schwarzenegger. Only Hong Kong audiences consistently prefer their own films, which pulse with a Chinese idiom – be it ghosts or *gongfu* (kung fu) – alongside aspects of Hollywood's successful formula: entertainment, action, a strong storyline, and a star system. These films are popular with predominantly, but not only, Chinese audiences everywhere.

In summary, at the beginning of this section it was posited that one way of defining national cinemas lay in their differences from Hollywood. This answer is incomplete. While Hollywood's influence was profound, the different historical backgrounds of Japan and China clearly shaped their industries. Within Asian scholarship, such differences are emphasized by explanations which place film within a context of rapid socio-cultural change and political struggle. But national cinemas may also be explained in terms of film language itself: narrative and aesthetics.

10.5   Narrative

What is involved in viewing a film from another culture? One answer is that we have to adjust our established ways of seeing. This section looks, first, at different story-telling techniques, or modes of narration, in Hollywood, Japanese and Chinese cinemas at different times in their histories. This is a way of formally decoding film, focusing on the text. We then look at how an audience's nationality and point of view can change the emotional response and ways of interpreting particular films. This way of reading is beyond the text; it is cross-cultural.

Modes of narration

In the case of Hollywood, American films were recognized as 'a classical art' just four decades after the beginnings of cinema a century ago. This included certain conventions that focus on telling a story realistically, but invisibly, through techniques such as continuity editing. Because of the pervasiveness of Hollywood, we have certain expectations about how filmic stories are told. This relates to narrative: 'a chain of events in cause–effect relationship occurring in time and space', schematized in Table 10.1 as a major part of film form (Bordwell and Thompson, 1990, p.55).

The classical Hollywood mode of narration is based on psychologically defined characters who struggle to solve a problem or to attain a goal, within a linear continuum of time and space. Story information fills the spaces and unambiguous story-telling is the primary formal concern (see Table 10.1). Films often begin with a rupture or enigma which is resolved in the classical 'happy ending', or in some other sense of closure. Hitchcock's *North by Northwest* (1959) is an example of classical film making, motivated by character, causally tight, and based around a mystery involving suspense and surprise until it is solved. The hero gets both the baddies *and* the girl in the end.

Socialist–realist film making in China represents a different mode of narration; it is based on historical materialism and soviet cinematic techniques rather than on Hollywood. Like Hollywood, however, these Chinese films are filled with story information, exhibit unambiguous closures, and are causally tight but around the logic of revolutionary progress rather than characterization. The forces of light (the revolution) take on the forces of darkness (capitalism, imperialism and feudalism) in

these films which heighten the drama through gestures and lighting from theatre, especially Beijing Opera, China's best known form of traditional drama. In the Cultural Revolution period (1966–76) the majority of the few films available were, in fact, of revolutionary model operas which subsumed all other art forms. Deng Xiaoping complained that Chinese art was reduced to 'a single flower blossoming'. New Wave Chinese cinema arose partly as a reaction to this stereotype, a desperate need to do something different, to explore film language away from the 'walking stick' of drama and opera.

In Japan, viewers and film makers tend to think in terms of what appears real to the senses and emotions. They expect to come away from a film more with a clear feeling than with intellectual or ideological understanding. The emphasis is on mood and tone, rather than on plot; on character, rather than on narrative. Japanese films show a concern with sequence but not necessarily with narrative sequence. In fact, they could adhere to a more illogical qualitative progression which links through association. A dramatic or tight closure is not so common.

This emphasis on mood is evident in the works of Ozu Yasujiro (1903–1963), called the 'most Japanese' of all film directors. He excelled in dramas of middle-class domestic life, a sub-genre of contemporary drama films. He disliked drama and obvious plots, claiming they bored him. In such films as

Table 10.1 *Film form[1]*

Formal system		Stylistic system
Narrative (narration or distribution of story information)	*Non-narrative*	*Patterned/significant use of techniques (codes)*
Story	**Categorical**	***Mise-en-scène*: what is filmed**
presented plus inferred information	grouping parts which organize knowledge	from drama, meaning to 'stage an event' in space/time
Plot	**Rhetorical**	setting, costume, lighting, figure expression/ movement combine in a stylistic system
everything visibly and audibly presented on-screen	persuasive argument to form opinion	look at characters and action plus spatial and temporal factors, such as composition and depth
Causality	**Abstract**	
takes place in time	abstract, visual, sonic qualities: shape, colour	**Cinematography: how it is filmed**
characters are usually the agents of action in classical Hollywood		cinematography means 'writing in movement' 'the photographic qualities, the framing and the duration of the shot'; camera movement, etc.
	Associational	shot = a take in shooting or one uninterrupted image in the final film
Time	image juxtaposition to suggest emotion	
story and plot time may differ, e.g. *North by Northwest*		**Editing: joining camera takes; techniques governing relations among shots**
		co-ordinating shots: fade-out, dissolve, wipe, cut
Space		continuity editing: cutting to maintain continuous narrative action
note on-screen and off-screen space		
		Sound: soundtrack combining speech, music and sound effects

[1] Film form refers to the system of relationships among parts of the film, e.g. beginning, end, pattern, techniques, in which the formal system interacts with the stylistic system within the total film.

Source: adapted from Bordwell and Thompson (1990, p.274)

Green Tea over Rice (1952), he avoided exaggerated action and complex movement, concentrating instead on the simple sadness and happiness of the Japanese middle class. He used intermittent shots of inanimate objects or seemingly unrelated natural scenes in 'poetic cutaways' or 'pillow shots', a phrase from classical poetry referring to techniques of representing another plane of reality, or a different internal logic. If you look at Table 10.1, then this mode of narration emphasizes stylistic patterns, split from the plot.

Desser (1988, pp.16–17) isolates three types of Japanese narrative, each linked to a major period of cinema. Ozu's work is an example of the transcendental, classical Japanese narrative. Desser distinguishes this from the psychological paradigm of later modern film makers, such as Kurosawa Akira in the 1950s, where there is more emphasis on individuals, linear time, and a faster pace, all reminiscent of Hollywood. Because of this, Kurosawa is considered by many to be the most 'Western' of Japan's classical film directors. New Wave cinema, such as Oshima's *Night and Fog in Japan*, rebelled against post-war humanism and introduced a narrative that reflected the alienation of Japan's youth.

China's New Wave exhibits aspects of all the above narrative styles. After three decades of isolation, the Fifth Generation directors consciously set out to be exploratory. They produced an art cinema – different in characterization, plot, theme, location, cinematography and style – which adapted a rich variety of narrative forms from their own tradition and from overseas. Thus, *Yellow Earth* (1984) cannot be read according to Hollywood narrative conventions, although it does use motifs from socialist–realism; overall, it gently unfolds like a landscape painting and works according to mythic seasonal time akin to Japanese transcendental narratives. Huang Jianxin's *Black Cannon Incident* (1985), conversely, resolutely sets itself in the problematic of the modern, with flashbacks emphasizing the alienation of ordinary Chinese in the system. Zhang Yimou's film *Judou* (1989) adopts a tight narrative which Chinese critics have likened to the inexorable logic of Greek tragedy. Other films use documentary styles, such as China's best-known Sixth Generation director, Zhang Yuan. This film movement has been called 'post-socialist' because it offers a pastiche and play with film language rather than placing itself in a single classical or modern, Chinese or Western, paradigm. It does, however, have much in common with art cinema, an international mode which emerged in Europe and was adapted by some Hollywood and Japanese film makers, such as Kurosawa.

Cross-cultural reading

Films tell stories which have meaning for their audiences. Hollywood films typically glorify and lavishly display an ideal American way of life. The same film or film tradition may, however, mean different things to different people, or peoples. Lu Xun's comment on American films as a means of stupefying colonized peoples is just one example. Later, under Mao, Hollywood was seen as the epitome of bourgeois decadence. Under Deng Xiaoping, numerous campaigns see Western culture as spiritually polluting.

This sort of verbal assault on Hollywood also came from the West where Marxists belonging to the Frankfurt School, for example, criticized the industrialization of film. In the 1940s, Hollywood during its heyday was castigated as 'a dream factory', 'Hollywood is engaged in the mass production of prefabricated daydreams. It tries to adapt the American dream that all men are created equal, to the view that all men's dreams should be made equal' (Powdermaker, quoted in Kerr, 1986, p.9).

This quote makes clear that Hollywood is about American dreams, ostensibly for '[hu]man[kind]'. It is a national cinema. It is sobering even for Australians – so habituated to Hollywood movies that they seem our own – to tour Tinseltown, see the locations of scenes in famous films, and be told by the guide that Hollywood is the centre of the world. The view from the periphery may be somewhat different.

Sato explains the Japanese response. In the pre-Second World War period, the optimism of American films was preferred over more gloomy European films. Even when Hollywood was being criticized as contaminating the Japanese before the Pacific War, the great director Itami Mansaku responded:

> The first thing we learned from American movies was a fast-paced life-style ... the next, a lively manner and a readiness to take decisive action. Lastly, we learned to take an affirmative, purposeful, sometimes even combative attitude toward life, and to value dearly our pride as human beings, fearing no man – in short, their first-class, tough philosophy on how to get on in the world.
>
> (Sato, 1982, pp.33–7)

With Americanization under occupation, the majority of Japanese youth thought of America as an ideal society because SCAP showed only positive films. Indeed, Sato attributes the Japanese economic miracle partly to the fact that 'thirty years ago Japanese boys made the startling discovery, through movies, that any American could own a car and a refrigerator, and they endeavoured to catch up'.

The Chinese responded to both Japanese and Hollywood movies. The most famous example is Lu Xun's reaction to seeing Japanese lantern slides, a precursor to film, of Japanese victories in the war against Russia early in the twentieth century. This was a favourite patriotic theme in pictures of the time. The slides showed the Japanese execution of a Chinese traitor in Manchuria during the war, with fellow Chinese apathetically standing around looking on. Lu Xun's response was the exact opposite of the Japanese. Disgusted, he left medicine in Japan for literature in China to change the spirit of the Chinese people. The rest is history: his stories, as Mao Zedong said, were the 'very road' for the culture of a new and independent China.

Despite this, American movies clearly had a seductive power over Chinese pre-war audiences and even post-revolution audiences if they had access. In the 1920s, a left-wing dramatist claimed films were one of mankind's three major achievements (the others being wine and music) because they created 'dreams in broad daylight' (Lee, quoted in Berry, 1991, p.7). More recently, one of the criticisms of Jiang Qing, Mao Zedong's wife, was that she secretly watched old American movies, particularly those featuring Garbo, while she was involved in running mass campaigns against the three main evils of the Cultural Revolution: American imperialism – which definitely included films – Soviet revisionism, and Chinese feudalism. This love–hate Chinese response is replayed in a 1990s Chinese television soap, *A Beijinger in New York*. A young Beijing man assaults the heart of corporate America, New York, to make his fortune and sample the wares so conspicuously displayed as desirable in films. The wares include money, discos, cars and white prostitutes whom he treats as commodities to be bought and used. This serial visually enacts Western feminist criticisms of Hollywood films as objectifying and fetishizing the female for male viewing pleasure. It was a Chinese blockbuster.

Chinese authorities as well as some highly-placed critics object to any filmic display of Chinese backwardness or exotica/erotica for the titillation of foreign audiences, just as they objected to Hollywood's display of the fruits of capitalism. This has been a major criticism of such directors as Zhang Yimou and led to the banning of many of his films within China. The authorities want to control how China appears to the West, as well as how the West appears within China. They are therefore enraged by Zhang Yuan's evasion of the censorship system by directly placing his films at international festivals. While censorship has softened since the Cultural Revolution, it is still a potent force which partly explains not only the narrative ambiguity in much Fifth Generation film but also what films will be released and where. Famous directors often bypass this by packaging their films as joint ventures with overseas partners, especially from Hong Kong.

In summary, there are different ways of understanding films from other cultures. The first focuses on narrative as part of film form. In its various national adaptations, the Hollywood formula is the most successful in terms of longevity and circulation. But, second, for ideological, political and cultural reasons, this has been rejected at various times across the Asia-Pacific. Asian cinemas have, instead, drawn on alternative modes of narration and ways of seeing, influenced by their own histories and by local or European, especially Marxist, traditions. They use film to tell their own stories. Film this century shows that Japan tried, and China insisted on, defining their own centrality within their own countries and within the region.

10.6 Aesthetics

National cinemas may be defined not only in terms of their histories, stories and modes of story-telling but also in terms of film style. Film is images and sound, involving the senses of seeing and hearing. This relates to aesthetics: the science of the conditions of sensuous perception. To test how you perceive and understand films from other cultures, we suggest that you borrow either or both of the famous films we focus on in this section – *Rashomon* (1950) and *Yellow Earth* (1984). Are they familiar, confusing, incomprehensible or just different? Can you learn to read them?

In this section, we use these and other films to look at film's stylistic systems (see Table 10.1), film imagery (*mise-en-scène*, cinematography and editing) and sound. This returns us to the theme of audience expectations – to instances where such famous films have ruptured national expectations because of radical stylistic changes, changes which have adjusted ways of seeing, both nationally and internationally. The point is that developments in film style – whether Asian, American or European – involve a complex transformation of national and international influences and responses. Film and audiences are not static.

Moving images

Film is light and sound. Photography means writing in light and, its extension, cinematography, means writing in movement. The primary and earliest film medium is therefore moving images. Artistic as well as literary traditions in different cultures have, therefore, influenced the ways in which filmic images may be framed and shot. Thus, Hollywood, Japanese and Chinese cinemas have all drawn upon ways to realize stories from the visual and performing arts, with some debate as to which of these is the primary force behind the development of film.

The answer is that, while both are important, the unconscious or deliberate selection of familiar artistic techniques or backdrops may result in a certain 'look' for a film or film movement. Thus, Hollywood strives for 'realism', based on naturalistic truth to historical fact and Aristotelian truth to the probable, through the use of techniques such as perspective and shadow-filled Rembrandtish lighting. However, the notion of realism is problematic because lighting, for example, primarily works to motivate the narrative in classical Hollywood and may change according to genre – high-key for comedies and low-key for horror and crime stories. In Chinese socialist–realist cinema, stylized operatic-style lighting was used on sets while Japanese films preferred the full, flat lighting of the *kabuki* stage. Thus, the performing arts, particularly story-telling and opera, were crucial influences in Japanese and Chinese film styles. But they were influences which were transformed by the film medium.

Rashomon, for example, is classified as a 'period drama' but it breaks all the conventions of this supposedly Japanese-style of film, influenced by the performing arts. While it is set in the Heian period, its content is not feudal, as expected of this genre, but a very modern commentary on the relativity and subjectivity of reality itself. When Kurosawa was asked why the film was so popular, he disingenuously said it was because it was about rape. But it is a rape – and murder – presented in flashbacks four times, in four different ways, and in four versions by the rapist (a bandit), the woman, her murdered husband and the only witness: a woodcutter. All lie, even the ghost of the husband, and although there is general agreement about the rape there is no agreement about the murder. The film does not give a definitive 'true' version and there was much confusion, even in the studio which produced it, as to what the film actually meant. Indeed, some enterprising theatres revived the *benshi* (the narrator in silent movies) to explain the narrative while the film was being shown. Richie (in Kurosawa, 1987, p.4) claims it is the mystery and 'elliptical intent' of the film which has captured audiences around the world; like both modern art and the tendency to retain the raw material in Japanese arts, the film 'gives us our original vision – that of children – and lets us observe rock as rock, wood as

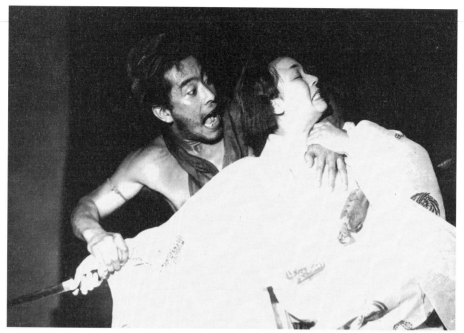

Rape and murder deep in the forest, and (below) the bandit, the husband and the woodcutter (Rashomon)

wood, and ... allows us to examine human behaviour undistracted by plot, undisturbed by logic'. Indeed, Kurosawa deliberately simplified the medium, returning to the aesthetic potential of the old silent black-and-white movies.

The confused reception was exacerbated by adventurous stylistic techniques, which highlighted the ostensible lack of meaning. The camera always moves. Commenting on his cinematographer's work, Kurosawa (1987, p.119) said that 'the introductory section in particular, which leads the viewer through the light and shadow of the forest into a world where the human heart loses its way, was truly magnificent camerawork'. The rape and murder take place in a dark, dense forest, giving the film its keynote: light and darkness, sunlight and shadows, to reveal the dark complexities of the heart. The film makers broke taboos such as actually filming the sun through the trees so that the film, influenced by French 1920s *avant-garde* films, is an exercise in cinematic impressionism.

There was a mixed response to the film in Japan and it was shelved after two or three runs. The studio reluctantly allowed it to enter the then premier film festival in Venice in 1951 and Japanese critics were shocked when it won first prize and then an Academy award. This was ultimately explained by deciding that foreigners liked exoticism rather than that they could understand a Japanese film, a prejudice shared by Chinese critics who berated Zhang Yimou's *Raise the Red Lantern* as exotic fare for foreigners. This underestimates the Western viewer. Richie (in Kurosawa, 1987, p.20) states that '*Rashomon* speaks to everyone, not just to the Japanese', especially as its analytical and speculative aspects appeal to Western reasoning. It still lives, being frequently re-shown in Japan and the West.

Yellow Earth was not popular or widely understood in China at all. The camera hardly moves; it was too slow and alienated audiences habituated over decades to stereotyped storylines and didactic endings. The authorities distributed only fifteen copies and criticized it for showing China's backwardness. As we said, it was Hong Kong audiences who rapturously recognized its quality in 1985.

At one level, the story is a cliché: a good looking Party official, collecting folk songs, visits a poor peasant family as they eke out a living in the middle reaches of the Yellow River, cradle of both Chinese civilization and the Chinese Communist Party. But rather than saving this family's children – from unwelcome marriage, drought or just plain hopelessness – the usual revolutionary happy ending is subverted by Party rules regarding membership and, despite promises, the official's late return to the village. Instead, the girl drowns trying to reach the revolutionaries in Yan'an and the Party official is filmed as a mirage, always coming but never arriving. The film returns peasants to their millennia-old intimacy with the land without the usual Party mediation in revolutionary stories; indeed, the Party is a mere passer-by. This subversion, play and ultimate rejection of the stereotype is part of the film's power and ambiguous endings became part of Fifth Generation cinema. The story is, however, carried not so much by the narrative but by images and sound. It stimulated a whole debate in China about film aesthetics.

Cuiqiao and Hanhan beside the river that nurtures and destroys them
(Yellow Earth)

Kurosawa (1987, p.116) said that *Rashomon* 'is like a strange picture scroll that is unrolled and displayed by the ego'. *Yellow Earth* has also been likened to traditional landscape painting, particularly the local Chang'an school which was influenced by the region's folk art. From this school, the film makers borrowed the high horizons so that the 'mother' land, shot as a warm yellow at dusk, fills the frame just as it fills peoples' lives. It dwarfs the characters who dot the landscape dressed in the red, black and white of folk art. The characters emerge from, and disappear into, the land, rather than exiting left or right. They are ultimately destroyed by it when drought descends. 'Empty' shots of sky, sun, loess and water – akin to the white spaces in traditional painting – have an active meaning in the film by depicting the human lives as inseparable from the vast, elemental and starkly beautiful landscape which both nurtures and destroys them. The film makers claim this as the unifying inner essence of the film which, as with the Japanese sense of mimesis, comes from a Daoist (or Zen) emphasis on the inner laws of nature rather than on the outward appearance of things.

This dwarfing or decentring of actors within a natural frame is also part of Japanese classical cinema. They do not tend to place a high value on frontality or on the typical shot/reaction shot along an invisible 180 degree axis which is a Hollywood convention. They are also reticent about the close-up. Kurosawa's stylistic changes involved breaking all these conventions in *Rashomon*.

In the case of innovative films, therefore, both foreign and home film audiences may need to adjust established ways of seeing. This is demonstrated by the local and overseas receptions of Kurosawa's *Rashomon* and Chen Kaige's *Yellow Earth* as well as Zhang Yimou's *Raise the Red Lantern*. Both *Rashomon* and *Yellow Earth* are unmistakable examples of their own national cinemas, yet they both departed from accepted conventions. Both are also part of international art cinema, challenging established notions of film style with deviations from the classical canon: an authorial voice, ambiguity, unusual angles, prohibited camera movements and character subjectivities. Both films are now considered masterpieces.

This cross-cultural appreciation also applies to Hollywood. It was not Americans but French who declared Hollywood film making a classical art. It was French members of the 1960s' New Wave who recognized the artistry of certain Hollywood directors, such as Hitchcock, while other French critics countered that this emerged from the classical tradition of American cinema itself. In short, the insider/outsider dichotomy does not necessarily work when viewing other national cinemas.

Sound

Sound, especially dialogue, unmistakably places a film within national, ethnic or linguistic borders. Because film is primarily a visual medium, the importance of comprehensible dialogue is often overlooked as a signature of a national cinema. Clearly, translated sub-titles detract from the immediacy which is part of film's power. But sound in film is more than speech; it is also music, sound effects and, equally important, silence. The soundtrack may augment or alter our perception of the images.

The power of sound to intensify an atmosphere and unify a narrative is evident in the final battle between bandits and samurai protecting a village in Kurosawa's *Seven Samurai* (1954), recognized as an international cinema classic. A combination of sound effects – the swelling drumbeat of horses' hooves, screams, whinnies, bows, swords, gunshots and sobbing – abruptly punctuate the background sound of wind and rain and dramatize crucial battle scenes across the whole village. Relentless rain at the Rashomon gate, once the great architectural symbol of feudal Japan, is filmed with black ink, augmenting the mood of cynicism and desolation in the opening scenes of *Rashomon* where three characters introduce the rape and frame the following story. Indeed, Anderson and Richie (1982, p.325) claim that a rain scene is almost obligatory in Japanese films, where it is used for full dramatic effect.

In *Yellow Earth*, songs and silence overlay the images. The Party official came to the region to collect folk songs but he never learns that the girl he romances about the revolution is the region's best-known singer. Her songs are hidden among other, more public, men's songs and reveal her heart only to the audience. In the last scene of the now empty land, the dead girl's disembodied song echoes in the silence, full of desire to be saved by the Party – which we now know it has manifestly failed to do.

In summary, Hollywood, Japan and China each draw on their own and other artistic traditions, transforming them into films whose styles belong to recognizable national cinemas or film movements. If we see an action-packed *gongfu* movie, with Chinese characters and Cantonese dialogue, we place it as Hong Kong cinema or cloned from Hong Kong. The originality of Japanese and Chinese cinemas, however, also lies in the ways in which different story-telling styles and traditional aesthetics combined with Western cinemas to allow new ways of looking at their own worlds through film. Film aesthetics and audience responses may differ but a formalist approach to film studies (as in Table 10.1) suggests we must first go through classical Hollywood before we can go beyond it to understand national and alternative cinemas (Bordwell *et al.*, 1985, p.385).

10.7 Conclusion

Classical (and contemporary) Hollywood's influence on national cinemas is profound, especially when we take a formalist rather than a historical approach to Asian cinemas. Hollywood certainly set standards for film making and viewing, with national cinemas presenting alternatives in stories, modes of narration and styles. It has been suggested that the very dominance of Hollywood stimulated nationalist film strategies to differentiate domestic products and compete in the international market, with Australia as one recent example (Bordwell *et al.*, 1985, p.371). If, however, we take the Asian approach of seeing film histories in the context of socio-cultural change this century, then cinema is part of the struggle for nationhood, the desire to see 'dreams in daylight' in one's own language and location. The Chinese called it 'new wine in old bottles'; that is, the film medium developed in the West is a bottle which, decanted, could contain the new wine of revolution. This nationalism is integral to the dynamic of Asia-Pacific cultures this century. While nation-states matter, the politics, economics and identities of national cinemas will also matter.

A parallel theme in this chapter is the international flavour of films, influences and audiences. Indeed, film may be considered the first global mass medium. It is true that all three countries have controlled film content to different extents and at different times. But Japan now owns part of Hollywood. China has taken control of its own culture but this will become more difficult with the 'deep democracy' of consumer choice in the new global information market – there are already problems in censoring the internet. Throughout the twentieth century, nations may have been at war but film makers, critics and audiences have also co-operated and learned across cultures. The simple fact is, however, that everyone in the region knows Hollywood but only the committed and curious know much about Japanese and Chinese films outside their home audiences.

This is set to change with the telecommunications revolution at the end of the twentieth century. This chapter suggests that national cinemas must ultimately be seen in a global context. The USA has dominated the twentieth century, but the struggle to control national media will continue and the Asia-Pacific is one region where it will be fought out. It is unlikely that the Chinese, in particular, will allow international conglomerates, unless Chinese, to control their media – whether film, television or new forms of telecommunications. Perhaps in the twenty-first century, with the rising economic power of Asian nations and new forms of media, there may be a different dominatrix.

Filmography

The Adventures of Robin Hood (USA, 1938) William Keighley and Michael Curtis.

The Beast from Twenty Thousand Fathoms (USA, 1953) Eugène Lourié.

Black Cannon Incident (*Heipao Shijian*, PRC, 1985) Huang Jianxin.

Broken Blossoms (USA, 1919) D.W. Griffith.

Children of the Atom Bomb (or *Children of Hiroshima*) (*Genbaku no Ko*, Japan, 1952) Shindo Kaneto.

A Chinese Ghost Story (Hong Kong, 1987) Ching Siu-tung.

Godzilla (*Gojira*, Japan, 1954) Honda Inoshiro.

(The Flavour of) Green Tea over Rice (*Ochazuke no Aji*, Japan, 1952) Ozu Yasujiro.

Harp of Burma (*Biruma no Tategoto*, Japan, 1956) Ichikawa Kon.

In the Realm of the Senses (*Ai no Koriida*, Japan, 1976) Oshima Nagisa.

Judou (PRC, 1989) Zhang Yimou.

King Kong (USA, 1933) Merian C. Cooper and Ernest B. Schoedsack.

Night and Fog in Japan (*Nihon no Yoru to Kiri*, Japan, 1960) Oshima Nagisa.

North by Northwest (USA, 1959) Alfred Hitchcock.

Raise the Red Lantern (*Dahong Denglong Gaogao Gua*, PRC, 1992) Zhang Yimou.

Rashomon (Japan, 1950) Kurosawa Akira.

Red Sorghum (*Hong Gaoliang*, PRC, 1987) Zhang Yimou.

Seven Samurai (*Shichinin no Samurai*, Japan, 1954) Kurosawa Akira.

Street Angel (PRC, 1937).

To Live (PRC, 1993) Zhang Yimou.

Yellow Earth (*Huang Tudi*, PRC, 1984) Chen Kaige.

References

Anderson, J.L. and Richie, D. (1982) *The Japanese Film: Art and Industry*, expanded edn, Princeton, Princeton University Press.

Berry, C. (ed.) (1991) *Perspectives on Chinese Cinema*, London, British Film Institute.

Bordwell, D. and Thompson, K. (1990) *Film Art, An Introduction*, 3rd edn, New York, McGraw Hill.

Bordwell, D., Staiger, J. and Thompson, K. (1985) *The Classical Hollywood Cinema, Film Style and Mode of Production to 1960*, London, Routledge.

Chow, R. (1995) *Primitive Passions: Visuality, Sexuality, Ethnography, and Contemporary Chinese Cinema*, New York, Columbia University Press.

Desser, D. (1988) *Eros plus Massacre, an Introduction to Japanese New Wave Cinema*, Bloomington, Indiana University Press.

Kerr, P. (1986) *The Hollywood Film Industry*, London, Routledge and Kegan Paul.

Kuhn, A. (1994) *Women's Pictures, Feminism and the Cinema*, 2nd edn, London, Verso.

Kurosawa, A. (director) (1987) *Rashomon*, Richie, D. (ed.), Rutgers, The State University.

Leyda, J. (1972) *Dianying, Electric Shadows, an Account of Films and the Film Audience in China*, Cambridge, Mass., The MIT Press.

Sato, Tadao (1982) *Currents in Japanese Cinema*, translated by Barrett, G., New York, Kodansha International.

Further reading

Cambridge University Press is publishing a new series on national cinemas, including Japan and China, which should provide an up-to-date reference (scheduled for publication in 2000).

See Bordwell and Thompson (1990) for a glossary of key terms. Most of these are everyday terms but not necessarily used with the precision required for reading about film.

Bordwell, D., Staiger, J. and Thompson, K. (1985) *The Classical Hollywood Cinema, Film Style and Mode of Production to 1960*, London, Routledge.

Clarke, P. (1987) *Chinese Cinema: Culture and Politics since 1949*, New York, Cambridge University Press.

Desser, D. (1988) *Eros plus Massacre, an Introduction to Japanese New Wave Cinema*, Bloomington, Indiana University Press.

Erlich, L.C. and Desser, D. (1994) *Cinematic Landscapes, Observations on the Visual Arts and Cinema of China and Japan*, Austin, University of Texas Press.

Erlich, L. and Ma Ning (1990) 'Course college file: East Asian cinema', *Journal of Film and Video*, vol.42, no.2, pp.53–70.

Kerr, P. (1986) *The Hollywood Film Industry*, London, Routledge and Kegan Paul.

Kuhn, A. (1994) *Women's Pictures, Feminism and the Cinema*, 2nd edn, London, Verso.

Noletti, A. Jr. and Desser, D. (1992) *Reframing Japanese Cinema*, Bloomington, Indiana University Press.

Acknowledgements to Maureen Todhunter for research assistance on this chapter.

The culture of politics

Stephanie Lawson

11.1 Introduction

Since the end of the Cold War, and the virtual demise of left/right ideological commitments as the primary point of reference for international political relations, the idea of 'culture' has emerged as a major candidate for filling much of the conceptual vacuum. It is now frequently used both as the major explanatory category for a host of political and economic developments as well as an important basis on which leaders from a number of non-Western regions have justified certain approaches to politics. This has been reflected very clearly in the contemporary 'Asian values debate' – especially where matters concerning human rights and democracy are at issue. A number of political leaders and academic commentators from the Asia-Pacific region have emphasized what they see as the crucial role played by culture in determining patterns of social, political and economic behaviour. Seen in its most positive light, 'Asian culture' is taken to be basically responsible for the remarkable economic growth, rising standards of living, increased longevity, and low urban crime rates that have characterized development in parts of the region. Thus Singapore's Prime Minister, Goh Chok Tong, says that correct economic policies are not all that is needed to preserve the living standards now enjoyed in the island state. Continuing success can only be assured by: 'a sense of community and nationhood, a disciplined and hard working people, strong moral values and family ties'. These values, he says, are related directly to 'Asian culture' which 'puts group interest above that of the individual' (Goh, 1994).

The achievements of places like Singapore are usually contrasted with a fairly negative image of the 'West'. The latter is depicted as a cultural or civilizational entity in social and economic decline. Goh Chok Tong's speech in fact spent more time on the apparent decline of the West than it did on the achievements of his own country. Other political leaders in the region such as Malaysia's Prime Minister, Dr Mahathir Mohamad, have also been very vocal in condemning this perceived trend in the West – highlighting drug use, urban crime, single parenthood, divorce, and homosexuality as serious social problems. In turn, these problems have been linked to Western political practices and institutions which are seen as undermining important values associated with respect and responsibility within the family, and cohesion, harmony and consensus in the broader society. More specifically, social problems in the West have been linked to an 'excess' of democracy which, according to its critics in some parts of Asia, has bred virulent forms of individualism and grasping materialism at the expense of positive community-oriented values and spiritual well-being. A similar exercise in imagery has been carried out by some political elites in the island states of the South Pacific region. This has given rise to an idealized social and political abstraction known as the 'Pacific Way' whose major proponents have frequently condemned Western democracy as inherently unfit for local consumption.

In assessments such as these, entities like 'Asia' and 'the West' are depicted as distinct monolithic blocs, each of which can be characterized according to certain cultural qualities. Although some proponents of the 'Asian values' or 'Pacific Way' theses believe it possible to blend the best aspects of Western and Asian or Pacific traditions, the terms in which the arguments are usually framed imply that 'Western values' are essentially incompatible with 'Asian values' or the 'Pacific Way'. These ideas have been supported by the 'clash of civilizations' thesis put forward in a 1993 article by the well-known US scholar of comparative and international politics, Samuel Huntington, and elaborated in a book-length version in 1996. His basic hypothesis, as set out in the original article, is that the fundamental source of conflict in the future will be cultural. He puts forward the idea of 'civilizational' entities which are defined as the highest cultural groupings of people and 'the broadest level of cultural identity people have short of that which distinguishes humans from other species' (Huntington, 1993, pp.22, 24).

Huntington goes on to identify a variety of broad civilizational groupings, including up to eight mega-groupings comprising Western, Confucian, Japanese, Islamic, Hindu, Slavic-Orthodox, Latin American and 'possibly' African (the people of the Pacific Islands are evidently not numerous enough to count). Any one of these could presumably come into conflict with any other. However, he draws the broadest line of potential conflict – and the most likely – between the West and 'the Rest'. According to Huntington, the main factors which mark the West off from just about any other civilizational entity are found in certain unique cultural concepts: 'Western ideas of individualism, liberalism, constitutionalism, human rights, equality, liberty, the rule of law, democracy, free markets, the separation of church and state, often have little resonance in Islamic, Confucian, Japanese, Hindu, Buddhist or Orthodox cultures' (Huntington, 1993, p.40). Cultural difference in Huntington's scheme also implies cultural determinism. While he notes that cultures can change, and that the nature of their impact on politics can vary, the 'major differences in political and economic development among civilizations are clearly rooted in their different cultures' (Huntington, 1996, p.29).

Huntington's ideas could just as easily have been put forward by any commentator supporting the 'Asian values' thesis, especially in the context of debates about human rights and democracy in the region. These are portrayed as essentially 'Western' ideas and therefore alien to 'Asian cultural values'. It has been suggested, however, that notwithstanding the increasing regularity with which the pan-Asian vision is being recited by some political leaders around the region, and which may seem to lend credence to Huntington's ideas, the crude culturalist argument that is put forward is 'both anthropologically naïve and politically paranoid' (Wright-Neville, 1995, p.4). This raises questions concerned not only with the relationship between culture and politics, but with the whole issue of cultural relativism. In addition, one of the most interesting questions of all that emerges is: what is 'the West'?

This last question is especially important when thinking about the place of countries like Canada, Australia, New Zealand and the USA in the Asia-Pacific region. Although they are certainly part of the broad geographic region, many would argue that their predominantly European cultural and political heritage places them in a quite different category from, say, the countries of other regional areas such as South-East Asia or the south-west Pacific. This is certainly the line taken by Prime Minister Mahathir in various dealings with Australia, and is reflected as well in his desire to exclude 'culturally non-Asian' countries from certain regional organizations such as the proposed East Asian Economic Caucus. But the implications of 'anti-Westernism' extend beyond the region as well and have the potential to seriously affect other relations. For example, in 1994 Mahathir became involved in a serious trade dispute with the UK following allegations in the British press of corruption surrounding a defence contract and British aid for the construction of a dam in Malaysia. Apart from placing a ban on the awarding of government contracts to British businesses, Mahathir engaged in some inverted racialist flourishes which drew on historic images of British colonial racism. He stated that Malaysians must, quite obviously, be corrupt 'because they are not British and not white' (quoted in Lawson, 1996a, p.122).

Such attitudes have been further encouraged by the eruption in Australia of the 'Pauline Hanson phenomenon' following the election of a renegade Liberal Party member to the Federal Parliament in 1996 who has since campaigned against further Asian immigration into Australia (as well as for major cuts in spending on programmes for Australian Aborigines). With the infamous 'White Australia policy' less than 30 years in the past and the current Prime Minister, John Howard, showing very weak leadership against Ms Hanson's position, Australia's image in the region has been badly tarnished despite concerted official efforts over the last few decades to promote a firm social basis for multiculturalism. The irony is that Ms Hanson has, like proponents of the Asian values thesis themselves and more sophisticated commentators like Huntington, focused much attention on alleged cultural differences between Asians and 'mainstream' Australians to justify her position.

In approaching all these issues we must start with the idea of culture itself, especially since some of the most important political questions derive from how culture is conceptualized in the first place. We then examine some aspects of the relationship between culture and the state in the Asian region, paying particular attention to how culture is understood in terms of national identity. Finally, we look more closely at the key features of the 'Asian values' debate and its implications for contemporary concerns about democracy and human rights. Although some reference will be made to similar issues in the island states of the South Pacific, it is not possible to deal as comprehensively with this part of the broad region simply for reasons of space. With respect to the conceptual aspects of the discussion, it should also be noted at the start that no firm answers to such questions as 'what is culture?' and 'what role does it play in political life?' will be provided. Indeed, one of the points of this chapter is to emphasize the virtual unanswerability of such questions. This is a valuable lesson in itself, especially if it increases the level of uncertainty about the extent to which we can ever assign cause and effect by reference to 'culture' in the study of politics.

11.2   The idea of culture

The idea of culture has a long and complex history, but we must confine ourselves to aspects of its conceptualization that are directly relevant to the issues outlined above. The best starting point is a particular perspective on culture developed largely within the discipline of anthropology. This perspective placed almost all matters concerning socio-political values, beliefs, practices and institutions within the framework of an over-arching conception of culture first put forward in 1871: 'Culture or Civilization, taken in its widest ethnographic sense, is that complex whole which includes knowledge, belief, art, morals, law, custom, and any other capabilities and habits acquired by man as a member of society' (Edward Tylor reproduced in Applebaum, 1987, p.37). Following this early influential definition, culture was usually thought of as referring to the entire way of life of a human community, rather than to one or other of its attributes. One major problem with using 'culture' to denote a distinct (but abstract) totality is that definitions of the totality itself – of the culture – inevitably tend to emphasize the idea of difference between so-called cultures, rather than any qualities that they may have in common (Firth quoted in Kroeber and Kluckholn, 1963, p.269). In addition, some perspectives hold that people 'behave differently as adults because their cultures are different'. It has also been argued that people are not only 'born into different habitual ways of life', but that they are destined to follow these ways 'because they have no choice' (Davis and Dollard quoted in Kroeber and Kluckholn, 1963, p.91).

Let us consider several major problems which emerge from these ideas about culture. First, conceptions which focus only on difference between groups invariably gloss over contradictions that may arise within groups. As societies have become increasingly diverse because of human population movements – a phenomenon that has become particularly widespread in the twentieth century – it is scarcely possible to speak any longer of discrete cultural groups living in discrete geographical spaces. Despite these obvious problems, many social scientists have continued to write as though cultures were clearly delineated entities with distinct boundaries. One scholar has recently pointed out that there has been a strong tendency among anthropologists to treat cultural groups (other than one's own) as if they were 'distinctive communities somehow set apart from modern history'. The same scholar also takes issue with other social scientists (mainly political scientists) who have used distorting top-down formulations in their treatment of culture that focus on the power of the state and formal institutions (Warren, 1993, pp.1, 4). Arguably, these sort of perspectives ignore the mass of people 'at the bottom' and hear authoritative expressions of culture only from those who have the power to make themselves heard, that is, from elites.

The second major problem is that the behaviour of either whole groups, or individuals within a group, is seen as more or less fixed in an overall cultural pattern that has been inherited from previous generations, will be lived out by the present generation, and passed on more or less intact to the next one. The most simplistic view would hold that people born into, say, an autocratic 'Confucian society', will so thoroughly absorb the 'Confucian value system' that they will forever live according to a certain scheme of filial piety, automatically accept their allotted sphere and duties in the family, pay due respect to their superiors outside the family, and generally obey political authorities without question, thereby playing their proper part in maintaining social stability, harmony and order. The overall result (at least according to this stereotyped view of Confucian society), must be a very static social order that reproduces itself without significant change generation after generation. However, nobody who is even marginally acquainted with the political and social history of countries in the so-called East Asian 'Confucian culture area' could seriously subscribe to such a view.

A third important issue is the extent to which culture may be equated with a value system. Another significant development in anthropological thought earlier this century has been extremely influential in shaping the way social scientists have approached this particular issue. The concept of a unique bounded culture inevitably gives rise to the view that such 'a culture' possesses its own unique frame of reference for all moral values – of what is right or wrong, good or bad, acceptable or unacceptable. Anthropology has long been imbued with the idea that different cultural groups and their moral codes should not be ranked in some kind of hierarchy, but treated with equal respect and judged only in terms of their own moral precepts and standards (rather than those of 'outsiders'). Thus the anthropological doctrine of cultural relativism, in summary, held that 'there is an irreducible diversity among cultures because each culture is a unique whole with parts so intertwined that none of them can be understood or evaluated without reference to the other parts and to the cultural whole, the so-called pattern of culture'. It follows that: 'Ethics, as part of a culture, cannot be understood or evaluated apart from the distinct world of the society to which it belongs' (Ladd, 1973, pp.2–3). It should be mentioned that the original doctrine of cultural relativism was extremely useful in opposing racism and acting as an antidote for chauvinistic forms of ethnocentrism. In relation to morality, however, the doctrine has posed some important problems for such issues as human rights because cultural relativism clearly implies ethical relativism, and it is this problem that underscores much of the contemporary debate about 'Asian values'.

Before leaving the general topic of culture and its treatment in social scientific thought, we should also look briefly at the concept of 'political culture'. This concept emerged within the discipline of political science (although it was influenced by anthropology as well), and has been quite influential in shaping perspectives on the relationship between culture and politics. It was originally used as a concept for addressing the problem of developing a 'democratic political culture' within societies at large. The impetus for this task was initially provided by the experience of Europe in the first part of the twentieth century which showed quite clearly that Western states were hardly invulnerable to doctrines such as fascism. Following the original formulation of ideas, however, the concerns of the political culture school were extended to political development in the 'new nations' of the decolonizing Third World.

The working definition of 'the political culture of a nation' adopted by its early proponents was 'the particular distribution of patterns of orientation towards political objects among members of the nation' (Almond and Verba [1965] 1989, p.13). This was not very different from previous studies in 'national character'. The latter concept had been taken to refer to relatively enduring personality characteristics and patterns of behaviour that predominated among the adult members of a given society. Although studies in both national character and political culture recognized that individual attitudes varied within a given national population, and that there were often significant sub-cultures, both were none the less based on the idea that the boundary of a political culture coincided with a larger political system, and in most cases this was the state. It followed that the entities in possession of a political culture were, in fact, states.

A major problem with the use of the political culture concept, at least in this way, is that it has lent itself to deterministic perspectives. A prime example is a major monograph on power and politics in Asia, the opening lines of which claim that:

> Throughout Asia today the drama of politics is being played out by leaders and followers whose roles are largely prescribed by culturally determined concepts about the nature of power ... Briefly put, my thesis is that political power is extraordinarily sensitive to cultural nuances, and that, therefore, cultural variations are decisive in determining the course of political development.
>
> (Pye, 1985, p.vii)

To summarize briefly, the general discussion in this section has aimed to raise the level of critical awareness about the complexity of issues surrounding conceptions of culture in general, and the relationship between culture and politics in particular. Special attention has been drawn to difficulties with earlier anthropological ideas about culture and the implications of these for cultural determinism and relativism – although I should add that anthropologists today do not necessarily endorse such ideas. At the very least, I hope this section has unsettled some of the more commonly accepted ideas about culture and its role in politics. What I have not done, of course, is provide anything resembling a definite answer to such questions as what culture actually is, and what role it might play in shaping political life. As suggested in the introduction, one purpose of the discussion has been to demonstrate just how problematic such questions are. This is important for approaching the next section in which we look more closely at how the idea of culture is implicated in perceptions of state and nation in the Asian region, and how these perceptions in turn influence ideas about political legitimacy and authority.

11.3   Culture and the state

In light of the issues introduced above, we shall now consider the nature of the modern sovereign state and its relationship to 'culture', especially since the state is another entity that is often depicted as some kind of totality with distinct boundaries. At the simplest level, states are legal/political units and few would argue with the proposition that they do in fact possess relatively clear – although by no means permanent – territorial boundaries. Each state (of which there are now close to 200 in the world) bears a distinctive name to denote the territory claimed as its sovereign space. Leaving aside questions concerning the artificiality of many territorial boundaries, especially those drawn by colonial powers, this seems fairly straightforward. What is more problematic is that each state is meant to encompass not simply a physical territory, but a 'nation' as well. This is clearly expressed in the widely used misnomer 'nation-state'. Keeping in mind that 'nation' is commonly defined in terms of a people who share a common, unique, cultural heritage, let us now very briefly consider the idea of a 'Chinese nation' and a 'Chinese culture'. Does the legal-territorial state of China encompass a single Chinese nation which is in possession of a single, coherent, homogeneous Chinese culture? And is such a culture sufficiently unique that it is clearly distinct from say, 'Korean culture', 'Thai culture', 'Singaporean culture', 'Indonesian culture', 'Papua New Guinea culture' and so on? Is there, in fact, any such thing as a uniform and unique 'national culture' in any of these places? And if so, on what exactly is it based?

The set of cases in which the boundaries of a state coincide more or less exactly with those of an identifiable ethnic or cultural group is extremely small. Indeed, it has been suggested that there is but one genuine case in the entire world – Iceland. The very idea of a 'national culture' is therefore highly problematic, and not just in the most obvious places like Papua New Guinea where around 800 different languages are spoken. But although most observers would admit that there are almost no states in the world whose borders contain a single 'nation' in possession of a unique and homogeneous culture, there is still a strong tendency, going back decades in disciplines such as international relations, to treat states more or less in this way, or at least to gloss over differences at the sub-national level as relatively unimportant. This has been supported to some extent by the work of the political culture school. As we have seen, although political culture theory has recognized that states may contain sub-cultures and minority groups, the theory has none the less tended to treat the state as the primary receptacle of a culture.

Another good example of this kind of thinking is evident in the work of the anthropologist, Ruth Benedict. Her well-known study, *The Chrysanthemum and the Sword*, is about 'what makes Japan a nation of Japanese' (Benedict [1954] 1994, p.13). I have suggested already that the idea that any state possesses some kind of identifiable 'national character' is simplistic to say the least – even in the case of Japan which appears to be relatively homogeneous. Simplistic ideas, however, especially in politics, are often among the most appealing, influential and powerful. We should therefore resist the temptation to think in terms of 'national cultures' which are bounded by lines on the map of states, and to consider instead the idea of intra-state cultural pluralism. In other words, we should consider differences, not so much between countries, as within them.

Japan is certainly *comparatively* homogeneous, especially *vis-à-vis* most other countries in the region. Indeed, it is widely regarded as one of the most homogeneous countries in the world. But the emphasis on the 'comparative' is very important because even in this instance, cultural homogeneity cannot be simply assumed. Apart from the fact that Japan is home to the indigenous Ainu people and to resident minorities from other countries in the region, the linguistic record in Japan indicates a cultural diversity among 'mainstream' Japanese that has not often been acknowledged. Japanese dialects, for instance, differ from each other even more than European languages such as Spanish and Italian, and 'standard Japanese' (a Tokyo dialect) did not emerge as the lingua franca until this century (Morton, 1996, p.52). This underscores the fact that the degree of cultural homogeneity evident today is of fairly recent origin. One writer points out that the use of the word *bunka* – as in the phrase *Nihon bunka* (Japanese culture) – is itself really very modern and did not make much impression on popular consciousness until about the 1920s (Morris-Suzuki, 1995, p.761).

More generally, it has also been pointed out that there is more than one Japan. Like virtually any other place in the world, Japan is a contested site and the 'various groups that make up its citizenry agree only in the most general terms on what constitutes its cultural, social, and political practices'. It is interesting to note, however, that both Western commentators and Japanese chroniclers have, at least until recently, tended to emphasize continuity and homogeneity over change and diversity, with an emphasis on what are assumed to be 'fundamental constants underlying Japanese culture and history' (Morton, 1996, pp.50–1, 72). The stereotyped views that many outsiders have of 'Japanese culture', and which have often been promoted within Japan by conservative groups as well, have therefore contributed to reducing the complexity of Japan to a uni-dimensional singularity in the name of a 'national culture'.

Another example of a relatively homogeneous country is the South Pacific island state of Tonga. But the question of cultural identity in Tonga is interesting from another point of view, and that concerns the extent to which 'traditional culture', even if it is almost totally homogeneous in some respects, must be decisive in determining political forms. Tonga has one of the most conservative political systems in the region. It is ruled by a monarch who presides over a parliament consisting largely of his own appointees and representatives of an hereditary aristocracy, while members elected by the people are in the minority. According to its supporters, the legitimacy of the present system is anchored in a body of traditional Tongan culture that goes back at least a thousand years. This system, however, has been under attack in recent years from a local pro-democracy movement which is seeking extensive institutional changes to ensure greater accountability and responsiveness. For this movement, the fact that the existing system is 'traditional' is not accepted as a bar to change and reform. Other critics point out that many elements of the present system have, in any case, been introduced via British influences and it is therefore inauthentic anyway. Questions of authenticity aside, the local pro-democracy movement refuses to accept that 'Tongan culture', as interpreted by the entrenched elites, will forever determine that ordinary Tongans must remain in a position of political subordination to an hereditary class of rulers (see Lawson, 1996b).

Another point worth emphasizing is that where expressions of national culture or shared national values occur in a political context, these are very often tied to issues involving political legitimacy. In Thailand, for example, the state religion of Buddhism constitutes 'a powerful element of both nationalist rhetoric and of social and political control', although this has not gone unchallenged by sects contesting official religious interpretations (Hewison, 1993, p.180). In the case of Vietnam, it has been pointed out that Ho Chi Minh successfully used selected aspects of Vietnamese history, tradition and culture to fortify the goals of national liberation and building socialism, as well as the historic and moral leadership role that the Vietnamese Communist Party had played in realizing them (Alagappa, 1995a, p.314). In other words, a unified vision of Vietnamese history, tradition and culture was used to serve the political purpose of rallying support for certain goals. That this has been largely successful is in spite of an actual diversity of experiences within Vietnam. As Vasavakul points out in her analysis of political legitimacy in socialist Vietnam:

> there is no single Vietnamese tradition, no single Vietnamese people, and no single Vietnamese peasantry: Vietnamese 'traditional' values vary from region to region, even from village to village … the concept of 'Vietnamese tradition' itself may be a construct created by power holders to legitimize their control of political authority.
>
> (Vasavakul, 1995, p.260)

Cultural diversity is much more visible in most other countries in the Asia-Pacific. This is a result not only of the presence of settler populations – usually from other parts of the region – but also because the territorial boundaries of modern states generally encompass more than one distinctive indigenous ethnic or cultural group. Such diversity unquestionably lies behind the strong emphasis placed on 'nation-building' by post-colonial regimes in many places. In turn, this has often resulted in the imaginative construction of official national unifying ideologies which seek to instil a common national ethos among their diverse citizenries. Historically, the perceived or alleged need for strong national unity has been further reinforced by Cold War fears – real, imagined or deliberately manufactured – relating to external threats and internal subversion. The three South-East Asian states of Indonesia, Malaysia and Singapore provide good examples of this and we shall therefore look at these in a little more detail.

Perhaps the best-known example of a national unifying ideology is Indonesia's official state philosophy of Pancasila. This philosophy is meant to unite a highly diverse population in common loyalty to the post-independent state bequeathed by Dutch colonialism. The diversity of the people populating the archipelago may be illustrated by reference to Indonesia's ethnic and linguistic pluralism. In addition to the largest ethnic group, the Javanese, who comprise almost half of Indonesia's total population of about 165 million, there are several lesser, but still significant groups such as the Acehnese, Bataks and Minangkabaus in Sumatra, the Sundanese in West Java, the Balinese, the Bugis and Makassar of southern Sulawesi, not to mention hundreds of other smaller groups as well as ethnic Chinese. This diversity is further complicated by a significant level of religious pluralism for although almost 90 per cent of the population is officially designated as Muslim, some of the groups receiving this designation practice highly syncretized forms which almost constitute distinct religions in their own right. And this additional dimension works to pluralize the Javanese as well, a group which might otherwise appear to be monolithic (Liddle, 1996, p.65).

Over the decades since independence, Pancasila has been rigidly institutionalized in an effort to rally this diverse population around a common set of principles. The Sanskrit word means literally 'five principles', and each of these are highly abstract: belief in God; Indonesian unity; humanitarianism; democracy; and social justice. Since 1985, all social and political organizations have been required to adopt Pancasila as their sole philosophical base. Furthermore, the denial or repudiation of Pancasila by any individual citizen is regarded as seditious. At the same time, however, cultural diversity within the state is explicitly acknowledged and reflected in the official state motto: Unity in Diversity.

But the degree to which expressions of 'cultural diversity' are permitted, especially if these were to become manifest in political activity, is obviously limited by the requirements of a 'national interest' which seeks to impose a high degree of political uniformity and obedience to the ruling party. One commentator reports that both President Sukarno and President Suharto have 'used it as an ideological weapon to delimit the boundaries of acceptable political contestation' (Liddle, 1996, p.79). So while a certain level of pluralism in 'harmless' cultural activities and practices is accepted, political pluralism is regarded as a challenge to the legitimacy of the government and a threat to the state itself.

Indonesia's close neighbours, Singapore and Malaysia, have also adopted national ideologies, although they have not been as rigidly institutionalized. There are also important contextual differences which have shaped their official expression. For one thing, the ideologies are based either explicitly or implicitly on the culture of certain dominant groups, namely the Malays in Malaysia and the Chinese in Singapore – or at least on what is assumed to be 'the culture' of these groups. In Malaysia, organized official efforts to propagate a National Cultural Policy (NCP) may be traced to a government-sponsored congress in 1971 that adopted three basic principles through which the policy was to be defined. First, it was to be based on the 'indigenous culture' of the region (that is, Malay culture); second, as a slight moderation of the first principle, suitable elements from other cultures were to be accepted; and third, to again reinforce the first principle, Islam was to be recognized as an important component. The emphasis on Malay culture and language and the religion of Islam may be seen as reflecting the determination of Malay political leaders to retain a paramount position over the large population of non-Malays. The latter is comprised largely of ethnic Chinese who number around 30 per cent of the population, as well as South Asians and some other minorities. One problem with the Malay emphasis is that it has reinforced very strongly the sense of second-class citizenship experienced by non-Malay citizens (Crouch, 1996, p.166).

The Singaporean context is different again. Here, ethnic Chinese comprise about 75 per cent of the citizenry with Malays and South Asians making up most of the remainder. Given the numerical, political, economic and social predominance of the ethnic Chinese, it is therefore not very surprising that Singapore's 'core national values' are often described in cultural terms as essentially Confucian. After all, Confucianism is Chinese (although, as we have seen, it is also often used to characterize a broader East Asian cultural area consisting of the two Koreas, Japan, and Taiwan as well as China). Singapore's 'Chineseness' – and the Confucianism that is often thought to accompany it automatically – is thus sometimes regarded as an interesting anomaly in an otherwise Malay-dominated sub-region of South-East Asia. But membership of the category 'ethnic Chinese' does not mean that one is automatically endowed with a Confucian world-view. In the case of Singapore's Chinese population it has been pointed out that, as an immigrant population drawn largely from displaced peasantry of southern China, the understanding of Confucianism that most Singaporean Chinese brought with them was, at best, a limited and 'distilled folk version'. Furthermore, the best educated among these immigrants were more likely to be influenced by the 'modernist' movements in post-1900 China 'in which Confucianism was ridiculed and rejected rather than followed' (Chua, 1995, pp.28–9).

The most important question, however, is not so much whether Singapore really is a 'Confucian society', but why an official programme of Confucianization was pursued by the government. What this means for the politics of culture and identity not only in Singapore, but in the wider region, represents one of the most interesting stories of the contemporary 'Asian values' debate. Indeed, the Singaporean political elite is often regarded as having instigated the original debate as far back as the 1970s. We shall next explore this historical development in terms of a phenomenon which has become known over the past two decades as the 'invention of tradition'. In relation to this, it should be noted that all traditions are 'invented' in the sense that they are socially constructed rather than naturally occurring phenomena, but the phrase has been used more specifically in recent years to denote a conscious exercise in construction that is deliberately designed to achieve certain social, economic or political ends.

As with Indonesia and Malaysia, the prime mover in the promulgation of national core values in Singapore has been the government. And, like its neighbours, Singapore has been dominated by a single government for decades – the People's Action Party (PAP) having been in power since 1959. In the earlier years of its rule, the PAP under Lee Kwan Yew instituted a programme of rapid economic development and modernization, and the relatively high standards of living now enjoyed by the majority of Singaporeans is testimony to the government's undoubted success in the economic sphere. At the same time, the government has made various attempts to reorient the 'values' of its population. At first this meant the repudiation of certain 'traditional' attitudes which might impede modern developmental objectives. By the mid 1970s, however, there was a change in thinking, and a new kind of rhetoric about the value of certain traditional values, especially 'Confucian values', began to emerge. By the late 1970s, more concerted efforts were being made to promote the 'cultural health' of the ethnic Chinese population through a 'speak more Mandarin' campaign. This language (which was spoken as a first language by fewer than 1 per cent of the ethnic Chinese population) was thought more appropriate for instilling a stronger sense of traditional 'Chineseness' and Confucian values than was the case with the more commonly spoken dialects of Hokkein, Cantonese, Teochew, Hainanese and Hakka. Mandarin was also thought to constitute a stronger buffer against the allegedly corrosive influence of the West.

These efforts were supplemented in the early 1980s by a new educational programme which involved the establishment of an Institute of East Asian Philosophies (IEAP). Its main official purpose was to promote the understanding of Confucian philosophy, especially among ethnic Chinese. The secondary school curriculum was also modified to make room for courses on religious knowledge and Confucian ethics. This was a direct response to Prime Minister Lee's concern about 'Westernization' and the need to strengthen traditional Asian virtues and values in school programmes. The religious education school programme, however, was later abandoned due to its apparent role in increasing religious tensions between various groups. In addition, the rhetoric associated with Confucianism has been modified over the years because of its exclusion of the non-Chinese sectors of the population. The IEAP itself was not actually dissolved, but transformed into an institute concerned with the study of the East Asian 'economic miracle' – although this miracle is, at least rhetorically, also now associated with Confucianism (see Khong, 1995, p.125).

Two interesting points emerge from this story. First, whereas 'Confucianism' was previously held responsible for economic stagnation, it is now being credited with predisposing societies to high levels of growth and development. This in itself should make us more wary of ideas about cultural determinism. Second, and as already mentioned, Singaporean Chinese have never had a particularly strong Confucian tradition, and to say that Singapore is 'traditionally' a Confucian society is very misleading. Also, up until the 1970s the government had, in the name of rational, modern economic development, done its best to eradicate whatever elements of 'Chinese tradition' had persisted to that time. The government's subsequent selection and promotion of the Confucian tradition – which of course is but one of a number of 'Chinese traditions' – therefore constitutes a classic case of the 'invention of tradition' for political purposes. As one commentator has wryly noted: 'The Confucian campaign was instituted by the ruling elite not because the citizenry was seeking a deeper understanding of its heritage, but rather because the leadership wanted to establish a set of cultural values it believed would further its policies' (Khong, 1995, p.125).

The more recent moderation of explicit Confucianization in Singapore, however, does not mean that the government has abandoned its efforts to inculcate certain social and political values in specific opposition to so-called Western values. Rather, it has become much more common to hear of a vaguely defined set of national 'core values'. Not surprisingly, these are very similar to what are promoted more generally in the region as 'Asian values'. In 1989, the Singaporean President, Wee Kim Wee, began an officially sponsored debate 'on national ideology' by announcing what its core values were to be: placing society above self; upholding the family as the basic building block of society; resolving major issues through consensus instead of contention; and stressing religious tolerance and harmony. These are scarcely different from the original set of values originally designated as 'Confucian'. The stress on community before self, and the importance of the family are much the same, and the ideas of consensus and harmony in the political and social spheres are the precise outcomes associated with obedience and duty in the Confucian scheme. On the announcement of the 'core values', the concerns previously voiced by the non-Chinese sectors were by no means put to rest. Said one Malay MP – from the PAP itself – the 'inherent nature of a national ideology and the heterogeneity of our society begs the question: whose values do we adopt?' (reported in Balakrishnan, 1989, p.37). In a society marked by a high degree of cultural diversity, this is indeed an important question to ask.

I have so far concentrated on 'deconstructing' some of the states in the region in order to demonstrate that it is almost impossible to find a case where a single culture is shared by all people within the borders of a state. I have also been concerned to show that expressions of 'national culture' are often carefully engineered and imposed from above – that is, by political elites – for clearly instrumental purposes. This does not mean, however, that 'the state' has failed to provide a focus of loyalty for numerous of its citizens, nor does it mean that nationalism has failed to make its mark as a significant force in the region. Far from it. The case of Japan in the late 1930s and 1940s stands as a prime example of just how powerful a force nationalism driven by the state can be.

Some have argued that (the experience of Japan excepted) nationalism in Asia has generally been a positive force: 'for peoples long victimized by colonialism, such sentiments mean empowerment, freedom and an assertion of national dignity'. Nationalism, according to this view, has therefore been 'an invaluable catalyst' for post-independence nation-building with Asian leaders over the past 50 years having unified and mobilized their 'freshly liberated peoples by reminding them of their traditional cultural or ethnic strengths' (*Asiaweek*, 9 February 1996, pp.22–3).

There is, however, much more to nationalism than this. As suggested earlier, a broad sense of nationalism has also worked to suppress many of the smaller cultural traditions and ethnic groups. And the rise of new nation-states in places like Indonesia, as well as the transformation of older ones such as Vietnam and Thailand, has put local cultural practices under considerable pressure:

> Right from the start, nationalists turned to traditional forms of cultural communication in order to spread their ideas, and once the new nation-states were established, they began to demand greater cultural orthodoxy to reinforce state identity. These demands of orthodoxy fell hard on ethnic minorities whose cultures were valued less than those of the dominant centre ... Even where minority and majority cultures are preserved in institutes of national culture, the vitality of these cultures has been stifled.
>
> (Mackerras, 1995, p.520)

So far from nationalism necessarily being a positive expression of a country's national cultural integrity or pride, it may well entail one group's domination over other smaller and weaker groups.

We turn next to the debate about 'Asian values', especially as this concerns such issues as democracy and human rights. As we shall see, certain ideas of 'Asian democracy' and an 'Asian' interpretation of human rights have been put forward by a number of political leaders in the region. A broad notion of Asian identity, connected firmly to some kind of cultural base, is of course essential to these ideas in that it serves as an important point of reference and legitimation for whatever model or account of democracy and/or human rights is put forward. Formulations of this kind have much in common with nationalist constructions of identity and so the kind of 'regionalism' evident in the process of conceptualizing an Asian identity in order to authenticate, for example, a specifically Asian model of democracy, may be seen as an extension of the nationalist device (see Lawson, 1996a, p.116).

11.4   The Asian values debate

Singapore's 'shared values' idea has provided a substantial basis for the wider Asian values debate. Indeed, the latter is in many ways simply a projection of the Singaporean debate onto the regional and international stages, and echoed with only slight variations by some other political leaders in the region. Moreover, the values which are promoted as 'Asian' and said to be shared widely across the region are still basically constructed from selected elements of the Confucian value system. One writer suggests that Lee Kwan Yew simply changed the name of his discourse from 'Confucian' to 'Asian', without really changing its substance because the former term was too restrictive. 'Asia', on the other hand, was an 'empty term' waiting to be filled (Callahan, 1996, p.10).

The general idea of Asian values has also allowed some authoritarian leaders to put forward a model of government called 'Asian democracy' as an alternative to 'Western democracy'. There is not the space to dwell at length on the details of this model (and in fact these details are not really discussed in much depth by its proponents) but the main features of 'Asian democracy' are usually set out primarily in contrast with Western forms. So while 'Western democracy' is characterized as based on dissensus, conflict, disunity and individualism, 'Asian democracy' is evidently imbued with such values as consensus, harmony, unity and community before self. When formulated in this way, the latter set of values may appear quite admirable and desirable, while the former appear to be just the opposite. But to accept these characterizations at face value is to yield too readily to the simplicity of the scheme. Any student of politics with even a modicum of insight into such ideologies as fascism, for example, can readily recall that ideas of harmony, consensus and unity, when harnessed to doctrines of organic statism under strong leadership, can produce quite abhorrent political consequences.

Given the relatively authoritarian perspectives of the proponents of 'Asian democracy', it is also unsurprising that civil and political rights are given a low priority in the model. This means significant limitations on the right of political oppositions to organize – indeed, on the right to oppose the government at all. At the same time, authoritarian leaders generally say that they give priority to social, cultural and economic rights. In contrast, the West is depicted as being concerned essentially with political and civil rights, which is taken to reflect individualistic approaches to rights in general. Both approaches are linked, respectively, to 'Western culture' or 'Asian culture'. As with some of the constructions considered earlier, the simplicity of the scheme is certainly appealing.

Another perspective on these issues is linked more explicitly to the international political context. Referring to the Bangkok Regional Preparatory meeting which preceded the World Conference on Human Rights in Vienna in 1993, one report said that: 'Human rights were no longer dismissed as a tool of foreign oppression but were promoted as a means of asserting Asian distinctiveness from Western dominated norms of social and political order'. To illustrate this point, it was noted that 'the weight China gives to certain rights, such as the right to subsistence over political and civil rights, demonstrates that vast differences remain between Chinese interpretations of international human rights documents and Western interpretations'. The report went on to suggest that even though 'the voices of Asian citizens are obstructed by the political control of the state', there might yet be 'a distinction rooted in Asian culture between some Western and some Asian cultural views of human beings' (see Bauer, 1995, pp.1–2). These views, however, are not necessarily – or even usually – shared by many non-governmental organization representatives from the Asian region. Indeed the NGO community generally is far more likely to reject culturalist positions and embrace more universalist approaches to human rights.

NGOs have become more influential in recent years and are now more likely to gain media attention as well. However, those with the power to make themselves heard most effectively are, as mentioned earlier, unquestionably those with the most political power. In this context, it is also interesting to note that there is at least one level at which a certain coherence does operate within the region in terms of culture, and that is at the level of political elites. In other words, one can identify certain 'cultural' commonalities among those promoting ideas such as 'Asian values' and the 'Pacific Way' in terms of an elite, regional political culture. Ironically, the elites participating in this regional culture are usually among the most 'Westernized' in terms of the language they use (English), educational background, life-style and income bracket. One well known critic of the Pacific Way has noted the extent to which this label denotes a 'club' for political elites operating through a number of Pacific Island institutions and bureaucracies. He argues that the Pacific Island elites themselves have become increasingly homogenized as a distinct class in their own right. This has come about largely through the adoption of Western life-styles at the expense of their own local cultures. Moreover, it has distanced them significantly from the ordinary people of the region (Hau'ofa cited in Lawson 1996b, pp.4–5). It is therefore seen as the height of hypocrisy for elites to resist demands for more democratic participation by appealing to the concept of indigenous cultural traditions which they themselves have largely abandoned.

There are some other obvious informal cross-national or transnational 'communities' that have emerged in the last decade or so, and which could also be described as having gone some way towards developing a certain culture among themselves. These include NGO communities, many of which have formed around common concerns and have often adopted a common (although not identical) approach to issues such as human rights and the environment. There are also powerful business communities. These sometimes have close links with governments but they are not necessarily synonymous with them. The increasing transnationalism of big companies also contributes to the process of building a certain cohesion into some business groups which transcends ethnic or national identities. More detailed discussions of business and economics must be left to other books in this series, but it is important to keep in mind that the development of certain patterns of behaviour and beliefs around business communities and their practices constitutes yet another aspect of culture, and further complicates contemporary issues concerning culture and politics in the region.

In summary, while it must certainly be acknowledged that 'cultural differences' do in fact exist and may be discerned across a considerable range of social, political and economic practices, we should maintain a critical perspective on all situations where the idea of culture is invoked. Certainly, much care must be taken in ascribing cause and effect where culture and politics is concerned. And as much care should be taken in identifying exactly what the unit or group is that is said to possess 'a culture'. For example, whereas the original formulation of the cultural relativist doctrine was in relation to the small-scale societies on which anthropologists usually focused, the frame of reference claimed by proponents of 'Asian democracy' or 'Asian human rights' is of course the whole entity known as 'Asia'. But since there is no single cultural tradition that can be said to apply to the whole of Asia, then there is no framework for a cultural relativist claim about 'Asian' democracy or human rights. Moreover, doctrines of cultural determinism are even less plausible in the context of the Asian values/democracy debate. For example, if 'Asian culture' is inherently incompatible with, or contrary to, the kinds of values that support democratic politics, then how is the record of democracy in many parts of Asia to be explained? This is best addressed via a brief review of the enormous variety of governmental forms found throughout the region which range from liberal democracies through to strong authoritarian regimes.

Japan has maintained a democratic form of government for half a century, even though it was imposed from outside on a conservative society with few apparent liberal elements of its own. More recently, South Korea and Taiwan have each repudiated authoritarianism even though authoritarian government had brought high levels of economic growth and a concomitant increase in standards of living. The cases of Japan,

Korea and Taiwan are especially noteworthy in light of some of the claims made about 'Confucian culture' and its apparently negative consequences for liberal political development, for in all three Confucianism is said to constitute an important and influential tradition – although again, it is not the only tradition in these places. Thailand's political history has certainly been volatile, but support for democracy under a constitutional monarchy is clearly stronger than any form of authoritarianism – especially that of a military regime. In Burma/Myanmar too there is little doubt that the preferences of ordinary people, if given free expression, would be for the pro-democratic (and previously democratically elected) leader, Aung San Suu Kyi, rather than the repressive State Law and Order Restoration Council (SLORC). In the Philippines there is strong support for constitutional government, especially after the experience of the Marcos years, even though democracy by itself is clearly not a simple panacea that is going to miraculously resolve the country's enormous social and economic problems.

If one is to make any broad statements about politics and government in the Asian region at all, then, it can only be in terms which stress considerable variety in political regime types. From the most repressive

Burmese opposition leader and chief of the National League for Democracy party, Aung San Suu Kyi, Rangoon, May 1996

regimes such as those of Burma and China (especially in the latter's rule over Tibet), to what is effectively an absolute monarchy in Brunei, to 'softer' forms of authoritarianism in places like Malaysia, to newly emergent democratic governance in South Korea and Taiwan, and to relatively long-standing democratic regimes in India and Japan, the Asian region displays an enormous range of political diversity which defies any attempt to reduce politics in the region to any one category. This is also just one of the reasons why it is impossible to leap to any firm conclusions about the relationship between politics and culture, especially in terms of the extent to which something called, say, 'Korean culture' let alone 'Asian culture', actually determines political behaviour and institutions.

One of the most useful general commentaries on these issues has been provided by Korea's long-time pro-democracy campaigner, Kim Dae Jung. First, Kim points out that doubts about the applicability of democracy in Asia have been raised mainly by the region's authoritarian leaders, and that most of their arguments about Asian culture and values are simply self-serving. Second, although he agrees that simply foisting alien systems of government indiscriminately on different societies cannot work, the more significant question is whether democracy is a system that really is so alien that it cannot work in the region. He further questions whether democracy has in fact been given much of a chance in places like Singapore at all, given the 'absolute intolerance of dissent' displayed by leaders there. Kim also argues that one can find significant elements of thought in philosophies around the region, including strands of Confucianism, Buddhism and the native Korean religion of Tonghak, that are as profoundly democratic as any of those of the West. Most importantly, however, he suggests that perhaps too much can be made of cultural factors. While undoubtedly important, culture alone does not determine the fate of a society, nor is it immutable. The biggest obstacle to democracy in Asia, he says, is not necessarily the cultural heritage of the region, but rather 'the resistance of authoritarian rulers and their apologists' (Kim, 1994, pp.189–94).

11.5   Conclusion

One of the main purposes of this chapter has been to emphasize the point that reference to 'cultural factors' in political contexts undoubtedly raises many more questions than it purports to answer. Certainly, it must be evident that 'culture' does not have nearly as much explanatory capability in terms of political practice and behaviour as some proponents of the 'Asian values' thesis might have us believe, and even this brief survey of 'culture and politics' in the Asia-Pacific region shows just how problematic any such attempt is. A critical approach to all these matters is therefore vital for developing a sophisticated understanding of how certain perspectives on culture are related to issues of political authority in the region, especially where the interests of political elites are at stake. As one writer has noted, a close study of contemporary politics in the region shows that 'culture' has emerged not so much as the context within which political relations and diplomacy between countries are shaped, but rather as a weapon to be used within the context of political relations and diplomacy (Wright-Neville, 1995, p.3). This indicates that there is an unambiguously instrumental dimension to the very idea of culture in contemporary politics – a theme which emerged quite clearly in our survey of culture, nationalism and the state, as well as in relation to the 'Asian values' debate.

Although I have not spent much time elaborating on the related theme of culture and politics in 'the West', I hope that I have said enough to make it obvious that to take this as a coherent category or point of reference for precise political analysis may be as problematic as 'Asia', especially when the idea of 'the West' is used as an oppositional foil for the construction of a contrasting 'civilizational' entity such as 'Asia'. This is important as well when considering relations between all the countries who claim membership of the wider Asia-Pacific region – and who are indeed members of such regional organizations as the Asia-Pacific Economic Co-operation (APEC) group. This group, and the wider geographic region itself, of course includes the USA, Canada, Australia and New Zealand. Although these countries and a large proportion of their inhabitants do share something in common that may be called 'cultural' because of their respective European-influenced heritage(s), they can hardly be lumped together as constituting a coherent 'Western' entity when it comes to a whole range of political, social, and economic issues and interests. One of the points in drawing attention to the 'Western side' is that the very same discourse tends to gloss over differences within the West as well, making the whole Asia/West dichotomy even more rigid. And apart from the fact that dichotomies are usually highly misleading, if not actually false, this type of thinking does not serve the cause of good political analysis. To accept the stereotypes and simplifications that are produced on both sides of the dichotomy with the aid of concepts such as 'culture' is to perpetuate the discourse of orientalism and all that it implies, as well as an equally problematic discourse of occidentalism.

References

Alagappa, M. (1995a) 'Seeking a more durable basis of authority' in Alagappa, M. (ed.).

Alagappa, M. (ed.) (1995b) *Political Legitimacy in Southeast Asia: the Quest for Moral Authority*, Stanford, Stanford University Press.

Almond, G.A. and Verba, S. (1989) *The Civic Culture: Political Attitudes and Democracy in Five Nations*, Newbury Park, Calif., Sage [first published 1965].

Applebaum, H. (ed.) (1987) *Perspectives in Cultural Anthropology*, Albany, State University of New York.

Balakrishnan, N. (1989) 'Pledge of allegiance: core values touted as antidote to Westernisation', *Far Eastern Economic Review*, 1 February, pp.32–7.

Bauer, J. (1995) 'International human rights and Asian commitment', *Human Rights Dialogue*, vol.3, December, pp.1–5.

Benedict, R. (1994) *The Chrysanthemum and the Sword: Patterns of Japanese Culture*, Rutland, Vt., Charles E. Tuttle [first published 1954].

Callahan, W.A. (1996) 'Rescripting East/West relations, rethinking Asian democracy', *Pacifica Review*, vol.8, no.1, pp.1–25.

Chua, Beng-Huat (1995) *Communitarian Ideology and Democracy in Singapore*, London, Routledge.

Crouch, H. (1996) *Government and Society in Malaysia*, St. Leonards, Allen & Unwin.

Goh Chok Tong (1994) 'Strong values the backbone of success', edited version of National Day Rally Speech reproduced in the *Australian*, 12 September.

Hewison, K. (1993) 'Of regimes, states and pluralities: Thai politics enters the 1990s' in Hewison, K., Robison, R. and Rodan, G. (eds) *Southeast Asia in the 1990s: Authoritarianism, Democracy and Capitalism*, St. Leonards, Allen & Unwin.

Huntington, S. (1993) 'The clash of civilizations?', *Foreign Affairs*, vol.72, no.3, pp.22–49.

Huntington, S. (1996) *The Clash of Civilizations and the Remaking of World Order*, New York, Simon & Schuster.

Khong, Cho-oong (1995) 'Singapore: political legitimacy through managing conformity' in Alagappa, M. (ed.).

Kim Dae Jung (1994) 'Is culture destiny? The myth of Asia's anti-democratic values', *Foreign Affairs*, vol.73, no.6, pp.189–94.

Kroeber, A.L. and Kluckholn, C. (1963) *Culture: a Critical Review of Concepts and Definitions*, New York, Vintage.

Ladd, J. (1973) 'Introduction' in Ladd, J. (ed.) *Ethical Relativism*, Belmont, Calif., Wadsworth.

Lawson, S. (1996a) 'Cultural relativism and democracy: political myths about "Asia" and the "West"' in Robison, R. (ed.) *Pathways to Asia: the Politics of Engagement*, St. Leonards, Allen & Unwin.

Lawson, S. (1996b) *Tradition Versus Democracy in the South Pacific: Fiji, Tonga, and Western Samoa*, Cambridge, Cambridge University Press.

Liddle, W. (1996) *Leadership and Culture in Indonesian Politics*, St. Leonards, Allen & Unwin.

Mackerras, C. (ed.) (1995) *East and Southeast Asia: a Multidisciplinary Survey*, Boulder, Lynne Reinner.

Morris-Suzuki, T. (1995) 'The invention and reinvention of "Japanese culture"', *Journal of Asian Studies*, vol.54, no.3, pp.759–80.

Morton, L. (1996) 'Japan' in Milner, A. and Quilty, M. (eds) *Communities of Thought*, Melbourne, Oxford University Press.

Pye, L.W. with Pye, M.W. (1985) *Asian Power and Politics: the Cultural Dimensions of Authority*, Cambridge, Mass., Belknap Press.

Vasavakul, T. (1995) 'Vietnam: the changing models of legitimation' in Alagappa, M. (ed.).

Warren, K.B. (1993) 'Introduction: revealing conflicts across cultures and disciplines' in Warren, K.B. (ed.) *The Violence Within: Culture and Political Opposition in Divided Nations*, Boulder, Westview Press.

Wright-Neville, D. (1995) 'The politics of Pan Asianism: culture, capitalism and diplomacy in East Asia', *Pacifica Review*, vol.7, no.1, pp.1–26.

Further reading

Foster, R.J. (ed.) (1997) *Nation-Making: Emergent Identities in Postcolonial Melanesia*, Ann Arbor, University of Michigan Press.

Friedman, E. (ed.) (1994) *The Politics of Democratization: Generalizing East Asian Experiences*, Boulder, Westview Press.

Ibraham, A. (1996) *The Asian Renaissance*, Singapore, Times Books International.

Laothamatas, A. (ed.) (1997) *Democratization in Southeast and East Asia*, Singapore, Institute of Southeast Asian Studies.

Leifer, M. (1996) *Dictionary of the Modern Politics of South-East Asia*, 2nd edn, London, Routledge.

Sheridan, G. (ed.) (1995) *Living With Dragons: Australia Confronts its Asian Destiny*, St. Leonards, Allen & Unwin.

Vatikiotis, M.R.J. (1996) *Political Change in Southeast Asia: Trimming the Banyan Tree*, London, Routledge.

Acknowledgements

Grateful acknowledgement is made to the following sources for permission to reproduce material in this book:

Tables

Table 2.1: Tate, D.J.M. (1979) *The Making of Modern South East Asia – Volume II, The Western Impact: Economic and Social Change*, Penerbit Fajar Bakti Sdn Bhd; Tables 3.1 and 3.2: United Nations Population Division, *World Population Prospects: The 1996 Revision*, by permission of the United Nations; Table 5.1: *Japan Statistical Yearbook*, 45th edn, 1996, Japan Statistical Association; Table 5.6: *The State of Hawaii – Data Book 1992: A Statistical Abstract*, State of Hawaii Department of Business, Economic Development and Tourism.

Illustrations

Cover: Hulton Getty; pp.12 and 33: Ron Giling/Panos Pictures; pp.42 and 79: Courtesy of J. Allan Cash Ltd; p.51: Courtesy of Sally & Richard Greenhill; p.119 (top and bottom): Courtesy of Colin Mackerras; pp.133, 170, 191 (top and bottom), 200 (bottom) and 248: Popperfoto; pp.142, 151 and 157: Pictures Colour Library; p.196: Courtauld Institute of Art; pp.199 and 200 (top): Hocken Library, University of Otago, Dunedin, NZ; pp.208, 213, 216, 222, 223 and 224: Courtesy of Ronald Grant.

List of contributors

Chilla Bulbeck taught women's studies and social sciences at Griffith University until 1998. She is currently Professor of Women's Studies at the University of Adelaide. Her publications in the area of women's studies in cross-cultural perspective include *One World Women's Movement* (1988), *Australian Women in Papua New Guinea* (1991) and *Re-orienting Western Feminisms: the Women's Movement in a Post-colonial World* (forthcoming).

Lucie Cheng is Professor of Sociology and of Urban Planning, University of California, Los Angeles, USA. She served as the Director of the University's Asian American Studies Center between 1972 and 1988, and as the Founding Director of the Center for Pacific Rim Studies. On leave from UCLA, she is the Founding Dean of the Graduate School for Social Transformation Studies, Shih-Hsin University, Taipei. She publishes in the fields of international migration, and gender and development.

Linda C. Erlich, Associate Professor of Japanese Comparative Literature and Cinema at Case Western Reserve University, has published articles and reviews about world cinema in *Film Quarterly, Cinema Journal, Cinemaya, Journal of Film and Video, Japan Forum*, and *Asian Cinema*, among others. Her co-edited anthology, *Cinematic Landscapes: Observations on the Visual Arts and Cinema of China and Japan*, was published in 1994. She received her doctorate from the Department of Drama and Theatre at the University of Hawaii, under an East-West Center grant.

Mary Farquhar is a senior lecturer in the School of Modern Asian Studies at Griffith University in Brisbane, Australia. Her research focus is Chinese culture, especially cross-cultural issues, literature and film. Her book on Chinese children's literature is being published by ME Sharpe, New York. She is a co-author of a work on Chinese cinema about to be published as part of a series on national cinemas by Cambridge University Press.

John N. Hawkins is Dean of International Studies and Overseas Programs at UCLA and a Professor of Comparative Education in the Graduate School of Education. He received his Ph.D. from Vanderbilt University in 1973. His research interests include education and politics, rural education, policy studies and project management, education and intergroup relations. His fieldwork has principally been in Asia with a focus on China and Japan. He has written or edited fourteen books and over 60 articles. His latest book is *Rethinking US–Japan Educational Exchanges* (SUNY Press, 1998) (with William Cummings).

Julia Day Howell is an anthropologist with over 20 years experience doing research on Indonesian studies, Asian religions and spiritualities, new religious movements, both in Asia and Western countries, and social change in complex societies. With a Ph.D. from Stanford University, she is now a senior lecturer at Griffith University's School of Asian Studies, Brisbane, Australia.

Terence T. Hull is Director of Graduate Studies in Demography, Research School of Social Sciences, Australian National University. A specialist in the demography of Asia, with particular emphasis on Indonesia, his work ranges over the cultural, political and historical dimensions of population issues. Most recently he has published contributions to Indonesian population literature including a book on prostitution, a history of public health initiatives, an innovative field study of maternal and infant mortality, and a study of the politics of family planning.

Jeyamalar Kathirithamby-Wells, formerly Professor of Asian History at the University of Malaya, Kuala Lumpur, now lectures and researches at Cambridge University, UK. Author of numerous articles, she contributed to Volume 1 of the *Cambridge History of Southeast Asia* (1992) and co-edited *The Southeast Asian Port and Polity: Rise and Demise* (1990). She is currently working on a forest history of West Malaysia.

Marian Katz is studying for a Ph.D. in sociology at the University of California, Los Angeles, USA. She has an MA degree in Asian Studies and has taught in China for four years before returning to pursue the doctorate.

Stephanie Lawson is Professor of International Relations (Asia-Pacific) at the University of East Anglia. She was previously a Fellow in the Department of International Relations, Research School of Pacific and Asian Studies, Australian National University. She has published numerous book chapters and articles on politics in the South Pacific and South-East Asian regions, as well as on broader issues concerning democratization, ethnic conflict, the politics of culture, and nationalism. She has also published several books, including an edited collection on the new agenda in global security. From 1993 to 1996 she was editor of the *Australian Journal of International Affairs*.

Colin Mackerras is Professor and Head of the School of Modern Asian Studies at Griffith University, Brisbane. He has also published some fifteen scholarly books and nearly 90 scholarly articles on Chinese and other East Asian affairs. His main academic research has been on China's minorities and theatre. His most recent major scholarly publications are: *China's Minorities: Integration and Modernization in the Twentieth Century* (1994); *China's Minority Cultures: Identities and Integration Since 1912* (1995); and *Peking Opera* (1997).

Richard Maidment is Professor of US Government and Politics at the Open University in the UK. He has published widely in the area of American Constitutional Law and has written several books on contemporary US politics. He also has interests in the field of American popular culture and in the construction of national identity.

David C. Schak is a Senior Lecturer at Griffith University. His areas of specialization include Chinese society and culture, social structure and organization, economic development, and socio-cultural change. He has written on dating as a new form of courtship, poverty, and beggars in Chinese society. His current research is in the area of Taiwanese business and management culture.

Stephanie Taylor is a Lecturer in Sociology at Goldsmiths College, University of London. She has recently completed a major project on nation and national identity focusing on the case of New Zealand/Aotearoa. Her research interests include discourse analysis and discursive constructions of identity with relation to place, including Europe. She comes from New Zealand and has lived in London for 20 years.

Anthony van Fossen is primarily interested in the international political economy of Oceania. He teaches interdisciplinary social sciences at Griffith University in Brisbane, Australia, and has published articles on such topics as race, class and geopolitics in Fiji.

Index

Note: page numbers in **bold** type indicate box references

Aborigines 92, 93, 94–6, 190–2, 198
abortion 3, 46, 53–4, 58, 172, 174–7
Adventures of Robin Hood 211
AFTA 234, 255, 260
agriculture 16–17, 19–23, 25–6, 35–6, 191–2
    cash-cropping 16–17, 168, 169
    in New Zealand 198–9
Al Banna 135
Allen, G.C. 155
Alternative Trading Organizations (ATOs) 179–80
Anderson, J.L. and Ritchie, D. 226
ASEAN Free Trade Area 234, 255, 260
ASEAN group, education 145–6
Asia-Pacific
    cinema 207–27
    convergence 8–11
    definition 39, 41, 202–3
    diversity 5–8, 30
    integration 15–16
    migration flows 70–2
    relevance of images to 187–8, 202–5
    women's movements 163–82
'Asian tigers', women in 164, 167–8
Asian values 1–5, 158–9, 231–4, 242–4, 245–50
    and Confucian values 147, 241–4, 245
    democracy and human rights 2, 231–4, 245–6, 247
    and education 158–9
'Asians', images of 203–5
assimilation (of migrants) 67–8, 69, 80, 84, 105–6
Asun 25–6
Aung San 29, 31
Aung San Suu Kyi 248
Australia 5, 9, 193, 233
    Aborigines 92, 93, 94–6, 190–2, 198
    demography 40, 43, 49, 54, 55, 175
    ethnic groups 91, 107
    land ownership 190–2, 198

    multiculturalism 84, 93, 98–9, 107–9, 111, 233
    'New Religions' 127, 131
    REL discrimination 89, 91, 92–9, 107–9, 111, 175
        'White Australia' policy 107, 233
    as settler state 9, 69, 74, 93, 107, 203
    trade unions 107–8, 111
    women in 166–7, 171, 181
authoritarianism 30–1, 245–6, 248–9

Bangladesh 132
Bank Mualamat Indonesia 7
Banks, J. 190
Barrios de Chungara, D. 171–2
Bavadra, A.K. 101
Beast from Twenty Thousand Fathoms 212
Beijing Fourth World Conference of Women 173–4, 177, 182
Benedict, R. 238
A Beijinger in New York 219–20
biculturalism 106–7
Black Cannon Incident 218
Boserup, E. 168
Botany Bay 190
Bougainville, L.A. de 194–5
Bridges, H. 109–10
Broken Blossoms 211
Brunei 31, 40, 125
Buddha Gautama 116
Buddhism 18, 24, 116, 118, 136–7
'Buddhist Light' mission 131
Budi Utomo 28
bumiputra 31, 102
Burma/Myanmar 7, 40
    authoritarianism 30–1, 248, 249
    Buddhism in 24, 31, 118
    colonial 20, 21, 22, 25–6, 29
business ethics 5, 7, 18–19, 31–2, 36

Cambodia 30, 31, 40
Canada 55, 84, 166–7, 233

population 40, 43
  as settler state 69, 203
cash-cropping 16–17, 168, 169
cassava 16, 20, 35
Cendana holdings 31
Chen Kaige 207, 218, 220, 224–5, 226
Chiang Kai-Shek 26, 28
child marriage 165
child prostitution 181
Children of the Atom Bomb 211
China 11, 22, 26, 29
  and Confucianism 8, 9, 18, 147
  trade and entrepreneurialism 7, 17, 18, 19, 22, 24
China (PRC) 4, 6, 8, 10, 11, 12
  cinema 209–10, 211–16, 219–20, 223–5, 226
  Cultural Revolution 7, 83, 123, 143, 216, 219
  education 4, 143, 150, 155
  emigration and diaspora communities 9, 18, 65, 82–4, 203–4
    Asian 70, 75
    in US 66, 70, 75, 78–80
  human rights 2, 11, 246
  population 39, 40, 41–2, 43
    ageing 56–7
    estimates of future 50, 52, 60–2
    fertility and One-Child Policy 42, 49, 50–2, 53, **175–6**
    sex ratios 53–4, 58, 175–6
  religion 4, 117–25 (*passim*), 137
    'Three Traditions/Religions' 118, 124
  women in 3, 54–5, 166–7
A Chinese Ghost Story 213
Ching Siu-tung 213
Chow, R. 208
Christianity 116, 118–20, 130–1, 189
  fundamentalist 103, 134, 136
  'home church' movement 125
  missionaries 26–7, 68, 120
  Pentecostalism 127
Christmas Islands 193
Chulalongkorm 36
cinema 207–27
  aesthetics 220–6
  backgrounds 209–15
  Chinese 209–10, 211–16, 219–20, 223–5, 226
  crosscultural 218–20, 223–5
  as global industry 208–9, 227
  influence of Hollywood 209–10, 211–12, 215
  Japanese 209–10, 211–15, 216–19, 221–3, 225, 226
  narrative 215–20
  New Wave 213–14, 218
  significance of 207–9

circumcision, female 172
citizenship 11, 94–100, 104, 108
Cochin China 22, 25
coffee 19, 20
colonialism 19–28, 46–9, 120, 189–92
  and Christianity 120
  colonizing and colonized women 163, 164–5, 172
  and images of emptiness 189–92
  and nationalism 25–8
  and population change 46–9
  reform and modernization 23–5
  socio-economic change 19–22
comfort women 28, 163, **170**, 180
Committee for Asian Women 179
Commonwealth Racial Discrimination Act (Australia) 107
communism 27, 28
Community Aid Abroad 179
community religions 117, 121
Confucianism/Confucian values 7, 8, 18, 116–17, 118, 235
  and education 4, 25, 147–50
  as unifying culture 241–4
Confucius *see* Kong Fuzi
contraception *see* fertility
Convention on Discrimination against Women 167, 171
Cook, Captain J. 190
core values 241–4
Cultural Revolution 7, 83, 123, 143, 216, 219
culture 7–8, 151–2, 172–3, 203–5, 208, 231–50
  Asian values 231–4, 245–9
  concept of national 237–8, 244–5
  determinism or relativism 232–3, 235–7, 243, 247
  diversity and differences 5–8, 171–8, 234–5, 237–9, 240–4
  and education 151–2
  familistic 7–8
  idea of 234–7
  and image 203–5
  'low-trust' or 'high-trust' 8
  significance of cinema 208
  state and 231–3, 236–45, 247–50
  and value systems 235–6
  women and differences in 172–8
Cummings, W. 151–2

Dalai Lama 123
Daoism 116, 118, 137
deforestation 3, 25–6, 35, 36, 169
democracy
  Asian 232, 233, 234, 245–6, 247
  in Japan 247–8, 249
  Western 232, 245
Deng Xiaoping 7, 214, 216, 218

Desser, D. 218
diaspora communities 65–7, 69–84
    Chinese 9, 18, 66, 70, 75, 78–80, 82–4
    concept and types of diaspora 72–4
    diversity 65–7
    Filipino 65, 70, 75–6, 77, 81–2
    Japanese 65, 66, 74, 76, 80–1
    in US 66, 69–72, 75–6, 78–82
    see also migration
discrimination, racial, ethnic and language 89–111
    citizenship and legal rights 94–9
    in Fiji, Japan and Malaysia 89–90, 92–3, 95, 96–7, 98–104
    with indigenous people as majority 93, 95, 96
    with indigenous people as minority 92, 94–6
    in new settler societies 92–6, 97–9, 104–10
    and unemployment 104–6, 108
    and unions 89–90, 93–4, 100, 103–4, 107–8, 110, 111
diversity 5–8, 30, 36
    cultural 5–8, 171–3, 234–5, 237–9, 240–4
    of diaspora communities 65–7
    of government 6, 31, 247–9
    population 43
domestic violence 164, 172, 177–8, **178**
domestic workers 66, 180
dowries 177–8
Dutch East Indies 20, 24

Earth Summit, Rio de Janeiro 3, 173
East Asia 5–8, 19–29, 30–6, 142–58
    colonial period 19–28
    diversity 5–8, 30
    Japanese imperialism 28–9
    and nationalism 25–8
    post-war 30–6
    pre-modern era 16–19
    role of women 33–4
East Timor 15, 40, 120
economic growth and development
    and education 4, 141, 155
    and state intervention 32
    under colonialism 21–2
    and women 168–9
education 3–4, 141–59
    Asian/Confucian values 4, 25, 147–50, 158–9
    and colonialism 23–4, 26–7
    and culture 151–2
    and economic development 4, 141, 155
    lifelong learning 142–3
    motivation 146–58
    North-East Asia 142–4
    private sector 158–9
    role of family 147–9

rote learning 148, 149–50, 152
    South-East Asia 145–6
    television in 156
    of women 151, 165, 168, 174, 175, 176
emptiness, images of 188–94
entrepreneurialism
    China 7, 17, 18, 19, 22, 24
    and migration 73, 75–6, 77
environment 3, 15, 35–6, 198–9
equality, sexual 171
ethics
    business 5, 7, 36
    as part of culture 236
ethnicity
    and Asian diasporas in US 78–80
    and colonialism 20–1
    ethnic grouping in selected countries 90–2
    and population policies 175
    see also diaspora communities; discrimination, racial, ethnic and language; migration
Europe
    East Asian colonialism 19–25
    migration 69, 70, 74, 92
    'New Religions' 127, 131
    pre-nineteenth century trade 17–19
exploitation of women 179–82

family 7–8, 18–19, 31–2, 147–9
    in business and politics 18–19, 31–2
    changing 10–11, 12
    and dual role for women 54–5, 165–6, 168
    familistic cultures 7–8, 148–9
feminism 2–3, 174–8
    see also women
fertility
    control of 42, 46, 49–52, 53, 62–3, 173–7
    falling 55–7
Fiji 103, 166, **178**
    ethnicity 9, 48–9, 91, 93
    population 40, 47, 48–9
    REL discrimination 89, 91, 92–9, 101–2, 103, 111
film *see* cinema
forestry and timber 3, 25–6, 35, 36, 169
Foucault, M. 202
France 193
Fraser and Neave 22
Fukuyama, F. 8
fundamentalism 103, 104, 132–6

galleon trade 16
Gauguin, P. 195
globalization
    cinema industry 208–9, 227
    economic restructuring and migration 65–7, 77, 82, 84–5

and working conditions of women 179–80
Godzilla 211–12
Goh Chok Tong 231
government
    authoritarian 30–1, 245–6, 247–8
    diversity 6, 31, 247–9
    migration policies 68, 86
    opposition to 6, 11
    policies on discrimination 96, 98, 101
    secularization of 122–5
Greater East Asia Co-Prosperity Sphere, Japan
    29, 31
Green Tea over Rice 216–17
Griffith, D.W. 211
group orientation 7–8, 148
Guam 27, 40
Guthries 22

Haji Samanhudi 28
Hall, J. 109–10
Hanson, Pauline 108, 233
happiness, images of 194–8
Harp of Burma 211
Hawaii 11, 27, 43
    'Big Five' companies 93, 109
    ethnicity 9, 92, 93, 94–6
    REL discrimination 89–90, 92–9, 109–10,
    111
hierarchy 4, 148–9
Hinduism 116, 117–18
Hitchcock, A. 215, 225
Ho Chi Minh 26, 239
Hollywood 209–12, 215, 218–20, 221, 226–7
'home church' movement 125
Honda Inoshiro 211–12
Hong Kong 4, 8, 19, 40, 147, 180
    cinema 213, 214
    status of women 166, 171
Hou Xiaoxian 213
Howard, J. 108, 233
Hsaya San 26
Hua Guofeng 51
Huang Jianxin 218
human development index (female) 171
human rights 2–3, 6, 11, 231, 233–4, 245–7
    and Asian values 2, 231, 233–4, 245–6
    universalistic approach 246–7
    and women's rights 2–3, 174–8
Huntington, S. 232–3

Iceland 237–8
Ichikawa Kon 211
images, Pacific 185–205
    of 'Asians' 203–5
    changing 198–203
    and constructs 201–5
    of early European explorers 188–92

East and West as opposites 201–2, 250
    of emptiness 188–94
    of happiness and sexual freedom 194–8
    nature of 186–7
    relevance to Asia-Pacific 187–8
In the Realm of The Senses 207
India 9, 48–9, 93, 117–18, 249
indigenous peoples 92, 93, 94–6, 97–9, 105,
    189–92
    citizenship and legal rights 94–5, 97–9
    'invisible' to early explorers 189–92
    as majority 93, 95, 96
    as minority 92, 94–6, 97–9, 105, 190–2
    and ownership of land 94, 105, 190–2,
    199–201
    sovereignty and self-determination 94,
    95–6, 105
    see also Aborigines; Maoris
individualism 7, 8, 148, 232, 246
Indo-China 20
Indonesia 3, 4, 10, 16, 20, 21, 31
    authoritarianism 6, 11, 31, 32
    education 4, 145, 166
    ethnicity 11, 83, 132–4
    fertility and birth control 48, 49, 52, 55,
    166
    nationalism/national identity 11, 26, 27,
    28, 124, 240–1
    Pancasila 31, 240–1
    population 39, 40, 43, 47–8, 52, 60–2
    religion 121, 123, 124, 125, 132–4, 240–1
        Islam 7, 39, 121, 124, 136
        other than Islam 121, 124, 129, 130,
        137
    women in 3, 54–5, 165–7
Indonesian Association 28
industrialization 10, 11–12, 35–6
infanticide 53–4
Institute of East Asian Philosophies (IEAP)
    242–3
International Monetary Fund (IMF) 169, 179,
    181–2
international traffic in women 179–81
Iran 132
Ishida Baigan 18
Islam 7, 12–13, 18, 116, 118–21, 132–6
    fundamentalism 103, 104, 132–6
    and politics 26, 27, 28, 135
    women in 3, 34, 136, 172, **173**
'Islamism' 135
Itami Mansaku 219

Japan 4, 7, 12, 17, 18–19, 28, 244
    cinema 209–10, 211–15, 216–19, 221–3,
    225, 226
    Confucianism 4, 118, 147, 148–9, 241,
    248
    democracy 247–8

diaspora communities 65, 66, 74, 76, 80–1
economic growth 142
education 4, 142–3, 147, 148–9, 150, 151–8
ethnic purity 90
inward migration 69, 96–7
millenarianism (Aum Shinrikyo) 138
national and cultural identity 11, 29, 238–9
population 40, 41, 42, 52, 54–5, 60–2
    ageing 55, 56, 58
REL discrimination 89–90, 92–101, 163, **170**
religion 117, 118, 120, 122–3, 128–9, 130, 138
unionization 4–5, 100, 111
war and occupation 28–9, 163, **170**, 211, 214
women in 3, 54–5, 151, 163, 166–7, 170, 171
zaibatsu 18–19
Jardine Matheson 22
Java 41, 46–8, 132–4, 138
    colonial 19, 21, 22, 23
    see also Indonesia
Jesuits 120
Jesus of Nazareth 118, 120
Jiang Qing 219
Jidou 218
Judaism 118

Kampuchea 15, 75
Kartini, Raden Adjeng 165
Kim Dae Jung 249
King Kong 212
Kinusaga 211
Kiribati 40, 193
Kobayashi, V.N. 152
Kong Fuzi (Confucius) 116–17
Korea 4, 26–7
    Confucian traditions 117, 118, 147, 149–50, 241, 248, 249
    education 147, 148, 149–50
    Japanese treatment of Koreans 90, 93, 97, 163, **170**
    religion 118, 120, 249
    see also South Korea
Koy, J.A. 103
Kuhn, A. 210
Kuomintang 27, 28
Kurosawa Akira 212, 218, 220, 221–3, 225, 226

labour diasporas 73, 75–6, 77, 78
labour force participation (women) 34, 166, 168–9, 176
labour shortages 55–6

land ownership
    in European terms 190–2
    indigenous peoples and 94, 105, 190, 199–201
    terra nullius doctrine 190
    women's 168
language 6, 7, 187–8, 242
    see also discrimination, racial, ethnic and language
Laos 30, 31, 40, 75
Lee Kwan Yew 1–2, 175, 242–3, 245
Leyda, J. 212
lifelong learning 142–3
Lu Xun 212, 218, 219

Magellan, F. 16
Mahathir Mohamed 1–2, 32, 103, 231, 233
maize 16–17, 20
Malaya 19, 20–1, 25, 29, 93
    growth of nationalism 27–8, 121
Malaysia 3, 4, 31, 32, 35, 36
    authoritarianism 249
    bumiputra 31, 102
    diversity 6, 11
    education 26, 145, 146, 166
    ethnicity 91, 92–9, 102–4, 145, 241
    nationalism and national identity 11, 27–8, 121, 124, 125, 132
    population 15, 40, 54, 167
    REL discrimination 6, 83, 89, 91, 92–9, 102–4, 111
        Malayanization 145, 241
    religion 31–2
        Islam 7, 103, 104, 121, 124, 132
        and nationalism 27–8, 121, 124, 125, 132
        other than Islam 121, 124
    women in 3, 34, 166–7, 173
Mao Zedong 7, 122
Maoris 92, 93, 94–6, 104–7, 190
    as tourist attraction 199–201
Marcos, F. 31
marriage
    age and rate of 54
    child 165
Marshall Islands 40, 193
Marxism and religion 121–2, 123
Matsushita 32
Mawdudi, Abu'l-A'la 135
Mead, M. 196–7, 201
Meiji government 117, 120
Melanesia 7, 9, 43
merchant capitalism 21–2
Mexico 40, 43
Micronesia 7, 9, 40, 43
'migrant states' *see* settler states
migration 9, 10, 21, 65–86
    Asia-Pacific flows 70–2

assimilation 67–8, 69, 80, 84
entrepreneurial/managerial 73, 75–6, 77
global economics and 65–7, 77, 82, 84–5
imperial/colonial 21, 73, 74
labour 73, 75–6, 77, 78
and nation-state 67–8, 69–72
professional/intellectual 73, 76–7, 84–6
rural–urban 10
serial international 66, 76–7
settlers or sojourners 74, 75–6
and technology transfer 85–6
through forced expulsion and exile 73, 74–5
types of 73–7, 78, 84–6
see also diaspora communities
millenarianism 132, 138
Mindon Min, King 24
missionaries 26–7, 68, 120, 164
Modernist Muslims 136
modernization theory 122
modernization, and tradition 11–13, 152–3
Mohammed (Prophet) 118, 120
Mongkut, Prince 24
Mongolia 137–8
Monte Bello Islands 193
Moon, Rev. Sun Myung 131
motherhood 174–5
multiculturalism
and migration 67, 70, 72, 84
in new settler societies 84, 92–3, 98–9, 107–9, 111, 233
multinationalism 67, 72
multiracialism 93, 102–3
Mururoa 193

Nakasone, Y. 99
nation-building
and education 3–4, 11, 145
and religion 31–2, 123–5, 239
Western concepts of nationhood 68
nation-state
image of 188
and migration 67–8, 69–70, 84
and national culture 237–8
and religion 121–5
national identity 11, 13, 123–5, 239–41
Hawaii 92
Indonesia 240–1
Japan 29, 238–9
Malaysia 124, 125, 132
New Zealand 105–6
Singapore 9, 175, 241–3
Thailand 123, 239
Vietnam 24–5, 28, 239–40
nationalism 25–8, 29, 237–8, 244–5
and cinema 212, 227
and colonialism 25–8, 121

and concept of national culture 237–8, 244–5
and Islam 26
and Japanese imperialism 29
and religion 26, 27–8, 121, 124
Neo-Modernist Muslim movement 136
Nestorian Christianity 120
Netherlands 17, 19, 21, 22, 23–4, 46–8
'New Age' movement 127
'New Religions' 127, 128–9, 130, 131
New Wave cinema 213–14, 218
New Zealand 92–9, 104–7, 111
bicultural or multicultural society 84, 92–3, 98–9, 106–7
changing images of 198–201
environment 198–9
ethnic groups 91
inward migration 9, 93, 105–6, 203–4
land and sovereignty claims 94, 105–6, 199–201
Maoris 92, 93, 94–6, 104–7
national identity 105–6
population 40, 43, 55
REL discrimination 89, 92–9, 104–7, 199–201, 203–4
as settler state 69, 92, 203, 233
unemployment 104–6
women in 166–7, 171
newly-industrialized economies (NIEs) 67, 115, 131
Night and Fog in Japan 214, 218
non-governmental organizations (NGOs) 246–7
North by Northwest 215
North-East Asia, education 142–4
nuclear testing 193–4
Nyuyen Truong To 25

opium 19, 20
'Orientalism' 201–2
orientation, group or individual 7–8
Oshima Nagisa 207, 214, 218
'others' 201–2
Oxfam 179
Ozu Yasujiro 216–18

Pacific Islands 7, 9, 43, 166, 246–7
religion 120, 121
Western images of 194–8
Pakistan 132
Pancasila 31, 240–1
Papua New Guinea 11, 40, 166–7, 238
wife-beating **178**
Pentecostalism 127, 134
pepper 16–17, 20, 21, 23
Pergau Dam 32
PERNAS 32

Pertamina 32
Peters, W. 106
Philippines 16, 20, 30, 31, 32, 248
    colonialism 19, 21, 22
    deforestation 35, 36
    education 146
    migration 77, 81–2, 83, 146, 180
        diaspora community in US 66, 70, 75–6, 81–2
        professional level 77, 81–2, 146
    population 40
    religion 7, 120, 121, 123, 130, 134, 138
    and US 22, 27
    women in 81, 166–7, 180–2
Philippines Sugar Commission (Philcoa) 32
Pitcairn 40, 43
political activism (women) 164–5, 166–7, 168
polygamy 165
Polynesia 7, 9, 40, 43
population 15, 39–63
    ageing 55–7
    colonialism and changes in 22, 46–9
    dangers of overpopulation 47–8
    demographic transition 49–52
    and fertility 46, 49–52, 55, 58–63, 174–7
    from 5000 BC to 2000 AD 44–6
    future projections 52, 58–63
    reproductive rights 174–7
    sex ratios at birth 53–4, 58
    and sustainable standards of living 61–3
Prekatan Perempuan Indonesia 165
professions
    and transnational migration 84–6
    women's entry into 165
prostitution 10, 20, 34, 180–1
    see also comfort women

Quezon, Manuel 27

race *see* discrimination, racial, ethnic and language
Raise the Red Lantern 223, 225
Ramabai, P. 165
Rashomon 212, 220, 221–3, 225, 226
reality, and image 186–7
Red Sorghum 212
refugees 73, 74–5
REL discrimination *see* discrimination, racial, ethnic and language
religion 115–39
    community 117
    diversity 6, 7
    emergent patterns 131–8
    and ethnicity 132–4
    expected decline 121–2
    fundamentalist 103, 104, 132–6
    Marxist view of 121–2, 123

millenarianism 132, 138
    modernization theory and 122
    and nationalism 26, 27–8, 121, 124
    'New Age' movement 127
    'New Religions' 127, 128–9, 130, 131
    revival of folk cults 137–8
    and social protest 132–4
    and the state 31–2, 121–5, 239
    'Three Religions' of China 118, 124
    universalistic 116–17
    see also Buddhism; Christianity; Daoism; Hinduism; Islam
rice 17, 19, 21, 25
rights of women 2–3, 174–8
Ritchie, D. 221–2, 223
    see also Anderson, J.L. and Ritchie, D.
Robinson, M. 150
Rohwen, J. 141
Rongelap Islands 193
rote learning 148, 149–50, 152
Rousseau, J.J. 194–5
Rozman, G. 148, 150
rubber 19, 20–1, 25
rural–urban migration 10

Said, E. 201–2
Samoa 40, 41, 167, 196–7
Sarawak 25–6
Sarit Thanarat, Field Marshal 32
Sato, T. 210, 219
Schiller, D. and Walberg, H.J. 155–6
secularization of government 122–5
self-concept 153–4
self-determination (indigenous people) 94, 95–6, 105
Sen, A. 2
settler states 69, 74, 92, 93, 94–9, 203, 233
Seven Samurai 226
sex ratios (at birth) 53–4, 58
sex tourism 170, 180–2
sex workers *see* comfort women; prostitution
sexual freedom, images of 194–8, 201–2
Shindo Kaneto 211
Shinto 117
Sihanouk, Prince 31
Singapore 4, 9, 19, 24, 32, 180
    authoritarianism 30, 249
    Confucian traditions/Asian values 147, 231, 241–4, 245
    discrimination and national identity 9, 175, 241–3
    education 146, 166
    population and fertility 40, 42, 54, 55, 166
    women in 166–7, 171
South Korea 8, 70
    authoritarianism 247–8, 249
    demography 40, 53–4, 55, 58, 167
    education 144, 155

religion 122–3, 137, 138
    women in 166–7, 171
    see also Korea
South-East Asia 7, 29
    education 145–6
    women in 33–4, 166–7
sovereignty (indigenous people) 94, 95, 105
Sri Lanka 118, 131
standards of living 61–3
Stark, R. 130
state
    and culture 237–45
    religion separate from 122–3
    see also nation-state; settler states
state intervention 32–3
Steamship Navigation Company (KNP) 24
sterilization 175
Stevenson Restriction Scheme 21
Street Angel 212
structural adjustment programmes 179–80
students (Japanese and American) 153–5
studio system (cinema) 211–15
suffrage (women's) 164–5, 166–7, 168
Suharto, Ibu Tien 34
Suharto, President and family 31, 34, 241
Sukarno, Megawati 6
Sukarno, President 26, 31, 241
Sumatra 21, 23, 121
Syarikat Islam 28

Tahiti 190, 194–5, 202
Taiwan 8, 19, 83
    authoritarianism 247–8, 249
    cinema 212–13
    Confucian tradition 241, 248
    demography 42, 53–4, 55, 58
    education 143, 144
    religion 131, 137
tea 17, 19, 20
technology transfer 85–6
television 32, 156
Tengku Abdul Rahman 26, 32
Terra Australis Incognita 188–9, **189**, 193–4
Terra Nullius 190
Thailand 4, 7, 21, 24, 26, 35, 36
    demography 24, 40, 54, 55
    early trade 17, 18, 24
    education 4, 145–6, 166
    monarchy 31–2, 123, 125, 239, 248
    national identity 11, 123, 239
    religion
        Buddhism 7, 18, 20, 32, 118, 123,
        136–7
        other than Buddhism 7, 117
    sex tourism 180
    women in 166
Theosophy Society 131
'Three Religions' of China 118, 124

Tiananmen Square incident 2, 11
Tibet 123
tin 20, 25
To Live 212
tobacco 16–17, 19, 21
Tonghak 249
Torrance, E.P. 156
tourism 9–10, 198–9
    sex 10, 170, 180–2
trade, pre-twentieth century 7, 9, 16–19, 22,
    24, 36
trade unions *see* unions
tradition, and modernization 11–13, 152–3
transnational companies 247
transnational professional class 84–6

U Nu 31
UN Decade for Women 163, 168, 169, 171–4,
    182
UN Development Fund for Women (Unifem)
    171, 179
UN Division for Women and Development
    171
UN International on the Protection of Rights
    of Migrant Workers 100
UN Universal Declaration of Human Rights 2,
    177
unemployment 104–6, 108
Unification Church, Rev. Moon's 131
unions 4–5
    and REL discrimination 89–90, 93–4, 100,
    107–8, 110, 111
United Kingdom 17, 48–9, 127, 131, 193
United Nations, women's representation in
    171
United States 8, 110, 193
    in Asia-Pacific 22, 26–7, 233
    Chinese diaspora community 66, 70, 75,
        78–80
    cinema *see* Hollywood
    demography 39, 40, 43, 49, 54, 55, 175
    education 149, 151–5
    Filipino diaspora community 66, 70, 75–6,
        81–2
    inward migration 66, 69–72, 75–6, 78–82,
        84–5
    Japanese diaspora community 66, 80–1
    as new settler society 69, 96, 203
    religion 127, 131, 134
    women in 166–7, 171
universalistic religions 116–17
urbanization 10, 12, 13, 22, 30
Ushiogi, M. 155

Vajiravudh 26
values
    Asian 1–5, 158–9, 231–4, 242–4, 245–50

Confucian 4, 25, 116–17, 147–50, 235, 241–4
    culture and value systems 235–6
    in education 4, 25, 147–50, 158–9
    national core 241–4
    Western 232, 243, 250
Vanuatu 41, 164, 166
    domestic violence **178**
Vasavakul, T. 239–40
veiling **173**
Vietnam 4, 17, 19, 24–5, 75
    authoritarianism 30–1
    Buddhism 7, 9, 118
    Confucianism 25, 117, 118, 147
    demography 40, 49
    education 26, 146
    nationalism/national identity 11, 24–5, 26, 28, 239–40, 244
    'well-being' of women 166–7
violence, gender-based 164, 172, 177–8, **178**

Wahabi movement 23
Waitangi, Treaty of 105
Walberg, H.J. *see* Schiller, D. and Walberg, H.J.
Wee Kim Wee 243–4
West 201–2, 231–2, 233, 250
    apparent decline 231–2
    Asia as opposite image to 201–2, 250
    concept of nationhood 68
    concept of 233
    images of Pacific Islands 194–8
    individualism of 7, 8, 232, 246
    influence of education in 26–7
    values 232, 243, 245, 250
wife-beating 164, **178**
women 2–3, 10, 20, 33–4, 54–5, 66, 163–82
    Beijing Conference 173–4, 177, 182
    in developing and developed nations 163, 164–71, 172
    differing cultures, differing goals 171–3, **173**, 174–8

    and domestic violence 164, 172, 177–8, **178**
    as domestic workers 66, 180
    dual role 54–5, 165–6, 168
    education of 151, 165, 168, 174, 175, 176
    exploitation 179–82
    female human development index 171
    fertility and fertility control 54–5, 174–7
    health of 166, 174
    and international agencies 168–9, 179–80, 181
    in Islam 3, 34, 136, 172, **173**
    labour force participation 34, 166, 168–9, 176
    and land ownership 168
    political activism 164–5, 166–7, 168
    rights of 2–3, 172, 174–8
    role in South-East Asia 33–4
    as sex workers
        comfort women 28, 163, **170**, 180
        prostitution 10, 20, 34, 180–1
        as spoils of war 169–70, **170**
    United Nations Decade for Women 163, 168, 169, 171–4, 182
    'well-being' 166–9
    women's movements 163–82
Women's Centre in Hong Kong 180
working conditions, of women 179–80
World Bank 169, 179, 181
World Conference on Human Rights 2, 246

Yellow Earth 207, 218, 220, 224–5, 226
Yen, James 26

zaibatsu 18–19
Zhang Yimou 212, 218, 220, 223, 225
Zhang Yuan 218, 220
Zhou Enlai 43, 47

PIER Collection
Program in International Education Resources
Yale University
306 Henry Luce Hall
34 Hillhouse Avenue
New Haven, CT 06520